CURES FOR CHANCE

Adoptive Relations in Shakespeare and Middleton

Cures for Chance

Adoptive Relations in Shakespeare and Middleton

ERIN ELLERBECK

UNIVERSITY OF TORONTO PRESS
Toronto Buffalo London

© University of Toronto Press 2022
Toronto Buffalo London
utorontopress.com
Printed in the U.S.A.

ISBN 978-1-4875-0878-4 (cloth)   ISBN 978-1-4875-3897-2 (EPUB)
                                   ISBN 978-1-4875-3896-5 (PDF)

Library and Archives Canada Cataloguing in Publication

Title: Cures for chance : adoptive relations in Shakespeare and Middleton /
   Erin Ellerbeck.
Names: Ellerbeck, Erin, author.
Description: Includes bibliographical references and index.
Identifiers: Canadiana (print) 2021023699X | Canadiana (ebook) 20210237082 |
   ISBN 9781487508784 (cloth) | ISBN 9781487538972 (EPUB) |
   ISBN 9781487538965 (PDF)
Subjects: LCSH: Shakespeare, William, 1564–1616 – Criticism and
   interpretation. | LCSH: Middleton, Thomas, –1627 – Criticism and
   interpretation. | LCSH: English drama – Early modern and Elizabethan,
   1500–1600 – History and criticism. | LCSH: Families in literature. |
   LCSH: Adoption in literature.
Classification: LCC PR3069.F35 E45 2022 | DDC 822.3/3–dc23

This book has been published with the help of a grant from the Federation
for the Humanities and Social Sciences, through the Awards to Scholarly
Publications Program, using funds provided by the Social Sciences and
Humanities Research Council of Canada.

University of Toronto Press acknowledges the financial assistance to its
publishing program of the Canada Council for the Arts and the Ontario Arts
Council, an agency of the Government of Ontario.

 Canada Council Conseil des Arts
for the Arts du Canada

ONTARIO ARTS COUNCIL
CONSEIL DES ARTS DE L'ONTARIO
an Ontario government agency
un organisme du gouvernement de l'Ontario

 Funded by the Financé par le
Government gouvernement
of Canada du Canada

 Canada

For Nicholas, Blaise, and Clio

Contents

Acknowledgments

I owe a great debt of gratitude to Lynne Magnusson, whose support and friendship have been unwavering. This book had its genesis in a class taught at the University of Toronto by Alexander Leggatt, to whom I remain thankful for his generosity and scholarly inspiration. Elizabeth D. Harvey and Holger Schott Syme helped shape the book in innumerable ways. Marianne Novy read parts of the manuscript in draft, and the book is all the better for her astute suggestions.

The friendships that I made at the University of Toronto have sustained me through academic life (and otherwise). Thank you to Alysia Kolentsis, Katie Larson, Jan Purnis, and Virginia Strain for your humour and conversation. I am fortunate to have excellent colleagues in the Department of English at the University of Victoria. For their support of my work, my particular thanks to Chris Douglas, Rebecca Gagan, Magda Kay, Gary Kuchar, Mary Elizabeth Leighton, Allan Mitchell, Stephen Ross, and Nicole Shukin.

I am grateful to my parents, Glenna and Ken Ellerbeck, and my brother, Quinn, for their constant encouragement.

Natalie Boldt and Heidi Rennert were dedicated research assistants.

The anonymous readers for the University of Toronto Press offered immensely helpful feedback on the manuscript. I would like to thank them, as well as the editorial staff at UTP. The guidance of Suzanne Rancourt, my editor, has been invaluable.

Any remaining errors or oversights are, of course, my own.

Research for *Cures for Chance* was generously funded by the Social Sciences and Humanities Research Council of Canada and the University of Victoria.

My thanks as well to the University of Toronto Libraries, the University of Victoria Libraries, the Harvard Library, and the Harry Ransom Center at the University of Texas, where I conducted my research.

A portion of chapter 1 is reprinted from "Adoption and the Language of Horticulture in *All's Well That Ends Well*," first published in *SEL: Studies in English Literature, 1500–1900*, vol. 51, no. 2, 2011, pp. 305–26. Much of chapter 4 was published as "Adoptive Names in Thomas Middleton's *Women Beware Women*" in *SEL: Studies in English Literature, 1500–1900*, vol. 57, no. 2, 2017, pp. 407–26. I acknowledge Rice University for permission to republish this material.

CURES FOR CHANCE

Adoptive Relations in Shakespeare and Middleton

Shaping the Family

Adoption, whereby parents take in children who are not, in the first instance, their own, is a resolutely human concern, although stories of animal adoption abound, as in the example of Romulus and Remus. To tell the story of adoption in early modern drama, however, I must begin neither with humans alone nor with animals, but with the vegetable kingdom – in particular, with grafted plants.

In early modern England, as in all societies, nature and culture were intimately linked, and many works of fictional and non-fictional literature took the natural world as their primary subject. Although English authors expressed interest in the natural world, much of the nature that surrounded them had already been altered by human hands, and faced further and continual manipulation. The "blessed plot" of England (Shakespeare, *Richard II* 2.1.50) was subject to deforestation on a large scale: in *The Commons Complaint* (1611), Arthur Standish noted the degradation of England's forests and the scarcity of wood "more within twenty or thirty last yeares then in any hundred yeares before" (1). Addressing King James, Standish chastised the English people for not preserving forests: "Little respect is taken but by your Maiesty, for the posterity and prosperity of your Kingdom; too many destroyers, but few or none at al doth plant or preserue: by reason thereof there is no Timber left in this Kingdome at this instant onely to repaire the buildings thereof an other age, much lesse to build withall: whereby this greeuance doth daily increase" (1). The quintessential English garden epitomized a culture in which nature was shaped and subsequently managed.[1] Manuals of gardening techniques proliferated so that readers might learn how to intervene in the natural world; horticultural practices now considered common were then seen as sources of mystery and possibility.[2]

In an image found in a treatise called *The Orchard, and the Garden* (1594), a horticulturalist is shown changing the form of a tree: he stands on a ladder and prepares a tree to receive a graft (Figure 1). The practice of grafting is demonstrated in three stages on three different branches, with the tree at once at the beginning, in the middle, and at the end of the procedure. The horticulturalist begins (as depicted in Figure 1) with the leftmost branch. He uses a knife to shave away the bark to clear a space for an incision. This incision is shown on the second branch; it takes the shape of an inverse V, allowing the wood at the peak of the V to be pulled away from the tree so that a scion – the shoot of another tree – can be inserted to feed on the sap of the host tree. Included on the third branch at the site of the incision is the piece of cloth required to bind and protect the completed graft. This branch also depicts the successful amalgamation of scion and stock. The fledgling, leafless shoot grows upward from the grafting site rather than following the path of the branch to which it has been attached: it is obviously both distinct from and yet still part of the host. The "strange bud," as the anonymous author of the treatise puts it, "hath prospered and joined himself" with the stock (14–15).

Readers at the time may have recognized this image: an earlier version appeared in Leonard Mascall's *A Booke of the Arte and maner, howe to plant and graffe all sortes of trees*, which was reprinted seven times between 1572 and 1599 (Figure 2). The figure of the horticulturalist distinguishes this particular version of the image from its predecessors; human intervention in the natural world is only implied in the older images. A still more striking aspect of the illustration is also the most puzzling, and it marks another departure from Mascall: the end of the third branch has been cut away and is shown falling towards the ground. This cut has been made after the scion and stock have been combined. The author explains, by describing the process in familial terms, that the last step is essential for the graft's survival: "for an especiall nourishment and keeping of the inner juice: then cut off the braunches round about it, that the mother may the better nourish the new son" (14). The metaphor is clear: the end of the branch is removed so that the "mother" tree does not have to divide its available nutrients. It can instead devote its resources to sustaining its "new son." Losing one branch but gaining another, the tree accepts and rears a slip; the horticulturalist's intervention produces a bond that did not previously exist.

The author's use of familial language and the comparison of grafting to the formation of a maternal relationship are in keeping with the etymological connection of grafting and adoption. "Adoption" derives from the Latin *adoptio*, which refers both to the practice of incorporating a person into a family and to the practice of grafting. The author of the treatise may or may not have known the etymology, but his choice of

Figure 1. *The Orchard, and the Garden Containing Certaine necessarie, secret, and ordinarie knowledges in Grafting and Gardening.* London, 1594, p. 7.

metaphor was apt: grafting and adoption are both attempts to alter that which exists in nature by combining unrelated things. The association of grafting with familial relation and adoption was not pervasive in early modern England. William Shakespeare uses it to great effect in *The Winter's Tale, Cymbeline,* and *All's Well That Ends Well,* but its success is partly due to the strangeness of the rhetorical figure. In this respect it differs from the dead metaphors of many current botanical clichés – a thorn in the side, a shrinking violet, a grassroots organization, a wall-flower. To describe grafting in familial terms was simultaneously old and new: it drew on a long-standing etymological and conceptual resemblance at the same time as it suggested the contemporary human capacity to transform the physical environment.[3]

But the differences between adoption and grafting are obvious and many; the metaphor of adoption in *The Orchard, and the Garden* is not a simple equivalence. Unlike the horticulturalist's visible joining of plants, adoption can be imperceptible. An adopted child is not, of course, physically attached to its family. Adoption's typical invisibility

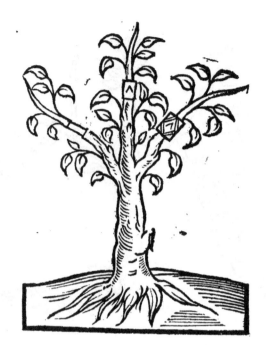

Figure 2. Leonard Mascall, *A Booke of the Arte and maner, howe to plant and graffe all sortes of trees*. London, 1572, p. 78.

made it potentially disruptive of societal norms. Like grafting, it revealed the extent to which the naturalized social order could be superseded, but it also demonstrated that this supersession could remain unnoticed. It allowed families to modify, either overtly or covertly, what was presumed to be the natural order. In a culture preoccupied with blood-based lineage, legitimacy, and succession, the organization of families along non-biological lines threatened to unfix patrilineality. It also disrupted what Marianne Novy has termed "a mythology of blood," by which she means the notion that personal identity and familial affection are products of biology ("Multiple Parenting in Shakespeare's Romances" 189). Perhaps unsurprisingly, adoption was not sanctioned legally in the period – it was not, in fact, inscribed in English law until 1926.[4] Although today we are used to thinking of adoption as an integral part of familial formation, and although adoption is found throughout early modern literature, it was usually imperceptible in early modern England.[5] And yet, as I will show, its invisibility off-stage was not a function of its scarcity but, paradoxically, of its omnipresence in a variety of typically unmarked forms. In addition to the comparison to grafting, the practice of adoption was understood and imagined in myriad ways. *Cures for Chance* thus considers how different figurations of adoption converge and diverge.

On the early modern stage, genre often dictated the depiction of adoptive practices and shaped their outcomes. Shakespeare's romances contain perhaps the richest and most recognizable collection of adopted characters. The romantic generic convention of families who are divided and then, often miraculously, reunited presents opportunities for children to be incorporated into adoptive families temporarily. *The Winter's Tale*, *Pericles*, *Cymbeline*, and *The Tempest* all include characters who establish ties to non-biological family members with varying degrees of success. In all cases save Marina's in *Pericles*, the new familial arrangements of adoptive children are seemingly permanent: their non-biological families are adoptive families rather than temporary foster families.[6] The lexicographer Randle Cotgrave defined "adoption" in *A Dictionary of the French and English Tongues* (1611) as "the conferring on fremme children all aduantages belonging to naturall ones" ("afiliation"). (He later explains that a "fremme" is a person who is "neither a dweller with, nor of kinne vnto, vs" ["estrangier"].) Cotgrave's definition provides a starting point for the identification as adoptees of characters who are afforded the advantages, and sometimes the disadvantages, of biological children, but who are not biologically related to those whom they consider their family members. Such advantages and disadvantages are various, ranging from the emotional to the financial. In some cases, adoptive parents and children on the early modern stage know that they are in adoptive relationships, while in other cases some parties are unaware of the missing biological connection. Cotgrave's definition also suggests adoption to be a practice in competition with nature itself; although adopted children are not "natural," they are made to seem so.

To describe the biological family as "natural" and the adopted family as "unnatural" is surely perilous. These terms are fraught, to say the least. "Nature" may be defined as "a state unaffected by human intervention; *spec.* (with reference to plants or animals) a wild condition that is not the result of cultivation, breeding, or rearing; (with reference to minerals or land) an uncultivated, unworked, or undeveloped state" (*OED*, P6.c). The etymological root of "nature" is the Latin *natura*, meaning "to be born." "Natural" relates to a "thing or object; something having its basis in the natural world or in the usual course of nature" (*OED*, N.6.a).[7] *Cures for Chance* considers adoption to be a human intervention in the natural world – one that recasts the family from a biological unit in which children are related to their parents by blood to one that is cultivated deliberately and that is not beholden to genetic ties. Discussing agrarian interference in the natural world, Charlotte Scott surmises that cultivation "imposes human patterns of control on an otherwise non-human world" (4). Although the human family is already very much part of the human world, *Cures for Chance* views adoption as a kind of cultivation that implements "human patterns of control" by placing in human hands the ability to choose relations. As Seneca the Elder declares in the *Controversiae* (c. AD 35), adoption is "the cure for chance" because it protects against the fickleness of nature (*Declamations* 1: 222).

Comedies and tragicomedies display varied models for adoption and for the family as the product of human agency. In these plays, heirship and financial considerations often determine how adoptive families are formed. In *A King and No King* by Francis Beaumont and John Fletcher, a childless monarch secretly adopts a boy, Arbaces, as his heir; Arbaces' claim to the throne is later jeopardized when his adoptive origins are revealed. Adoption as a strategy for inheritance is used to comical effect in Ben Jonson's *Volpone*, which involves a competition between fortune-hunting would-be adoptees. Some early modern comedies feature impoverished mothers who deliberately place their infant children with wealthy families for a better chance at social and material success. Such cases may not appear to be straightforward instances of adoption because the adoptive parents do not necessarily know that they are raising someone else's offspring, but the children may nonetheless form strong attachments to their adoptive families. In John Lyly's *Mother Bombie*, children have been inserted surreptitiously into affluent households. When they learn about their birth identities, they are horrified by the idea of reverting to their biological roots: Accius proclaims that he will "not swap [his] father for all this!" (5.3.2169), while Silena asks "do you thinke I'le bee cosned of my father?" (5.3.2170). Concern about loss of economic status is implicit in their protests: the wealthy children do not want to become impoverished. Thomas Middleton's *No Wit, No Help Like a Woman's* portrays an affluent child who is exchanged for a poor one by a cunning wet nurse. Economic considerations also govern Jonson's *The New Inn*, in which the host's adopted son, Frank, is in fact a girl in disguise. Frank's mother places the child in the host's home because she cannot provide care; in a final twist it is revealed that the host is actually Frank's biological father and was therefore never an adoptive parent at all.

Lest it seem that adoption occurs only for economic reasons or to permit the comical confusion of identities, I note that some characters seek urgently to take in children and to raise them as their own. In

Shakespeare's *A Midsummer Night's Dream*, for instance, Oberon and Titania compete for custody of the Indian boy. In *All's Well That Ends Well*, the Countess asks Helena to be both her daughter-in-law and her adoptive daughter. Such characters form public and affectionate bonds with the children whom they wish to adopt. The degree to which emotional ties were established among family members in the early modern period is a topic of long-standing historical debate. Following Philippe Ariès, who argued in *Centuries of Childhood: A Social History of Family Life* (1962) that high rates of infant and child mortality encouraged parents to become emotionally unattached to their offspring, Lawrence Stone suggested in *The Family, Sex and Marriage in England 1500–1800* (1977) that the frequent death of children "made it folly to invest too much emotional capital in such ephemeral beings" (105). Revisionist historians such as Alan Macfarlane, Linda Pollock, Ralph Houlbrooke, and Steven Ozment have since argued against Ariès's and Stone's assertions, emphasizing familial closeness rather than distance through the use of archival evidence such as letters and family papers.[8] Adoption presents a unique case for examining familial affect because adoptive familial bonds are not innate, but are instead typically established deliberately; the practice demonstrates that familial bonds might be based solely on affection rather than on consanguinity. As John Merbecke makes clear in his *Book of Notes and Common Places* (1581), the adoptive bond is primarily emotional: "Men do call children adopted, those which be not naturall children to them which doe choose & accept them for their children: but they are it onelie by the loue & fauour of him which taketh them for his children, & giueth them such right, as he might giue to his naturall children" (15). "Loue & fauour" are substituted for blood. Dramatic examples of adoption afford the opportunity to examine to what degree ties of affection are imagined as being forged between an adopter and an adoptee.

Tragedies often foreground the ostensible weakness of adoptive ties, and show that the desire to adopt is misguided. In *Othello*, Brabantio declares that he would "rather adopt a child than get it" (1.3.190). He seeks to eliminate the uncertainty he perceives in his natural progeny – namely Desdemona, of whose behaviour he does not approve – and to acquire confidence in a family that could be said to be premeditated.[9] Although Brabantio's preference for adoption has classical antecedents and is, in a sense, a venerable position, his desire to disown his innocent daughter is destructive. In Middleton's *The Revenger's Tragedy*, the inability of two families to merge – for characters to accept each other as kin when they have been made related by marriage – leads to death. Whereas in comedies identities that have been obscured by adoption can still be clarified, in tragedies adoption can utterly dissolve identity. Middleton's *Women Beware Women*, for example, stages the result of the disorder and confusion of identity that a perceived adoption can cause. In that play, Isabella's belief that she is adopted and her subsequent alteration of her identity lead her to engage in an incestuous relationship. Generic conventions tend to cause adoption to be portrayed as a practice full of possibility or one that can intensify despair.

Cognates of Adoption in Early Modern England

The regular appearance of adopted characters on stage reflects the omnipresence of adoption-like practices in early modern England. Although there was no legal mechanism for adoption, a culture of adoption outside the law was cultivated, and non-biological, pseudo-familial attachments were forged continuously.[10] Several institutions were related to adoption, and involved the exchange of children between households. The most obvious case is the tradition of service, or "fostering out," in which a child was sent into another household in a position of service or as an apprentice.[11] As Stone observes, "some very fragmentary census data suggest that from just before puberty until they married some ten years later, about two out of every three boys and three out of every four girls were living away from home" (*Family* 107). Children were often put into service in the households of their relations, but they could also be placed with unrelated families of comparable or higher social status. According to Houlbrooke, although for upper-class children "formal education began in or near the home, between ages seven and thirteen they were commonly sent away from home to another household or to board in or near a school of good repute" (150). While an Italian visitor to England in 1551 suggested that fostering out revealed "the want of affection in the English," the practice was not derided by the English themselves (qtd. in Gottlieb 162). Fostering out was a fundamental aspect of the composition of households. Servant-children became part of their receptive families, however temporarily, and moralists argued that they should be treated as such.[12] Alan Bray discusses friendship in early modern England in similar terms, claiming that it sometimes took on the character of kinship. In particular, he posits that "sworn" brotherhood constituted a kind of ritual kinship that transformed friends into symbolic family members (104). In such cases, an oath – a distinctly human expression – created a kinship network that was wider than the strictly biological (214).[13]

Wardship was another well-established tradition, and its royal abuse was a concern for nobility: the underage sons and daughters of deceased noblemen in some cases became wards of the reigning monarch, who could then control their finances and arrange their marriages. There is evidence dating back to the reign of Henry I that wardships and marriages were for sale (Hurstfield 5); a nobleman would have known that "the control of [his heir's] marriage might well pass out of the family and be bought and sold like merchandise" (134). The Court of Wards was established in 1540 to manage the process of wardship, and by Queen Elizabeth's time an increasingly rigid system of oversight was in place. However, as Joel Hurstfield observes, ultimately "the wards were the queen's wards and she alone could dispose of them at her will and pleasure" (90). King James, an advocate of wardship, was petitioned about the practice, but allowed it to continue.[14] As Hurstfield remarks, "there can have been few noble or gentle families whose genealogy does not bear the inescapable marks of one or more feudal wardships" (145).

Wet-nursing likewise removed children from the family home, although for a considerably shorter time. Despite warnings from doctors who opposed the practice on the grounds of the babies' health, and despite the opposition of the Church, wealthy women sent children to the homes of hired nurses for twelve to eighteen months in order to relieve themselves of the burden of breastfeeding.[15] It was feared that wet nurses could pass on their own characteristics through their milk to suckling children.[16] Breastmilk was believed to be made of blood and was therefore thought to shape and influence the infant who ingested it. In *Child-Birth or, The Happy Delivery of Women* (1612), Jacques Guillemeau wrote that "it were fit that every mother should nurse her owne child: because her milke which is nothing else, but the bloud whitened (of which he was made, and wherewith hee had beene nourished the time hee staide in his Mothers wombe) will bee always more naturall, and familiar unto him, than that of a stranger" (1). Raised for a time by their milk mothers, children were, in effect, temporarily adopted into the households of influential "strangers."[17] As Valerie Fildes observes, "any discussion of infant and child care" in the period "must include the important role of surrogate mother which was played by wet-nurses during the impressionable years of early infancy" ("English" 169).[18]

Despite medical and religious objections, wet-nursing was sometimes necessary, and some saw it as a kind of communal obligation in cases of special need. The clergyman and natural historian Edward Topsell believed that "every woman being in health of bodie and minde, is bound by the word of God to nurse her owne children" (*Reward* 301). However, he also allowed that "in causes of weakenesse in the woman, danger to the child, or sicknesse in either of both, it is not only a dutie of necessitie, but of conscience, to nourish and cherish the children of other" (303). The fates of orphaned and abandoned infants depended on wet nurses who were not likely working out of a "dutie of ... conscience," but who nonetheless formed the front line of a system of temporary, informal adoption overseen by individual parishes.[19] Such children were sent out to nurse at the expense of the parish and were typically given as a surname the name of the parish in which they were abandoned – for example, "Thomas Staneing a nurs childe of the parish of Saint Mary Staneing in London" (qtd. in Fildes, "English" 152). In the burial records of orphans and foundlings who did not survive infancy, the names of wet nurses are often mentioned, as in an example from the parish of St. Botolph without Aldgate: "Marie a chylde that was founde in the streete beyond the widowe carltons Dore in the high waye neare a Dunghill whose father and mother was not knowne beinge nursed by henrie Mawkenews wyfe in Barnarde Alye" (qtd. in Forbes 192).[20] Once parentless children had been weaned, their home parish also paid for foster care until they were old enough to work or to be apprenticed.[21] The quality and length of such care, however, appear to have been varied and uncertain.

In addition to the support provided by parishes, there were institutional measures in place to care for orphaned and abandoned infants that also mimicked adoption. Christ's Hospital in London was founded in 1552 to house homeless children. The hospital sent out infants to be suckled in both London and the country, many of whom are noted in parish burial records as being "a nurse child, foundling from the hospital," or "a nurse child from the Hospital" (qtd. in Fildes, "English" 148).[22] These foundlings were frequently breastfed alongside the children of wealthy Londoners by wet nurses who took in any charges that they could find (152).[23] The hospital was limited in its capacity for care, however, and eventually became an educational institution that accepted only older children.[24] The London Foundling Hospital was established in 1739 as a direct response to the number of abandoned babies and children in London, many of whom were left to die in the city's streets.[25]

The Adoptive Family and Human Agency

The elasticity of the family structure captured the imagination of early modern playwrights, who depicted on stage a wide range of familial formations. *Cures for Chance* shows how early modern English theatre envisioned a world of dynamic familial relations. Dramatists questioned the inevitability of the biological family and proposed new models of familial structure, financial inheritance, and gendered familial authority. My study elucidates ways in which adoptive relationships were defined, described, and envisioned on stage. In the plays with which I am concerned, families and individual characters create, alter, and manage familial relationships. My interpretation of the plays focuses on the human capacity to change the natural world. I examine the public performance of relations that alternately bind characters together and hold them apart. Understanding adoption and its portrayal illuminates aspects of the complex history of artistic attempts to comprehend individual identity in the social world. My overarching argument is that dramatic representations of adoption test conventional notions of the family by rendering the family unit a social construction rather than a biological certainty, and that in so doing, they evoke the alteration of nature by human hands that was already pervasive in the early modern period. Playwrights conceptualized the manufactured family; the plays in question express the fantastic possibilities, as well as the dangers, of understanding familial relation in non-biological terms.

Cures for Chance attends to families and to the ways in which their composition might be understood according to what Lawrence Buell terms "the environmental imagination" (1). Situating family studies alongside studies of the environment in literature, I demonstrate that, like the natural world, bloodlines can to some extent be bent to human will. While feminist literary criticism has often viewed the domestic sphere as a realm of patriarchal oppression and confinement for women, I emphasize the agency of women in, and the transgressive potential of, adoptive relationships. Building on Wendy Wall's efforts in *Staging Domesticity* to "rescue domesticity from being the sordid spot of retrograde values that feminists sometimes take it to be" (9), I show that dramatic plots involving adoption often figure domestic space as a site of opportunity in which characters can make and remake their worlds. Early modern intersections of nature and culture have not yet been fully explored. Because adoption circumvents reproduction, the portrayal of adoption obliges audiences to reconsider ideas of nature and kinship. Adoptive relationships also bear upon the understanding of the human capacity to intervene in the natural world and can provide insight into the period's interest in the relation between art and nature. *Cures for Chance* thus aligns a consideration of the disruptive force of the modification of the domestic sphere with ideas about the human modification of nature.

Marianne Novy's analysis of adoption and multiple-parent families in Shakespeare's romances is the most notable exception to the rule that little attention has been paid to the representation of adoption in early modern literature.[26] My own study, which draws on her insights, extends Novy's analysis by examining more broadly the cultural and literary significance of adoption as practice and trope. Because, as I have noted, adoption was neither illegal nor formally sanctioned, it has proven resistant to systematic investigation. To an extent, early modern adoption has been explored in studies of literary apprentices, wards, foundlings, bastards, and changelings, but whereas the emphasis in such studies often lies on birth families, or families from which such characters were separated, my focus rests on the taking in of children by non-biological parents – the incorporation of children into new families and the concomitant reconstitution of the family.[27]

Shakespeare and Middleton portray the unstable family in especially vivid ways; I have chosen to examine the composition of the family in selected works by these playwrights. Both concentrate on human control of nature, reproduction, and familial relation, but their treatments of such themes differ in notable ways. My examples from Shakespeare depict the introduction into families of abandoned, kidnapped, distressed, or orphaned children, and compare adoption to practices that alter and adapt nature. Shakespeare's plays often view adoption as it was seen in the classical world. Middleton's representations of adoption, in contrast, deal typically with issues of reproduction and are based in cuckoldry and bastardy, or in fictional genealogies. He stages, for instance, the makeshift composition of the family in a corrupted urban environment. Middleton also focuses on the economic and linguistic repercussions of altered familial relationships. His plays offer a more cynical perspective on familial formation, one that does not necessarily champion the modification of nature and that is more characteristic of the Jacobean period.

In what remains of this introduction, I examine early modern political and religious influences on adoption, as well as classical antecedents of the practice. I then provide historical examples of adoption in England. I conclude by suggesting metaphorical affinities between adoption and literary production. Then, in chapters 1 and 2, I investigate Shakespeare's treatment of adoption in relation to the natural world. Shakespeare looks to the plant and animal worlds for examples of adoption, or for models of parenting and familial formation. First, a chapter on Shakespeare's use of the grafting metaphor in three plays – *The Winter's Tale*, *Cymbeline*, and *All's Well That Ends Well* – further examines literary examples of the previously overlooked cultural importance of horticultural metaphors of adoption. It explores ways in which early modern culture explained adoption by depicting it in figurative language. Shakespeare uses the established early modern lexicon of grafting to consider issues of belonging and biological inheritance. Chapter 2 shows how in *Titus Andronicus* the natural world – the world seemingly beyond culture – offers models of the family for humans. I concentrate on Lavinia's statement that "ravens foster forlorn children" (2.2.153). Lavinia uses this element of folklore to beseech Tamora to assume the role of the compassionate but fickle raven by disregarding her sons and taking pity on her. In the Roman setting of the play, fosterage and adoption have particular resonances such that Lavinia's request is especially potent. The chapter demonstrates how the play associates proper Roman conduct and virtue with adoptive practices, and uses animals as images of such proper conduct. I examine Roman adoption, as well as classical, biblical, and early modern narratives about the adoption of humans by animals. In chapters 3 and 4, I explore Middleton's interest in the surreptitious alteration of familial bonds. To a far greater degree than Shakespeare, Middleton is concerned with the economic and social consequences of interfering with bloodlines. Chapter 3 focuses on infertility in *A Chaste Maid in Cheapside*, and on the practice of adoption as a strategy for navigating the social world. The cynical outlook on the manipulation of nature in *A Chaste Maid in Cheapside* differs from the tone and mode of Shakespeare's comedies and romances. In the satire of Middleton's city comedy, familial constitution and social convention are decoupled: the play suggests that the dense and populous city provides an abundance of opportunity for illicit behaviour. The urban environment allows characters to violate social expectation by disentangling parenthood and reproduction. Their behaviour is typically debased, their goals ignoble. The play ultimately proposes that paternity can be divorced from biology in the interest of economic constancy. As a result, Middleton exposes potential ruptures in the family and undermines the stability and permanence of genealogy. Finally, in chapter 4, I investigate familial relation as a source of linguistic power in *Women Beware Women*. Strategies of what Erasmus in 1522 termed "adoptive" naming offer female characters, in particular, the chance to transcend their perceived familial roles (57). These strategies also, however, permit an incestuous union between two characters who initially believe themselves related. The play therefore emphasizes the linguistic constitution of kinship and its ability to grant particular speakers linguistic authority. *Women Beware Women* also posits the destruction of idealized, biological kinship as an act of power. Livia's lie about Isabella's origins prompts Isabella to refashion her life.

The Spirit of Adoption

In early modern England, family life was in many ways characterized by adoption, but the concept of adoption was understood according to prevalent political and theological metaphors. Facing a succession crisis in which she was expected to produce a biological heir, Queen Elizabeth styled herself as an adoptive mother. During her first Parliament in 1559, the Speaker of the House of Commons urged the queen "by Marriage [to] bring forth Children, Heirs both of their Mother's Vertue and Empire" (qtd. in Coch 423). In response, Elizabeth envisioned herself as the parent of her people; she replied that she was content for the time being to be "a good mother of my Contreye" (qtd. in Coch 423).[28] In 1563, she assured her subjects that "though after my death you may have many stepdames, yet shall you never have any a more mother, than I meane to be unto you all" (Marcus et al. 72). Although Elizabeth was not the first female monarch to suggest that she was an adoptive mother to her kingdom, she used the metaphor to deflect attention from her lack of biological children.[29]

Elizabeth's metaphors of adoption complemented and perhaps derived from the Christian tradition; the term *adoption* is used in the Bible to refer to spiritual adoption, or the taking in of believers by God. The Book of Romans asserts the eternal adoptive relationship between God and humankind:

> For as many as are led by the Spirit of God, they are the sons of God.
>
> For ye have not received the spirit of bondage again to fear; but ye have received the Spirit of adoption, whereby we cry, Abba, Father.
>
> The Spirit itself beareth witness with our spirit, that we are the children of God:
>
> And if children, then heirs; heirs of God, and joint-heirs with Christ, if so be that we suffer with *him*, that we may be also glorified together. (8.14–17)[30]

The "Spirit of adoption" establishes a filial relationship to God. Such a bond replicates the paternal-filial bond between God and his son Jesus Christ, and makes humankind his "joint-heirs." In the Book of Galatians, Christ himself is figured as an agent of adoption sent to bring his followers into a familial relationship with God:

> But when the fullness of the time was come, God sent forth his Son, made of a woman, made under the law,
>
> To redeem them that were under the law, that we might receive the adoption of sons.
>
> And because ye are sons, God hath sent forth the Spirit of his Son into your hearts, crying, Abba, Father.
>
> Wherefore thou art no more a servant, but a son; and if a son, then an heir of God through Christ. (4.4–7)

God has sent his son so that Christ's followers understand what it means to be children of God. Adoption is transformative: once a servant, the believer becomes a son and heir, inheriting the same share of God's love as Christ. Spiritual adoption creates a sibling relationship among all of the faithful, and between them and Christ; through adoption, all Christians become part of a single family. Spiritual adoption notionally diminishes the mortal emphasis on earthly blood relations.[31]

That early modern writers likewise described relations to God in adoptive terms suggests the widespread understanding of Christian faith as a process of adoption. Observing that "God adopteth vnto himselfe his elect," Merbecke declares that God adopted man not because he "had not an other sonne (for he had his onlie begotten sonne Christ in whom he was well pleased)," but because he did not have other children: "for through *Adam* we were all made strangers vnto him" (15). According to Merbecke, God sent "his naturall and legitimate sonne" into the world so that he could "adopt vnto himselfe, manie children out of our kinde" (15). Spiritual adoption here involves the creation of an extended family and the combination of utterly distinct entities. Adam's banishment from Eden marked humans as dissimilar in kind from God and Christ; God's adoption of believers implies conversely that two kinds can be joined in communion. Pamphlets such as Thomas Granger's *A Looking-Glasse for Christians* – with the lengthy subtitle *or, The Comfortable Doctrine of Adoption Wherein Euery True Beleeuer May Behold his Blessed Estate in the Kingdome of Grace* (1620) – suggest that authentic familial connections can be formed by adoption. Granger states that God gives his followers "the spirit of sonnes, by whom we call him (abba) Father, euen as naturall sonnes doe their parents" (B4). Echoing the Book of Galatians, Granger describes spiritual adoption as freedom from slavery: once adopted, "the seruant or bondman ... liueth no longer to his former Masters, but to his Adopter, not in seruitude, but in freedome, not in slauish, but in son-like feare, *viz.* awfull reuerence and loue" (B2). In his estimation, the Christian adoptive bond occasions genuine familial feeling; the adoptee escapes bondage and is instead subject to the bonds of familial affection. Queen Elizabeth similarly uses the rhetoric of adoption to describe herself as belonging to God's family:

> O Lord, my God and my Father, I render undying thanks unto Thy divine Majesty with my mouth, with my heart, and with all that I am, for the infinite mercies which Thou hast used toward me – that not only hast made me Thy creature, made me by Thy hands to be formed in Thy image and similitude; and hast by the death and passion of Thy only Son Jesus Christ reconciled me with Thee, adopted me, and made me Thy daughter, sister of Jesus Christ Thy firstborn and of all those who believe in Thee. (Marcus et al. 156–7)

Because of her likeness to God and because of Christ's sacrifice, she becomes not only God's adopted daughter but also the sister of Christ and all believers. In her own formulation, adoption makes her God's second child after the "firstborn" Christ.

Why, given the prevalence of Christian rhetoric of adoption, was formal adoption not encouraged in early modern England? Jack Goody argues in *The Development of the Family and Marriage in Europe* (1983) that the medieval Church disallowed, primarily for economic reasons, the adoption of heirs.[32] Goody observes that in the fourth century the Church began a massive effort to increase donations and bequests. Christians were encouraged to leave their land and assets to the Church rather than to their children, and the Church advocated the condition of heirlessness (99).[33] By discouraging practices, including adoption, that allowed childless couples to designate heirs, the Church ensured that it would receive the possessions of its childless members upon their deaths. It espoused a view of the family as a unit based on "'natural' kinship, on 'blood' relationships, on 'consanguinity,'" and one "created by the union (*copulatio*) of men and women, that is, by a physical act" (101). If wealth was to be circulated within the family, it had to be passed from parents to children; "heirs who were not 'of the body'" were disallowed (101).[34] Adoption was an unacceptable strategy for the transmission of capital.

One of the pioneers of such thinking was Salvian, a fifth-century Gaulish writer intent on comprehending the fall of the Roman Empire as God's punishment of man. In the third of *The Four Books of Timothy to the Church*, he insists upon the religious implications of inheritance. Salvian states that he understands why parents might want to leave a portion of their wealth to their children, "provided they are good and holy" (321). Even parents who bequeath something to "evil and corrupt" children may be partially excused for neglecting the Church, given that they often cite "parental love," "the ties of blood," and the authority of "nature itself" as reasons why they must provide for their offspring (321). But in Salvian's estimation, those who prioritize earthly inheritance cannot ultimately be saved because their behaviour demonstrates that they value their children above God (321). He reserves special scorn for the childless who acquire heirs deliberately. Those who "seek out others to whom they bequeath the substance of their own wealth" are "wretched and most unholy people" (322). In finding unrelated benefactors, "they ascribe to them some faint title to blood relationship. The nominal parents make them as their adopted sons, so that the offspring of perjury takes the place of those offspring who are non-existent" (322). Adoptees, according to Salvian, are the children of lies who fill a void unnecessarily.

But adoption, of course, still took place in various forms. Kristin Gager suggests that the concept of spiritual adoption may have encouraged the practice of adoption in early modern France: she proposes that "the Christian theology of 'adoption through baptism' might very well have aided in sustaining adoption traditions for families interested in having a non-natal child to stand as their heir" (69). The notion of adoption was common even if it was not legally enshrined, and in France as in England, adoption could be translated from the world of the Church to everyday life. Gager finds evidence of several informal adoption contracts drawn up for inheritance purposes in early modern France (1–35). A lack of records, however, renders adoptive practices in England largely invisible.[35] As John Boswell observes, adoption continued to be doctrinally significant but somewhat covert in its social expression: "As a theological idea [adoption] remained an important element of Western religious thought ... but almost no one in medieval Europe idealized it as a social reality. Neither parent nor child wished to acknowledge that a family relationship was not biological" (431). If an adoption took place, it did so quietly and nearly imperceptibly; adoptive parents "almost invariably pretended the child was a biological heir" (431).

The diminished and secretive status of adoption in the early modern period is surprising not only because of the importance of adoption in the Christian tradition, but also because of the social importance of adoption in ancient Rome, where it took place in everyday life. Romans appear to have cared little about the role that nature played in forming the family, and yet they were also concerned with imitating, to a point, normative generative processes; adoption was recognized as an equivalent means by which to create a family, so long as cases met certain criteria. According to the *Institutes* (AD 161), Roman civil law enshrined the principle that adoption should mimic natural reproduction insofar as possible (Peppard 54). Most Roman adoptees were adults. There was, however, a required gap of eighteen years between adopter and adoptee such that it was at least plausible that the parent-child relationship might have existed naturally (Lindsay 218). Cicero, disgusted by a case of politically motivated adoption in which the adopter was younger than the adoptee, commented that the adoption "set nature at defiance" (qtd. in Huard 745).[36]

Roman adoption followed two distinct legal procedures: *adrogatio* and *adoptio*. *Adrogatio* involved the adoption of a legally independent, or *sui iuris*, person. The adoptee voluntarily submitted to the *patria potestas* of the man who became his non-biological father. *Adrogatio* legally terminated the adoptee's relation to his natal family. The practice was public:

it required "the authority of the people" as expressed through a mandatory inquiry by the college of pontiffs into the admissibility of the adoption (Gardner, *Family* 126–30).[37] A sanctioned adoption ensured that the adoptee was considered the equivalent of a *filius familias*, or a son under paternal power, conceived in a lawful marriage.[38] Conversely, private adoption, or *adoptio*, was conducted before a magistrate and involved the adoption of a person who was still *in potestate parentis*, or under the authority and legal control of the biological parent. The child was given in *adoptio* by the *paterfamilias*, the highest-ranking male family member, and was taken up as a *filius familias* by his new, adoptive family.[39]

Roman adoption took place primarily for practical reasons. As Jane F. Gardner notes, its initial purpose appears to have been to allow people without heirs of their own (*sui herdes*) to acquire an inheritor of their patrimony (*Family* 202). Adoption compensated for childlessness. Roman citizens with biological children were not forbidden to adopt, but most adoptions seem to have been undertaken by those without children to ensure familial continuity (202).[40] Boswell observes that "social critics from Isaeus (fourth century B.C.) to Seneca commented on the fact that the rich could not lack heirs, since they could buy them if they failed to beget any" (115).[41] The adoption of family members, whether close or distant, was far more common than the adoption into families of outsiders (Dixon 112). In addition to securing the transfer of property and the preservation of lineage, adoption in imperial Rome could be politically motivated. Julius Caesar, for instance, adopted Octavian as his heir (44 BC). Octavian then adopted Tiberius, who became emperor upon his death in AD 14. Similarly, Nerva adopted Trajan (AD 97) who then adopted Hadrian (AD 117) (Lindsay 209). Such adoptions within the imperial family were often publicized and celebrated with the issue of a new coinage.[42] Portraits and commemorative statues also guaranteed that knowledge of the family status of these new heirs was widespread (Peppard 69).

Adoptive Families in Early Modern England

If the rule was that adoption in early modern England took place quietly, there were of course exceptions. Sir Thomas More is perhaps the most famous adoptive father of the time. He took in an infant girl named Margaret Giggs, whom he treated publicly as his own child although it was widely known that she was not biologically related to him.[43] Giggs and Margaret More, More's eldest child, were born within a short time of one another and were both nursed by Giggs's mother, who was a neighbour of the Mores (Guy 15). When Mistress Giggs died not long after Margaret More was weaned, Thomas More decided to adopt Margaret Giggs because her father could not care for her on his own (Guy 15). In letters quoted by his sixteenth-century biographer Thomas Stapleton, More, writing in the third person, addresses his correspondence "to his dearest children and to Margaret Giggs, whom he numbers amongst his own" (qtd. in Guy 98), and "to Margaret, Elizabeth, Cecily his dearest daughters, and to Margaret Giggs as dear as though she were a daughter" (qtd. in Guy 100). Although More distinguishes Margaret from his biological children, he considers her to be part of his family. She appears in the More family portrait painted by Hans Holbein the Younger in 1527, and was the only family member to attend More's execution.[44] In Holbein's preparatory sketch for the portrait, Giggs is described as "cognata," or as a relation by blood to the Mores (RCIN 659104). More also had a stepdaughter, Alice, and took in two other children through formal wardship procedures, both of whom eventually married his biological children.[45] In *Utopia* (1516), More envisions an ideal society in which adoption was practised regularly. For instance, male children whose professional interests did not align with those of their biological fathers could be adopted: "Ordinarily the son is trained to his father's craft, for which most feel a natural inclination. But if anyone is attracted to another occupation, he is transferred by adoption into a family practising that trade" (52). In both his own life and in his fictional ideal world, More imagined the family as mutable.

Relatively high death rates meant that many children, like Margaret Giggs, were orphaned or were left without a sustainable living arrangement. They were lucky if their parents had made plans to have them adopted by a friend or relative. The alderman William Carre of Newcastle is an illustrative example. In his will of 1572, he gave instructions for the adoption of his six children by members of his extended family. He stated that his father should raise one of his sons, his mother one of his daughters, and his brother, aunt, nephew, and son-in-law one other child each. The adoptive parents were "to bring [the children] up in the faithe and feare of god. And as there owne to whome I will gyve them as frelye as god haith sente or geaven them to me" (qtd. in Raine 381). In Carre's terms, his children are like gifts to be exchanged between family members; they are not bound to Carre and his wife alone.

Childless couples sometimes adopted distant relatives to acquire heirs, despite the Church's position on the practice. Such heirs might be expected to carry on the family business. For example, Thomas and Lucretia East adopted Lucretia's orphaned nephew Thomas Snodham and employed him as an apprentice so that he could carry on their music publishing business. Thomas East had many apprentices over the course of his career – including the playwright Henry Chetle – but he does not seem to have considered any of them to be adopted sons in the way that he did Snodham: Snodham is identified in East's will as his adopted son rather than as his nephew (J. Smith 15, 9).[46] East bequeathed the business and his property to his wife with the provision that it would pass to Snodham after her death. His will also stipulated that in the meantime, Snodham should have full control of the business (J. Smith 123–4).[47] Snodham eventually became an important printer of music and plays, including the first edition of Ben Jonson's *The Alchemist* (1612).

Children were also at times placed for adoption for economic reasons, even if they were from families of relatively high social standing. Jane and Dorothea Helena Rupa, the daughters of the financially troubled Bohemian Baron Rupa, were adopted by the English diplomat Sir Thomas Roe (1581–1644) and his wife Eleanor, who did not have biological children (M. Brown 166). As Roe's biographer notes, the adoption appears to have been relatively temporary since the girls kept the last name of Rupa and only lived with the Roes for five years (Brown 276). Both girls left England to serve as ladies-in-waiting to Elizabeth Stuart, Queen of Bohemia. But it is clear that the Roes became "very attached" to their adoptive children (276). In letters to Thomas, Elizabeth provided the adoptive father with details of the well-being of his girls and referred to them variously as "your daughter" and "your daughter Rupa" (Akkerman 771, 944). She clearly considered the girls to be the children of the Roes, although she was aware of the circumstances of their adoption.[48]

Adoption, Fiction, and the Theatre

In "A Gratulatory to Master Ben Johnson, for His Adopting of Him to Be His Son" (c. 1630), Thomas Randolph thanks the famous poet and playwright for assuming the role of his literary father. Randolph had apparently been selected by Jonson to be one of the "sons" making up the Tribe of Ben, the group of writers who considered themselves akin to Jonson in ability and style.[49] The adoption, according to Randolph, established him as the beneficiary of Jonson's poetic legacy:[50]

I WAS not born to Helicon, nor dare
Presume to think myself a Muse's heir.
I have no title to Parnassus Hill
Nor any acre of it by the will
Of a dead ancestor, nor could I be

Ought but a tenant unto poetry.
But thy adoption quits me of all fear,
And makes me challenge a child's portion there.
I am akin to heroes, being thine,
And part of my alliance is divine,
Orpheus, Musæus, Homer too, beside
Thy brothers by the Roman mother's side;
As Ovid, Virgil, and the Latin lyre,
That is so like thee, Horace; the whole quire
Of poets are, by thy adoption, all
My uncles; thou hast given me power to call
Phoebus himself my grandsire; by this grant
Each sister of the Nine is made my aunt. (ll. 1–18)

The practice of adoption affords Randolph (and, by extension, Jonson) a model for conceptualizing poetic influence. Jonson's creation of a literary family – and his role as a progenitor of poets – ensures that he will have literary successors whose talents are imagined to be derived from those of the great writers of the past as well as his own. Randolph had no previous claim to Mounts Helicon or Parnassus, classical sites of poetic inspiration. However, through his newly established relation to Jonson, whom he believes belongs legitimately to the "family" of authors that includes Horace, Homer, and Virgil, he becomes part of a literary genealogy that includes even the gods of antiquity. The adoption grants Randolph an imaginative network of relatives upon whose authority his own poetry can stand. With the newfound "power to call" Phoebus his grandfather and the muses his aunts, he can reshape his artistic identity. In accounting for the transmission of artistic inspiration and aptitude, Randolph also elucidates a facet of adoption that was esteemed by classical authors in particular: adoptive families are composed deliberately and therefore rely on choice rather than biology. As Randolph proclaims later in the poem, he is the "son of [Jonson's] adoption, not his lust" (l. 30).[51] Randolph's adoption is literary in two senses: he is both an author who will now write in the style of Jonson, and someone who has been written into Jonson's family line.

The prevalence of adopted characters in early modern drama perhaps owes something to the literary and theatrical qualities of the practice itself. The fact that children can be chosen rather than born into a family underscores adoption's close association with fiction and drama.[52] Adoptees and their families act out relations that are presumed to be innate; that is, like players on the stage they perform the roles of parents, children, and siblings when those roles are not dictated by biology.[53] Adoption's theatrical nature meant that it was frequently viewed as a form of familial relation that could not produce the equivalent of biological offspring. William Clerke, for instance, maintained in *The Triall of Bastardie* (1594) that adopted children could not be considered legitimate because they were artificial. Adoptees were only "a bare immitation of nature," Clerke stated, and there was no place for them in England (39). On the early modern stage, however, adoption's imitative quality, like the theatre itself, presents the opportunity to envision the formation and transformation of identity.[54] As Barbara Diefendorf observes with a nod to Stephen Greenblatt, the family is of "profound importance ... as an element in and context for 'Renaissance self-fashioning'" (668). The adoptive family allows for an even greater negotiation of familial identity that accounts for tensions between a character's individuality, his or her ties to a birth family, and his or her merging with an adoptive family. The theatrical adoptee poses a challenge to the seemingly fixed nature of lineage-based identity; the suppleness of adoptive familial bonds is then a reminder of the transformative nature of theatre itself.

In accounting for individual and familial identity, *Cures for Chance* contemplates how adoption shapes social life. Considering the family as the product of human intervention rather than as only the result of biology, it shows how social relations are managed and sustained. The plays in question, which present a range of potential responses to adoption and varied discourses of familial relation, have in common an insistence on the human resolve to shape environments.

Chapter One

Shakespeare's Adopted Children and the Language of Horticulture

… enfans, qui comme tendres plantes enracinées en un jardin, sont contraintes de tirer aliment du suc qui s'y présente.

… unborn children, who like tender plants rooted in a garden, are forced to extract nourishment from the sap that comes to them.

Jacques Duval, 1612[1]

In Shakespeare's *All's Well That Ends Well*, the Countess takes Helena into her care after Helena's father dies. The Countess then announces her connection to her newly adopted ward. Blurring the boundaries of biological and adoptive parent-child relations, the Countess informs Helena that she is her mother, although the audience knows that she is not her biological parent: the Countess places the girl "in the catalogue of those / That were enwombed mine," or those who were contained in her womb, thus identifying Helena as the equivalent of a birth child (1.3.138–9).[2] But as she attempts to describe their attachment further, the Countess begins to speak in the language of horticulture instead of the language of the womb. In trying to persuade Helena of their closeness, the Countess states that "'tis often seen / Adoption strives with nature, and choice breeds / A native slip to us from foreign seeds" (139–40). She uses a botanical metaphor to express to Helena the artificial familial bond that she understands to exist between them. By creating a mixed family that blends together, adoption, the Countess suggests, works in much the same way as the art of grafting. Just as a gardener grafts a slip, or a scion, to a stock that is not its own, adoption joins a child to a new family. In her remark to Helena, the Countess also emphasizes the power of choice in adoption, insisting that foster parents choose their adopted children rather than give birth to them naturally. In fact, by selecting Helena, the Countess competes with nature and proposes alternative ways of understanding relations between parents and children.

It is these artificial familial bonds and the horticultural lexicon with which Shakespeare describes them that I examine here. As an example of the ways in which early modern gardeners manipulated the natural world, the practice of grafting collapses any rigid distinction between nature and culture. It serves in *The Winter's Tale*, *Cymbeline*, and *All's Well That Ends Well* as a metaphor for the splicing of families, in which a child belonging genetically to one family is adopted by another. The plays therefore align the creation of families of mixed biological origin with this then-novel modification of nature. The grafting metaphor suggests within the context of the plays that legitimate families might be synthetically produced, or based on non-biological ties. But *The Winter's Tale* and *Cymbeline*, both romances, treat adoption somewhat differently than *All's Well That Ends Well*, a comedy.

Shakespeare refers to grafting in several plays. For instance, the vexed Queen in *Richard II* prays that the gardener's grafted plants will never grow (3.4.101); King Henry in *Henry IV, Part 1* imagines young Hal as grafted to the "rude society" with which he associates (3.2.11–17); and Buckingham in *Richard III* envisions a polluted England's "royal stock graft with ignoble plants" (3.7.126). In these examples, all drawn from history plays, grafting is a metaphor for social decay and political corruption; grafting clearly suggests harm to the nation. The gardening technique receives its most detailed and constructive treatment, in contrast, in romances and comedies that involve adopted children.[3] In *The Winter's Tale*, Perdita is aligned ironically with the grafted gillyvors that she so despises because she is herself a "grafted" child: she is fostered by the shepherd after she is abandoned and is therefore attached to a familial stock that is not biologically her own (4.4.79–108). Similarly, *Cymbeline* uses as its principal metaphor the re-grafting of missing, adopted children – described on the tablet that Jupiter leaves for Posthumus as "lopped branches" – onto their biological "old stock" (5.3.204–5). However, Shakespeare's use of the grafting metaphor for adoption in *All's Well* is a distinct case. The play does not involve a lost, stolen, or abandoned child of mistaken identity who is cultivated by a family poorer than its own, but instead concerns an orphaned young woman who is openly adopted by someone of higher station. The Countess describes herself as a grafter in order to express her desire to create a blended family. The play consequently invites its audience to consider whether Helena's figurative graft will be successful, and, in so doing, questions early modern assumptions about the formation of families.

The homological thinking that structures Shakespeare's rhetoric of adoption compares human life to plant life. The particular comparison of human reproduction and botanical reproduction is not unique to Shakespeare, but rather has its origins in classical literature and the Bible, in which horticultural metaphors often describe human propagation. Shakespeare's own understanding of grafting likely derives from these antecedents, as well as from the abundance of horticultural pamphlets published in the early modern period. By using the metaphor of grafting to describe unconventional familial formation, Shakespeare both casts adoption in recognizable terms and imbues it with the sense of advancement and experimentation that accompanied the horticultural practice; the metaphor connects a child to the novelty and possibility that the grafting of plants connoted. An adopted, grafted child straddles two worlds – that of nature and that of artifice – and its identity is not clearly fixed but mutable. Shakespeare's use of these metaphors introduces into a shifting cultural and social milieu the prospect of new modes of generative possibility – modes that enhance, and perhaps also potentially destabilize, the biological order. Grafting was an augmentation of nature that both mimicked natural creation and threatened the integrity of the natural order. At once full of ambitious promise and dangerously subversive, this horticultural technique allows us to understand how alternative practices of human reproduction were simultaneously necessary and profoundly alarming.

In this chapter, I first examine early modern attitudes towards grafting, noting what horticulturalists held to be its principal tenets. I then consider the classical origins of grafting, the eventual extension of the practice into metaphorical use, and the potential to forge bonds between people that the metaphor represents. Shakespeare's use of the grafting metaphor for adoption, I contend, is part of a long tradition of describing the family in arboreal terms. *The Winter's Tale*, *Cymbeline*, and *All's Well* envision the possible additions and substitutions that adoption might make to a family tree, although each play differs in its evaluation of the success of an adoptive bond. While the two romances – which each feature children who have both adoptive and biological sets of parents to contend with – do not determine whether adoption fails or succeeds, *All's Well*, a comedy, depicts the successful grafting of an orphaned child into a new family. It is perhaps, then, the very nature of the romance genre – with its convention of birth families lost and rediscovered – that prevents Shakespeare from portraying the definitive grafting of a child onto an adoptive stock in *The Winter's Tale* and *Cymbeline*.

Grafting signifies a type of propagation that exists apart from "natural" proliferation.[4] Shakespeare uses grafting to displace and question forms of biological reproduction. Adoption, described through the metaphor of grafting, negates the need to create genealogical children. As a substitute for biological reproduction, the plays instead employ a kind of procreative writing: children are incorporated into their adopted families by being grafted, or written, into them.[5] While *The Winter's Tale* and *Cymbeline* depict fathers as grafters, *All's Well* presents women as horticulturalists. By linking botanical propagation to human familial formation and female gardeners, the play ultimately rejects a heteronormative model of procreation, despite the fact that children in the early modern period could not, of course, be created in any other way. Both the Countess and Helena employ the grafting metaphor, placing the power of alternative familial generation in female hands. Helena is not only an adopted daughter but also eventually a wife who joins herself to a new familial stock; the horticultural image of the graft illuminates her marital and adoptive attachments alike. Emotional, adoptive attachment in *All's Well* ultimately acts as a substitute for blood. Children in the play are not required, as this chapter's epigraph suggests, "to extract nourishment from the sap that comes to them" in their mother's wombs; instead, they might take their sustenance elsewhere.

"Diverse Colours, and Diverse Savours": Early Modern Grafting

The comparison of adoption to grafting hinges on the fact that both practices mimic biological creation. That is, they both imitate and intervene in what is seen to be a natural process. In its most basic form, grafting involves the insertion of a scion from one plant into the stock, or stem, of another. In order to graft scion to stock, the base of the scion must be trimmed to a quill-like point and a slit must be created for it in the receptive plant. The insertion of the scion into the stock allows for the circulation of fluid and nutrients between the two plants and ensures that the scion is fed by its host. Connected by the gardener's skill and a ligature, or tie, the two plants gradually merge and grow together. Grafting is an asexual form of reproduction, meaning that the part of the plant that grows as a result of the graft is not a cross between scion and stock, but is rather the scion itself, kept alive by its new base. The created plant is an amalgamation, wherein elements of two distinct plants consist in a new, singular form. But in order for a successful graft to take place, the joined plants must be closely related. A slip from a citrus tree cannot, for instance, be joined to the stock of a chestnut tree, but slips from a variety of citrus fruit trees might be grafted onto the stock of a lemon tree.

Leonard Mascall complains in *A Booke of the Art and maner, howe to plant and graffe all sortes of trees* (1572) that the English were slow to take up the horticultural arts already flourishing in France and Italy (A3v–A4r). Medieval Continental Europeans showed enthusiasm for the grafting of intricate and unlikely trees. Although gardeners were often aware that the joining of disparate types of trees might not always result in successful grafts, they attempted these horticultural feats nonetheless. For instance, Petrus de Crescentiis, an Italian agriculturalist writing around 1305, noted that it is "a great beauty and pleasure to have in one's garden trees variously and marvelously grafted, and many different fruit growing on a single tree" (qtd. in Thacker 85). Horticultural guides such as the French *Ménagerier de Paris* (1393) taught readers how to graft their own marvels, allowing them to create "grapes without pips," for example, by slitting a stock in the moonlight (qtd. in Thacker 85). Although grafting in England can be dated to the medieval period,[6] the practice did not become popular until the fifteenth and sixteenth centuries, when there was new interest in the cultivation of fruit trees (Henrey 1: 55). As England became progressively more affluent, high-quality dessert fruit – introduced through trade with horticulturally advanced countries on the Continent – came into demand (Webber 29). Apples and pears had long been grown in England for the production of cider and perry, but gustatory fruit – the varieties of sweet, flavourful apples and pears that we recognize today – was not widely available. Rather than import fruit from the Continent at great expense, the aristocracy introduced foreign, superior grafts to existing trees (Webber 29). Henry VIII later encouraged the commercial production of fine fruit and hired Richard Harris, a fruitier, to collect grafts from abroad. Although he was particularly interested in pippins, a type of apple, Harris also cultivated cherry and pear grafts, making New Garden, the king's orchard at Teynham in Kent, the epicentre of large-scale fruit growing in England. Grafts from New Garden were sent for from all over the country (Webber 31–3).[7]

Horticultural innovation became increasingly common in England, making mastery of grafting essential for English horticulturalists.[8] Writing a tract to husbandmen in 1530, John Fitzherbert declared that

> it is necessary / profytable / and also a pleasure to a husbande to haue peeres / wardeynes / and apples of dyuers sortes. And also cheryes / fylberdes / bulleys / dampsons / plummes / walnuttes / and suche other. And therfore it is couenyent to lerne how thou shalt graffe. (xliiii r)

The list of expected results from grafting was ever-expanding, and the combination of different types grew more ambitious. Rebecca Bushnell notes that early modern English gardening manuals show us men (and some women) not content with the status quo, jostling each other in the markets, experimenting, grafting and pruning, envisioning new designs – and, of course, writing and printing books ... These books not only disseminated the changing practices of gardening in the sixteenth and seventeenth centuries; they helped to shape that practice and the image of the English man and woman's garden as a place of dreams. (47–8)

Readers of these manuals were led to believe that grafting was not a simple practice, but rather one that could offer complex and surprising outcomes. Giambattista Della Porta's *Natural Magick* (1658), translated anonymously from the Italian *Magia naturalis* (1558), held that "not onely every Tree can be ingrafted into every Tree, but one Tree may be adulterated with them all" (58). The implication was that horticulturalists could and should create anything. In this vein, the anonymous English author of *The Craft of Graffing and planting of trees* (1563), for example, asserted that an elm branch grafted to an apple tree would bear apples (A1v). Similarly, Thomas Hill promised in *The Profitable Arte of Gardening* (1574) that it is possible to make one tree stock put forth fruits "of diverse colours, and diverse savours," and provided readers with the instructions to do so (87). Hill later published *Naturall and Artificiall Conclusions* (in 1581) and taught readers to make "an hearb to growe, which shall have many savors and taste" (38). Many early modern botanical writers adopted this optimistic stance on grafting, conveying their sense that horticulture made innovation possible. Mascall, writing in 1572, even supplied directions for altering the shapes of fruit: "To make an Apple growe within a glasse, take a glasse what fashion ye list, and put your Apple therein when he is but small, and bind him fast to the Glass, and the Glass also to the tree, and let him growe, thus ye may have Apples of divers proportion, according to the fashion of your glasse" (77). The experimental spirit that pervades these horticultural works indicates a focus on change, and the celebration of artifice.

In *De Augmentis Scientiarum* (1623), Francis Bacon explains that various seemingly incompatible fruit trees could be made to grow together, and that plants and fruit can, with assistance, take on new forms. He hails horticulture's potential for combination and augmentation, noting that "the artificial does not differ from the natural in form or essence, but only in the efficient; in that man has no power over nature except that of motion; he can put natural bodies together, and he can separate them; and therefore that whatever the case admits of uniting or disuniting of natural bodies ... man can do everything" (427).[9] For those, like Bacon, who believed that the management of nature held endless opportunities, horticulture was a means of initiating new kinds of creation. Even when horticultural literature – such as the anonymous *The Orchard, and the Garden* (1594) – advocated a cautious approach to grafting, the hope that something innovative might transpire was always present. *The Orchard, and the Garden* suggests initially that the fanciful trees imagined by Hill, Bacon, and others are not possible:

> You must have still regard that you imp kind upon kind, as apples upon apples, peares upon peares: for he that graffeth strange upon strange; as peares upon apples, and apples on peares, and such like, although it be done often for pleasures sake, yet will it not last: for the naturall nourishment is so that it will hardlie nourish a strange kind of fruit. (9)

Elaborate grafts are pleasurable, according to the author, but have no hope of survival. Implicit in this set of instructions is the idea of compatibility: as grafting literature became more sophisticated, there was an ever-increasing interest in ensuring that the uniformity of type was upheld, and that grafting experiments did not become uncontrollable. And yet, towards the end of *The Orchard, and the Garden*, the author asserts that although grafting kind with kind is important, the truly persistent and experimental gardener might have luck in mixing "contrary kinds," and could end up creating "many wonders" (20). Although recognizing that imping "strange upon strange" will not create a lasting and healthy tree, the author holds out hope that the secret knowledge of grafting might yet produce something entirely new.

The belief that something novel might come from grafting fuelled debates about the technique's legitimacy, prompting some authors of horticultural treatises to defend grafting and horticulture more generally as arts sanctioned by God.[10] Mara Miller observes that gardens have always held "an ambiguous status in a number of different respects – between poles of 'art' and/or the 'artificial' on the one hand and 'Nature' on the other, between art and craft, and between fine and applied art" (72). Horticulture pits human skill against God's or Nature's creations; early modern horticulturalists believed that whatever combination they could envision might take literal shape through grafting. In effect, they positioned themselves as nature's masters.[11] Della Porta, for instance, states that "Art, being as it were Natures Ape, even in her imitation of Nature, effecteth greater matters then Nature doth" (73). He describes how, through grafting, fruit can be produced at a new pace and can be grown to resemble anything its creator chooses. The horticulturalist, or "magician," as Della Porta terms him, "takes his sundry advantages of Natures instruments, and thereby either hastens or hinders her work, making things ripe before or after their natural season, and so indeed makes Nature to be his instrument" (74).

Art was often linked to horticulture. Dissatisfied with what the natural world had to offer, the horticulturalist could improve upon nature through grafting in much the same way as a poet, as Sir Philip Sidney asserts in his *Defence of Poesy* (1595), in verse "doth grow in effect another nature, in making things either better than nature bringeth forth, or, quite anew, forms such as never were in nature" (78). In *The Art of English Poesy* (1589), George Puttenham likewise compares poetry to horticulture, championing both as means to alter the natural world. Claiming that the gardener and poet both assist nature, Puttenham notes that "art is an aid and coadjuter to nature ... as the good gardener seasons his soil by sundry sorts of compost" (382). Puttenham, like Sidney, also believed that poetic and horticultural art could even surpass nature:

> The gardener by his art ... will embellish the same in virtue, shape, odour, and taste, that nature herself would never have done, as to make the single gillyflower, or marigold, or daisy, double, and the white rose red, yellow, or carnation; a bitter melon, sweet; a sweet apple, sour; a plum or cherry without a stone; a pear without core or kernel; a gourd or cucumber like to a horn or any other figure he will – any of which things nature could not do without man's help and art. (383)

Here Puttenham envisions the gardener and the poet as comparable creators. Horticultural art makes it possible to fashion that which did not exist previously through skill and invention, just as the poet makes fictional improvements to the world. In creating "a plum or cherry without a stone," or making a "sweet apple sour" – both results attributed to grafting – the gardener-poet generates something new and fantastic, modifying that which is ostensibly natural to suit his or her creative vision.

"The Adopted Stock": Classical Sources and Familial Metaphors

Those who wanted to learn the secrets of grafting looked to ancient texts for information. Hill, for example, acknowledges "the authors out of which this worke of Gardening is gathered" and lists Pliny the Elder, Cato, Theophrastus, and Aristotle, "among sundrie others," as sources for his text (*Profitable* A.i.). While none of these authors accounts for the origin of grafting, their views laid the foundation for early modern horticultural understandings of plant propagation and the interaction

between stock and scion. Some classical authors esteemed the interdependent nature of grafting – a scion relies upon its host stock for
survival – while they simultaneously emphasized the mystery and pe-
culiarity of the art. Virgil, for instance, describes in *Georgics* (c. 29 BC)
the joining of two species of trees into one:

> ... *nec longum tempus, et ingens*
> *exit ad caelum ramis felicibus arbos,*
> *miratastque novas fronds et non sua poma.*

> ... it isn't long before
> A new great tree is towering toward the sky,
> Exulting in its boughs, and full of wonder
> At its foliage and its fruit, so unfamiliar. (53)

Observing that a grafted tree becomes a visual hybrid wherein two distinct species can be identified, and imagining the tree's own admiration for its synthetic duality, Virgil celebrates one tree's cultivation and
support of another. In his *Natural History* (c. AD 77), Pliny the Elder
likewise describes grafting in terms of influence. He notes the sense of
combination and interrelation involved:

> *Peculiaris inpudentia est nucibus insitorum quae faciem parentis sucumque*
> *adoptionis exhibent, appellate ab utroque nucipruna.*

> Plums grafted on a nut-tree show a remarkable effrontery, displaying the
> appearance of the parent tree and the juice of the adopted stock; they take
> their name from each, being called nut-plums. (316–17)

The nut-plum is a combination of both species, according to Pliny. Although the fruit looks like a regular plum, it is flavoured by its adopting stock. Fostering is inherent in grafting, as Pliny contends, because
the stock, supporting its newly grafted scion, nurtures something alien.
In his observation of nut-plums, Pliny assigns parental and adoptive
characteristics to their old and new stocks. He thus renders grafting, a
complex practice, in recognizable terms by associating it with familial
relation and adoption.

Ancient authors frequently envisioned human life, plant life, and animal life as analogous. Aristotle, for example, refers to plants as rooted
animals, just as Anaxagoras before him describes them as a kind of animal secured in the soil.[12] In "On the Nature of the Child" (c. 400 BC), one
in a series of embryological treatises, the Greek physician Hippocrates

represents the development of human embryos in arboreal terms.[13] As embryos grow, he explains, "in due course the bones at their extremities branch out just as in a tree it is the tips of the branches which are last to shoot forth twigs" (331). The branches of trees mature in the same way as a "child's fingers and toes become differentiated" (331). Hippocrates then turns to an explanation of grafting. Through the use of simile, he ties the development of an embryo in a womb to the growth and nourishment of plants in the soil. He observes that just as an embryo depends upon its mother for its nutrition, so plants growing in the earth receive their nutrients from their surroundings (334). Concluding that grafted slips, like all other trees, draw nutrients from the ground rather than from the stocks of the trees onto which they are grafted, Hippocrates asserts that grafts maintain their natural characteristics. That is, he argues that the grafted fruit is fashioned by the conditions of the soil out of which it grows, not the stock onto which it is transplanted, and that "the process of growth in plants and in humans is exactly the same" (341).

Although the connection between embryological development and artificial plant propagation may strike modern readers as somewhat unusual, Hippocrates asserts that he "could hardly avoid giving a complete account of the subject" of "trees and their fruit" in his embryological treatise (340). The comparison of human breeding and horticultural development aligns artificial proliferation and natural reproduction. Hippocrates thus questions the extent to which a plant's or a person's characteristics are influenced by biological and environmental factors. The description of the technique of grafting in a treatise on embryonic development complicates any assumption that biological factors are deterministic. Readers might contemplate what might happen when plants are displaced from their native soil or are combined with different stocks.

I am less concerned with why exactly Hippocrates compares embryos and trees, however, than with what this analogy meant to those who inherited it. The metaphor linking the human and the horticultural was passed down to early modern authors and allows for an investigation of the ways in which metaphorical language is used to formulate and understand the world.[14] In ancient times, metaphor was recognized as useful for naming things that were newly conceived or yet to be understood. "In naming something that does not have a proper name of its own, metaphor should be used," Aristotle counsels (*On Rhetoric* 224). As Henry Peacham observes in the early modern period, metaphors "give pleasant light to darke things, thereby removing unprofitable and odious obscurite" (13). Puttenham also notes under his "causes" of metaphor that the device is used out of "necessity or want of a better word" (263). Rendering the unfamiliar familiar, metaphor explains a novel or obscure concept in common terms. Writing in the late twentieth century, Paul Ricoeur views metaphor as invigorating. "Metaphor is that strategy of discourse," he notes, "by which language divests itself of the function of direct description in order to reach the mythic level where its function of discovery is set free" (247). Allocating to one idea the sign of another, more well-established idea, metaphor forges new logical pathways. In Ricoeur's model of metaphor, poetic language has a re-descriptive, rather than a simply descriptive, function. Metaphor enables people to describe reality indirectly, he suggests, and to remake it how they choose.

Pliny's familial metaphor re-describes grafting, creating an alternative way to explain and envision the practice. He produces a conceptual connection between familial relation and horticulture. Familial metaphor is thus used by Pliny to render horticultural practices intelligible, whereas horticultural metaphor in the early modern period is used to elucidate the complexities of familial relation. The early modern family tree, for instance, is a metaphorical expression of genealogical connection, demonstrating lineage by specifying a person's ancestors through the recognizable referent of a tree: consanguineous relations are identified as they branch out from a common stock. The exact origins of the family tree are unknown, but the image dates at least to the twelfth century, when Jesse trees, artistic representations of the genealogy of Christ, became popular. Styled after the metaphorical account of Christ's descent from Jesse in the Book of Isaiah, which states that "there shall come forth a rod out of the stem of Jesse, and a Branch shall grow out of his roots" (11.1), Jesse trees map the family in arboreal terms. In these images, a stock typically grows from the supine Jesse's abdomen. Christ's relatives are shown as branches of this stock; Mary and her son are located at the top of the tree.

A somewhat similar chart probably predates the Jesse tree: the *arbor iuris*, another antecedent of the typical European family tree, was devised in the sixth or seventh century and used in medieval law. Created to give lawyers a map of family members who were closely related, the document was used to solve matters of inheritance in civil law (Wilkins 62–3).[15] A series of columns joins relatives by extending above, below, and to each side of a person named at a central point in the diagram. The term *arbor* is used only figuratively to suggest a tree's branches; there is no arboreal decoration.[16] Later, canonists used a model of familial relation similar to the *arbor iuris* to illustrate permissible marriages between relatives (Wilkins 63). Boccaccio's *De Genealogia deorum gentilium* (1360) is the first known secular representation of familial relation that uses the image of a tree. The text, illustrated by thirteen trees that show the lineage of the classical gods, contains, as Ernest H. Wilkins notes, "the first non-biblical genealogical charts in which stems, branches, and leaves appear" (61).[17] After Boccaccio, and in keeping with the imagery of the Jesse tree, European families were often documented using tree structures. The family tree uses a botanical model to establish and represent relation. The influence of the family tree permeates early modern familial discourse: the terms *stock* and *root* are commonly used to indicate the source of a line of descent; a *branch* refers to the portion of a family derived from a particular ancestor; and the terms *scion* and *slip* are used for descendants.

Shakespeare's use of the grafting metaphor participates in and perpetuates the horticultural discourse of the period, and likely derives in part from the metaphor of the family tree. He envisions adoption through the grafting metaphor because "natural," or biological, families are already imagined through the metaphor of the tree. To describe adoption in terms of grafting extends the metaphor of the family tree. Grafting represents a different method of familial production and conveys the possibility that people who are not related by blood or marriage might become part of the same family tree. By deploying a set of natural and genealogical associations, Shakespeare's horticultural metaphor explains adoption while allowing audiences to see the potential for unusual familial formation.

The Winter's Tale: Horticultural Manipulation and the Art of Survival

There has to date been a rich critical discussion about art, class, bastardy, and marriage in relation to grafting in *The Winter's Tale*, but Perdita's specific status as an adopted child has not yet been scrutinized in light of the play's horticultural concerns.[18] Critics have typically overlooked the relevance of the grafting debate between Perdita and Polixenes (4.4.70–108) to Perdita's position as an adopted child.[19] Perdita is a kind of "grafted" girl, brought up in Bohemia by one family but belonging biologically to another.[20] Her negative opinion of the combination of two stocks of flowers (4.4.81–4) is therefore ironic, given that she is herself figuratively attached to a familial stock that is not naturally her own.[21] Grafting in *The Winter's Tale* draws attention not only to the amalgamation of people from different classes, but also to the competing roles of nature and nurture in the development of an adopted child. Perdita's encounter with Polixenes at the sheep-shearing festival presents her adoption in horticultural terms, comparing her rearing to the careful cultivation of a hybrid plant. At issue is not only whether Perdita's biological characteristics dominate those that she might acquire from her adoptive parents, but also whether she will be more attached to her birth family or to her adoptive family once her biological identity is revealed. The grafting debate alludes to Perdita's familial circumstances and prompts the audience to evaluate them: we are, in effect, asked whether Perdita's adoptive graft is successful.

Robert Greene's *Pandosto* (1595), the source text for *The Winter's Tale*, does not mention grafting, but it does devote a significant portion of its narrative to tracing the effects of adoption on both children and parents. Although Mopsa is at first jealous of the child whom her husband Porrus, a shepherd, brings home, and believes that the girl is his illegitimate daughter, she eventually reveals that she hopes that God, "seeing they could get no children, [has] sent them this little babe to be their heir" (201). Unable to produce children of their own, Porrus and Mopsa adopt the girl in order to expand their family. "Both of them [begin] to be very fond of [the baby]" (201), and they raise her in ignorance of her status as an adopted child. Fawnia, the child, calls her adoptive parents "Dad" and "Mam," and is so skilled at rural life that the family's sheep prosper under her care (201). Possessing a child's devoted love for her parents, she "honour[s] and obey[s] them with such reverence" (201) that all of their neighbours note her exemplary behaviour. Fawnia's affinity for country life, however, gives way to her biologically determined characteristics when she reaches the age of sixteen, and "her natural disposition [does] bewray that she [is] born of some high parentage" (202). The question of how well an adopted child might be amalgamated with an adoptive family is thus present in the foundational material for Shakespeare's play.

From the beginning of *The Winter's Tale*, grafting expresses an idyllic sense of connection and community. When Leontes and Polixenes are reunited, it is said that, having "trained together in their childhoods," they "rooted betwixt them then such an affection which cannot choose but branch now" (1.1.22–5). The two men, it is implied, formed an attachment early in life and entwined their figurative roots. As a result, their affection now "branches" like the limbs of a tree that has been grafted successfully. Leontes and Polixenes refer to one another as "brother" and were raised, as Polixenes reminisces, "as twinn'd lambs that did frisk i' th' sun, / And bleat the one at th' other" (1.2.67–8). The grafting metaphor creates a sense of artificial, non-biological, pseudo-familial attachment – in this case through friendship that is described in pastoral terms.[22]

The play's focus on the idealization of the natural world and its potential to foster brotherhood between those who are not actually related suggests that a natural environment permits attachment. As the bond between Leontes and Polixenes breaks down, however, so too does this vision of the natural world as protector and joiner. Convinced that his friend is the father of the child that his wife Hermione carries, Leontes discounts her baby as a bastard and orders Antigonus to bear the child – young Perdita – to "some remote and desert place" (2.3.175) outside his kingdom where she will be left "(Without more mercy) to [her] own protection / And favour of the climate" (2.3.177–8). While Leontes and Polixenes were entwined with each other in childhood, the young Perdita is left without any kind of support.

Although she is deserted and must rely on "favour," or chance, Perdita survives because she is cared for by the shepherd. She forms with him what appears to be an enduring familial bond: the shepherd treats her as his daughter and Perdita lives unaware of her biological origins. While the shepherd thinks that "some scape" (3.3.71) or indiscretion can be read on the baby's face when he finds her, and seems to believe that some illicit "behind-door-work" (3.3.74–5) was involved in her generation, he accepts her. He is thereby presented in direct contrast to Leontes, who has just rejected Perdita because of her supposed illegitimacy. To the shepherd, Perdita is not as warm as those who begot her (3.3.75–6) – an opinion that recalls Leontes' remark that Hermione and Polixenes' actions are "too hot" (1.2.108) and that implies that he does not burden the child with what he assumes are its parents' sexual transgressions (Leggatt 153). Accepting her as a blessing, a "[thing] new-born" (3.3.113), he decides to take her in before he discovers the gold that is bundled with her. As Marianne Novy observes, the shepherd is thus unlike his counterpart in Greene's *Pandosto*, who takes up the abandoned baby only after discovering that she comes with financial benefits (*Reading* 68).[23] In *The Winter's Tale*, the shepherd's willingness to incorporate a foreign child into his family underscores the play's fascination with familial hybridity. Much of the play's later action is occupied by an examination of Perdita's attachment to her new relations, as is made apparent in the famous argument that takes place at the sheep-shearing festival.

The dramatic irony of the garden debate between Polixenes and Perdita, the supposed shepherdess, occurs, as critics often note, because although the king disapproves of the relationship between his son and a low-born woman, he approves of the horticultural practice of marrying "a gentler scion to the wildest stock" in the crossbreeding of plants (4.4.93). Polixenes, of course, takes the side of the debate in favour of combination in order to provoke Perdita: he has come to observe his son at the sheep-shearing festival precisely to stop the combination of a base stock (Perdita) and a noble scion (Florizel).[24] And while Perdita herself is prepared to change ranks by marrying Prince Florizel, someone of a higher station (as far as she knows), she condemns the mixing of plants that Polixenes endorses. Perdita appears to believe, as Montaigne does in his essay "Of the Caniballes," that humankind has, by its inventions, "surcharged the beauties and riches of [Nature's] works" and has "over-choaked hir" (*Essays* 102).[25]

Laurie Shannon argues that Perdita's exchange with Polixenes provides metaphors "by which notions of both friendship practice and the counselor's craft may be further specified" (*Sovereign* 215). Polixenes, she maintains, "essentially theorizes the process that results in friendship's 'artificial body' – two bodies are literally incorporated by being grafted into one" (*Sovereign* 216). While grafting is used initially to describe friendship, the argument between Perdita and Polixenes, I propose, is far more suggestive of a familial analogue. Such an interpretation can be illuminated by examining horticultural metaphors of the family. In an effort to prove the shepherdess hypocritical in her detestation of grafting and her willingness to marry his son, Polixenes argues that grafting can "mend nature" (4.4.96) and that "the art itself is nature" (4.4.97). He insists that a "bark of baser kind" can conceive a "bud of nobler race" (4.4.94–5). Polixenes' comments allude to social standing and invite a comparison of Perdita's two fathers. "Bark of baser kind," in this context, refers to the stock of a tree. As I have noted previously, however, the term *stock* was also frequently used figuratively to indicate "the source of a line of descent" (*OED*, N.3.a). Typically, then, the stock, or the tree itself, referred to the family patriarch. The notion that a base stock can foster a noble bud therefore draws attention to the possibility that the care that the noble Perdita has received from the base shepherd has fostered her growth in a way that her royal, biological father could not have.[26] Raised by a loving shepherd who has ensured that she thrives, Perdita fares far better in rural Bohemia than she would have in the dangerous court of Sicilia.[27]

The idea that a delicate scion could be better cultivated by a robust stock was a well-known tenet of grafting since the time of Theophrastus (a successor of Aristotle). Theophrastus, often considered the father of horticulture, recommends the amalgamation of fine scions with base stocks in order to produce enhanced fruit. Transferred from a superior but delicate tree, such scions flourish because they take nourishment from a rougher and healthier stock. As Theophrastus observes, "the scion is better fed because the stock is strong," and the scion's transplantation therefore allows it to thrive (68). Shakespeare seizes on the implications of this principle. *The Winter's Tale* applies theories of grafting to familial formation, suggesting that Perdita's upbringing in Bohemia is a graft that strengthens her development. "Art" is claimed to "mend nature," and adoption is shown to repair the damage caused by the birth family. The shepherd grafts Perdita to his family tree, allowing her to survive.

Perdita is not, however, joined seamlessly to her adoptive family; her blood-based nobility is evident despite her humble upbringing. Rather than fulfill her role as hostess at the sheep-shearing festival, Perdita instinctively acts as though she should be treated as a guest, and the shepherd scorns her for dereliction of duty (4.4.55–69). His "old wife," he claims, was "both pantler, butler, cook, / Both dame and servant" at once, taking every opportunity to make her guests comfortable (4.4.56–7). Expecting his adopted daughter to behave like her deceased adoptive mother, the shepherd has not anticipated that Perdita might act in keeping with her noble origins. Other characters also comment on her unusually noble qualities. Polixenes declares that "nothing she does or seems / But smacks of something greater than herself, / Too noble for this place" (4.4.157–9), and Florizel observes that "she is as forward of her breeding as / She is i' th' rear' [of his] birth" (4.4.581–2).[28] Her graft to the shepherd's family has not fundamentally changed her underlying characteristics, which are presumed to be biologically inherited. As Susan Baker notes, however, the shepherd can likely ascertain Perdita's noble birth when he first finds her because of her fine clothes and gold, and, as a result, he may raise her with different standards in mind, thereby influencing her behaviour (312). Ralph Austen, a writer of gardening and husbandry treatises, admired the fact that "*Grafts*, and *Buds* should retain their own natures, and not be altered into the nature of the Stock whereon they grow, but have power to digest, change, and assimilate this harsh and sower sap, into their own sweet and pleasant natures, and bring forth fruits accordingly" (54). Perdita's biological nature is not greatly altered by her environment. The extent to which the play finally endorses the concept of a blended, adoptive family is therefore somewhat ambiguous, as Perdita does not always seem to merge with her new surroundings. Although she is raised in rural Bohemia, the Sicilian court shines through in all that she does.

The reintroduction of Perdita's birth family further complicates the question of belonging. Once it is established that Perdita is the daughter of Leontes and Hermione, she suddenly finds herself with two families, one biological and one adoptive. Shakespeare at first appears to imply that the two families might be united. The shepherd's son suggests that Perdita's birth and surrogate families are now indistinct from one another when he reports that, upon their meeting, Leontes and Polixenes called the shepherd "brother." He also states that Florizel called him "brother" and the shepherd "father" (5.2.140–5). As Novy observes, this brief dialogue suggests the "utopian possibilities of an extended cross-class family of biological and adoptive parents" ("Multiple Parenting in Shakespeare's Romances" 193). The three families – those of the shepherd, of Leontes, and of Polixenes – at first seem to be one. It is then reasonable to expect, given the shepherd's son's report, that all of Perdita's family members would be present at the play's recognition scene and family reunion. Perdita's adoptive family is absent, however, when Paulina unveils Hermione, and the princess is ultimately left with her biological relatives. Leontes and Polixenes are reunited and are again described in terms of their resemblance. It is reported that "there was casting up of eyes, holding up of hands, with countenance of such distraction, that they were to be known by garment, not by favour" (5.2.47–50); in other words, they are distinguishable only by their clothing, not by their physical features. The audience, however, is left unconvinced that the shepherd's family can be fused to Leontes and Polixenes. The shepherd's son's story – of a blended family based on both biological and adoptive familial relation – is potentially progressive (as opposed to conservative), but it is only reported and never staged. Excluded from the play's final scene, the shepherd and his son fade from view.

Grafting introduces an element of human design into the world of plants. It turns nature into a garden of possibilities. Through the use of horticultural metaphor, *The Winter's Tale* expresses the novel potential of an unusual familial combination: Perdita is allowed to survive because she is a grafted child. But the play's dynamics of language and character oblige the audience to ask whether certain grafts might fail to take, and if the unlikely familial combination of certain people is destined to end poorly. Although Perdita once appeared to accept the shepherd as her father, her devotion to the shepherd and his son remains uncertain at the play's close. Before she discovers that the shepherd is not her biological parent, Perdita cries out "O my poor father!" when she fears that he might be condemned to death by Polixenes (5.1.201). Such concern, however, disappears after her reunion with Leontes and Hermione; Perdita is silent on the subject of her adoptive family in the final moments of the play. The shepherd and his son are also guilty of this apparent willingness to forgo adoptive ties. They were previously eager to report Perdita's adopted status to Polixenes in order to avoid any connection to her and her crime of aspiring to marry a prince (4.4.820–2). They believe that if they can dissociate themselves from Perdita biologically and prove that she is, as the shepherd's son states, "none of your daughter nor my sister" (4.4.821–2), then they can avoid being punished for her transgressions.[29] Adoptive bonds are not necessarily lasting.

Cymbeline: Re-grafting and the Preservation of Stock

Like *The Winter's Tale*, *Cymbeline* envisions familial combination through grafting, but instead uses re-grafting – the reparative grafting of displaced scions onto their original stock – as its principal metaphor. Any alteration of the supposedly natural states of either plants or humans in *Cymbeline* is shown to be dangerous or temporary. The play uses a metaphorical reversal of horticultural practices to signal the restoration of familial and social harmony. Kidnapped by Belarius when they were infants and raised as his children, Cymbeline's sons, Guiderius and Arviragus, are brought up outside the royal court into which they were born. Whereas grafting imagery in *The Winter's Tale* emphasizes Perdita's possible attachment to the shepherd's family and her position between two families, in *Cymbeline* it implies that Guiderius and Arviragus must be reunited with their birth father in order to bring calm to the troubled royal family. Visiting the king's son-in-law Posthumus in a dream, the god Jupiter reveals the requirements for the resolution of the young man's various predicaments. Peace will be brought to the royal family, Jupiter tells Posthumus, when the "lopped branches" of a "stately cedar" that have been "dead many years, shall after revive, be jointed to the old stock, and freshly grow" (5.3.204–5). By the play's close, it is clear that Cymbeline is the cedar tree and that his missing sons are the branches that have been "dead," or have been taken from him. Jupiter claims that the "jointing," or grafting, of the branches/ princes back onto their biological stock will ensure that they are revitalized.[30] Grafting imagery is thus employed to express the re-formation of the blood family, not the splicing and combination of various unrelated family members; the play demonstrates that the reconstruction of Cymbeline's family tree involves the restoration of a presumably unadulterated tree, rather than envisioning a newly blended family tree. *Cymbeline*, therefore, appears to endorse a view of adoption that holds that children will fare best with their biological families. Like *The Winter's Tale*, however, the play does, for a time, present a compelling image of the adoptive family.

Cymbeline conceptualizes in botanical terms children who form familial bonds with those to whom they are not biologically related. Posthumus, for instance, who has been Cymbeline's ward since infancy, is imagined as being cultivated by the king. The First Gentleman describes how Cymbeline "breeds [his ward], and makes him of his Bedchamber" (1.1.42). The care and education that the king awards Posthumus, the First Gentleman notes, "in's spring became a harvest" (1.1.46). That is, the successful "breeding" of Posthumus yields a crop, or is fruitful. This metaphor for the ward's edification and development is repeated in reference to the two kidnapped princes. Belarius observes that the "valour / That wildly grows in them [the princes], but yields a crop / As if it had been sowed" (4.2.178–80). This second use of the metaphor produces the opposite effect of the first. Whereas Cymbeline's cultivation of Posthumus' talents results in the boy's improvement, Belarius does not need to cultivate the princes at all. They are left to grow in the wild, but mature as though they were carefully tended. "Sowing" here is not viewed as a manipulation of the princes' natures, but is rather a manifestation of what is "naturally" theirs by birth.[31] Guiderius and Arviragus are thus resistant to the environment in which they find themselves and, like Perdita, they develop as though they were still attached to their biological family. Belarius' influence as their adoptive father might, of course, shape them more than he admits. The princes hold within them some combination of the untamed and the refined, as Belarius observes: they are at once "wild" and "sowed." They are, by their very positions as royal children adopted into a pastoral family, like hybrid plants that combine two varieties into one.

In addition to its emphasis on describing the development of children in botanical terms, *Cymbeline* exhibits, from its beginning, a fascination with the interdependence and interconnectivity of blood relatives. It establishes the "naturalness" of biological relation and asserts that biological relatives belong together. In the play, blood relations – particularly parents and children – are shown to be almost symbiotic, as though family members were physically and emotionally reliant on one another, each living or languishing depending on the condition of their relations. Before audience members are introduced to Posthumus, they are told about his lineage and family history. Unable to "delve him to the root" (1.1.28), or to trace his genealogy to its origin, the First Gentleman in Act 1, Scene 1 attempts to give an account of Posthumus' ancestry. He focuses on the military accomplishments of Posthumus' father, Sicilius. It is soon revealed, however, that Sicilius is dead, having "quit being" (1.1.38) after the battlefield deaths of Posthumus' two brothers. Posthumus was, at the time of his father's death, still in the womb. "Old and fond of issue" (1.1.37), Sicilius doted on his children; when they died, he could not live without them. The play thus presents the notion that what physically affects a child will eventually also physically affect that child's parents. Although Posthumus has never known his father, his attachment to him is inscribed in his name: "Posthumus Leonatus" denotes the fact that he was born after his father's death.[32] Later in the same scene, Cymbeline, expressing his anger at his daughter, Imogen, echoes Sicilius' physical reliance on his children. Believing that his daughter "shouldst repair [his] youth," or bring his youth back to him, but that she instead "heap'st / A year's age on [him]" (1.1.132–3) because of her disobedience in marrying Posthumus, Cymbeline implies that Imogen shortens his lifespan. Her defiant actions affect him physically, causing him to age.

Just as parents are shown to be physically dependent on their children, siblings in *Cymbeline* are endowed with an intrinsic ability to recognize one another and to sense relation. Raised in a cave in the hard pastoral of the British woods, Guiderius and Arviragus believe that they are the biological children of Belarius, their kidnapper. The boys treat Belarius as their father and venerate the memory of Euriphile, the nurse they believed to be their mother (3.3.103–5). Despite their ignorance of their blood origins, however, the princes are able to sense that they are biologically related to Imogen, their sister, even if they do not know how to express their understanding.[33] Upon first meeting Imogen disguised as the male page Fidele, and inadvertently expressing a confused romantic interest in his own sibling, Guiderius announces that he would woo the boy if he (Fidele) were a woman (3.6.66–7). Arviragus, however, correctly identifies the connection to the page as love between siblings – although he has mistaken sister for brother – by declaring that he will "love him as [his] brother" (3.6.69). The princes each establish an instantaneous bond with the supposed stranger who wanders into their cave. The brothers go so far as to privilege Fidele's life over the life of the man whom they think is their biological father. Although he does not know why he loves Fidele, Arviragus is sure that if he had to choose between Fidele or Belarius, he would single out "[his] father, not this youth" for death (4.2.24). While this decision appears to be counterintuitive – because Arviragus would rather sacrifice his blood relative than someone whom he believes to be unrelated – it is clear to Belarius (and to the audience) that the boy knows intuitively that Belarius is not his biological father. In an aside, Belarius praises his adopted son's choice, acknowledging that Arviragus' instinctual rejection of someone unrelated to him is confirmation of his "breed of greatness," his royal status (4.2.25). When he learns that Guiderius and Arviragus "at first meeting loved" Imogen (5.4.379,) although they did not know her as their sister, Cymbeline exclaims "O rare instinct!" (5.4.381). The outburst epitomizes the play's position on familial relation: blood relatives are innately aware of their connection and act in each other's best interest. Depictions of this instinctive recognition anticipate the reunion of biological family members in the play's final scene, which deploys the metaphor of a reassembled family as a re-grafted tree that will "freshly grow" (5.3.206).

Negative examples of gardening and cultivation permeate *Cymbeline*. References to horticulture suggest that any attempt to interfere with nature, or to use nature to an inappropriate end, can be hazardous. The Queen's gardening practices, for example, attest the evils associated with the manipulation of the natural world. Although she has been taught by the physician Cornelius "to make perfumes," to "distil," and to "preserve" flowers for medicinal purposes (1.5.13), the Queen instead uses her knowledge of plant life to ill effect: she gathers flowers in order to extract their poisonous essences. Bushnell observes that early modern housewives collected plants in order to prepare cosmetics and medicine for their households. It is therefore "odd," Bushnell surmises, "that in this play this housewifely function ... evokes a sense of danger" (120). The Queen's gardening, I suggest, is made dangerous to offset the more acceptable "natural" tending of plants that takes place at the play's conclusion, in which the horticultural metaphor of re-grafting ostensibly portrays gardening in a positive light. Re-grafting is depicted favourably precisely because it is a reversal of artificial practices. It represents, in this particular case, a restoration of the natural, biological family – although, of course, re-grafting is still a human intervention. Cymbeline's metaphorical re-grafting of his children is an affirming example of the manipulation of nature because it is not a manipulation at all; blood is reunited with blood as Cymbeline's family is re-established.

Elsewhere in the play, Shakespeare alludes to the Book of Ezekiel when he refers to the princes as the detached branches of a tree.[34] In Ezekiel, the branches of a great cedar are decaying, and in an effort to repair them, God breaks them from the tree and transplants them to a mountaintop where they will thrive.[35] Shakespeare's use of the biblical tale differs from his source in that the survival of Guiderius and Arviragus is ensured by their being restored to their original, figurative tree. The image of the grafted tree in *Cymbeline* also echoes both the Jesse tree and the Book of Romans, chapter 11.[36] Robin Moffet notes that the grafted tree is "constructed so that it will recall familiar biblical ideas and images without suggesting any one obvious line of interpretation" (217). By presenting Cymbeline's family reunion as a re-grafting with biblical overtones, the play assigns it an almost religious significance.

It remains a question, however, whether the restoration of the princes to Cymbeline's family tree is successful. Like Perdita in *The Winter's*

Tale, Guiderius and Arviragus display affection for their adoptive father before they learn that they are in fact biologically related to another
man. Assuring Belarius that they share in the risk that he takes when
he speaks to Cymbeline in the final scene, the princes assert their bond
with their supposed father (5.4.314–15). Although the boys grow up
longing to live in the court and resent living in their "cell of ignorance"
in the woods (3.3.33), they respect Belarius as the only parent they have
ever known. When it is revealed in the final scene that Guiderius and
Arviragus are the sons of Cymbeline, the adoptive family ceases to exist
as such, but Belarius is forgiven for kidnapping the boys and is called
"brother" by Cymbeline (5.4.399) in much the same way as the shepherd's son in *The Winter's Tale* reports that he and his father are accepted
into the royal family. Belarius is allowed back into the court without
punishment for his actions and appears, at least momentarily, to become part of a new, blended family.

It is clear, however, that such a hybrid family cannot exist. Cymbeline
will now be the boys' father: using a phrase that suggests rebirth, he
claims that he is "a mother to the birth of three" children (5.4.369), including the newly returned Imogen.[37] Yet the silence of Guiderius and
Arviragus in this final scene is telling: they never address Cymbeline
as their father, and they speak only to state that they know Imogen.
Although the princes report to Cymbeline that they "at first meeting
loved" their sister (5.4.379), they do not verbally express the same sentiment about him. Arviragus does, however, acknowledge Posthumus,
telling Cymbeline that Posthumus helped them – Arviragus and Guiderius – in battle "as [he] did mean indeed to be [their] brother" (5.4.423),
and that they are overjoyed that he is in fact their brother by marriage.
Similarly, Imogen tells Belarius – who also acted as her adoptive parent
in the woods – that he is her "father too, and did relieve [her] / To see
this gracious season" (5.4.400–1). Amid the expressions of goodwill and
the acknowledgment of pseudo-familial relation, the princes' silence
before Cymbeline is striking. Although the final scene could be staged
to show the princes' excitement upon their reunion with Cymbeline,
this sentiment is not conveyed by the dialogue itself. While the play
metaphorically re-grafts the boys to their biological father and family
tree, whether they wish to form a family with Cymbeline remains unclear. Such uncertainty suggests the possibility that re-grafting is unfea-
sible without some kind of change having occurred in the intervening
period of transplantation.[38]

While *Cymbeline* suggests that blood relatives belong together, its
conclusion leaves biological relation on somewhat unstable ground.
Purity of stock is restored as the princes return to their blood family,

but such a return is perhaps not entirely desired by them. Relatives are not as easily interchanged as scions are grafted, or re-grafted, onto a stock.[39] More so than *The Winter's Tale*, *Cymbeline* endorses adoptive familial bonds, although it ultimately favours the biological family. It also, like *The Winter's Tale*, features fathers as the horticulturalists, or the shapers of their families. The shepherd, Belarius, and Cymbeline graft and create – or re-create, in the case of Cymbeline – their relations as they see fit. They thus stand in contrast to the female horticulturalists of *All's Well That Ends Well*.

All's Well That Ends Well: Female Agency and the Grafted Family

Female power in *All's Well* has been a long-standing critical concern. In particular, feminist critics have often noted Helena's significant agency. In an important discussion of the play's use of the bed trick, for instance, Julia Briggs observes that Helena's desire for Bertram "drives the play's action forward" and demonstrates "transgressive overtones" (302).[40] Barbara Traister similarly suggests that Helena's skill as a physician lends her an authority that is remarkable for a female character (333–4).[41] Other scholars, however, have emphasized the ways in which Helena's transgressive powers are mitigated by the play's generic conventions. Jean Howard argues that all of Helena's actions take place "safely within the ideology of wifely obedience" (51) and that she is embedded in a plot of "patriarchal ruin and repair" (44). Kathryn Schwarz likewise contends that Helena's loyalty to Bertram reinforces patriarchal values. However, Schwarz also insists that Helena's actions foreground the extent to which the preservation of patriarchal ideology relies on the active and willing participation of women. Helena's "constant will," she maintains, works "primarily and indispensably to secure heterosocial relations" (205), but her deliberate and sustained reinscription of the norms upheld by marriage and comedy is "too audible" (210) and thus underscores the workings of patriarchal ideology (221). Schwarz concludes that while Helena restores patriarchal hierarchy through her acquiescence to Bertram's demands, "any victory of normative relations is always, at least potentially, pyrrhic" (227).

Following Schwarz's contention that Helena's failure to invert patriarchal norms does not negate her ability to draw attention to patriarchal ideology, I suggest that although Helena ultimately grafts herself into the role of the obedient wife and mother, metaphors of grafting assert female agency and the possibility of evading typical methods of familial formation. The Countess's agency in her adoption of Helena is frequently overlooked. Carolyn Asp, for instance, acknowledges the Countess's significant role and describes her as "a kind and caring woman, a validator of Helena's desire," but determines that her effectiveness is limited and that she "accepts her position of dependence within the patriarchal order" (182). I maintain, however, that the Countess challenges the patriarchal order through her adoption of Helena and her use of horticultural metaphor. *All's Well* features female grafters and, to a degree, excludes men from familial formation, thereby circumventing heteronormative and biological methods of procreation. Women in the play cannot dispense altogether with heteronormative reproduction, but the Countess and Helena use the grafting metaphor to emphasize their agency.

William Painter's *The Palace of Pleasure* (1566) – a translation of Boccaccio's *Decameron* (ninth story, third day) and the most likely English source text for *All's Well* – concerns Gilleta, "a Phisitions doughter of Narbon" who has lost her father and who loves Beltramo, Counte of Rossiglione (145).[42] Shakespeare omits some of the details of Painter's text – Helena does not, for instance, bear Bertram twin sons who are presented at the play's conclusion – but he also makes some additions, the most notable of which is the character of the Countess of Rossillion. The Countess not only provides Helena with a family by adopting her after her father's death, but also acts as a foil for the King, who takes her son Bertram as his ward. She is a creator and indicator of synthetic familial bonds; Shakespeare's addition of the Countess is crucial to the play's portrayal of family relation.

All's Well has a distinctly generational focus. As many critics have observed, the Countess introduces birth as a notable theme in the play's opening line: "In delivering my son from me, I bury a second husband" (1.1.1).[43] By using an image of childbirth to allude to her husband's death and her son's departure, the Countess asserts her identity as mother. Over the course of the play, however, she modifies the standard, biological definition of the term *mother*. As I have noted, the Countess creates an adoptive bond with Helena, emphasizing the organic nature of her feelings with the metaphor of a slip, grown from "foreign" seeds, becoming "native" to its new stock. She insists on the success of this amalgamation and on the familial ties that it produces. Her understanding of familial relation assumes that wards and adoptive children are the social and familial equivalents of biological children; she imagines the adopted child growing into and becoming a part of its adoptive family.

In several places, the play characterizes the Countess as an innovative, non-sexual genitor. The Clown, for instance, wants to marry and asks the Countess for her permission, insisting upon the importance of having biological children. He believes that he will "never have the blessing of God till [he] have issue a' [his] body" (1.3.22–3) and that "barnes are blessings" (1.3.23–4). Desperately anxious to reproduce, he is the play's comical example of faith in the significance of natural generation. Paroles, whose argument with Helena over the uses of virginity is likewise comical, also emphasizes the naturalness of biological reproduction. A woman should not preserve her virginity, he states, because no virgin was ever conceived by a virgin: "to speak on the part of virginity is to accuse your mothers" (1.1.134–5). Accentuating the male role in propagation, the Clown and Paroles draw attention to the physicality of reproduction. The Countess, in contrast, imagines adoption as an unconventional, social way of becoming a mother to Helena – even though Helena, of course, had biological parents, as the play makes clear. Although she never gave "a mother's groan" (1.3.142), or felt labour pains, the Countess claims Helena as her own grafted child (1.3.139–41) – a child gained without male involvement.

In the first interview between the Countess and Helena, the women struggle to define the terms of their relationship. Upon her ward's entrance, the Countess announces, "I am a mother to you" (1.3.133). Helena, unwilling to accept this term, responds by calling her guardian "mine honourable mistress" (1.3.134). Replacing the language of relation with that of social deference, she excuses herself from being considered part of the Countess's family. The Countess insists on eliminating any reference to social standing and maintains that she is not a mistress but a mother (1.3.134). Helena's reaction to the term "mother" is violent – the Countess notes that Helena looks as though she has seen a serpent (1.3.136) – and the Countess answers by explaining their bond with the grafting metaphor, thus assuring her ward that she can become a part of the Rossillion family through adoption. Despite the Countess's efforts, however, Helena returns to social position and states that Bertram cannot be her brother because she is "from humble, he from honoured name" (1.3.151). It soon becomes clear that Helena is also afraid to accept the Countess as her mother because she worries that their adoptive bond might doom her relationship with Bertram, with whom she is in love, to be sisterly: "He must not be my brother" (1.3.155). If Helena were to become the Countess's daughter, her social position would be equal to Bertram's, but she would then also be a member of his family. Helena treats the adoptive bond seriously enough to fear that a union with Bertram might be incestuous.[44]

The Countess, it is important to note, knows of Helena's desire to marry Bertram; the Steward has informed her of it (1.3.101–16). With Helena's aspiration in mind, the Countess makes it obvious that she wants Helena to be both her adopted daughter and her daughter by marriage. She concludes their interview by assuring Helena that she might become her daughter – without being Bertram's sister – by becoming her daughter-in-law (1.3.162). The similarity between the terms *daughter* and *daughter-in-law* – designations which were often interchangeable in the early modern period – informs much of the dialogue between the women.[45] Helena, for instance, tells the Countess that she weeps because she is not her daughter. She also implies, however, that she weeps because she is not yet married to Bertram and therefore not the Countess's daughter-in-law (1.3.148–9). Although she appears to share a close bond with the Countess, Helena does not at first see herself grafted into the Countess's family as an adopted daughter; she imagines herself as a potential daughter through marriage.

Throughout the play, however, the Countess considers Helena her natural child rather than her daughter-in-law. She emphasizes her affective bond with her ward and even distances herself from her biological son as a result. When she learns that Bertram has abandoned his new wife and run off to war, the Countess highlights her attachment to Helena. She is adamant that Helena share her grief at the loss of her husband with her surrogate mother: "If thou engrossest all the griefs are thine," the Countess states, "Thou robb'st me of a moiety" (3.2.65–6). Helena's failure to share her sorrow deprives the Countess of an equal part of that feeling. Claiming that her adopted daughter means as much to her as her birth son, the Countess renounces Bertram on the grounds that he has wronged Helena: "He was my son, / But I do wash his name out of my blood / And thou art all my child" (3.2.66–8). The extremity of this statement – the assertion that Helena is now "all" the Countess's child, or her only child – reveals the mother's deep attachment to her adoptive daughter. "All" might also suggest that the Countess considers Helena to be entirely her child, or equivalent to a biological child. Although Helena and Bertram are married, the Countess does not think of Helena only as her son's wife and does not disown her alongside her son, but instead views her separately as her own child. Later, as she prepares to coax Bertram home, the Countess restores the balance between her two children, treating them equally in claiming that she does not have "skill in sense / To make distinction" between them (3.4.39–40).

The King views his ward in altogether different horticultural terms. He declares his power to deal with Bertram as he pleases. Although he welcomes Bertram to the court by stating "my son's no dearer" (1.2.76), marking him as the equivalent of a family member, the King does not demonstrate affection for his ward as the Countess does hers. He tells Helena that he has "both sovereign power and father's voice" (2.3.54) over his wards at court, establishing his authority to allow her to choose whichever ward she might like for a husband. When Bertram refuses Helena, the King assures Bertram of his power in horticultural language:

> We, poising us in her defective scale,
> Shall weigh thee to the beam; that wilt not know
> It is in us to plant thine honour where
> We please to have it grow. (2.3.154–7)

Although Bertram is unworthy of Helena and is subject to the King's command, the cruelty inherent in this guardian-ward relationship is evident.[46] The King's use of a controlling horticultural metaphor stands in contrast to the Countess's kinder treatment of Helena, where "choice breeds" the adopted child into the family (1.3.140). Unlike the Countess who sees Helena as a grafted slip, the King views Bertram as a seedling that he can plant at will, one that he does not need to graft but that can be forced to take root wherever he sees fit. The distinction between planting and grafting echoes an earlier episode. The King, remembering Bertram's father's effective style of speaking, tells Bertram that the Count's words were "scatter'd not in ears" but were instead "grafted" to them "to grow there and to bear" (1.2.54–5). G.K. Hunter notes that Shakespeare frequently puns on "ears" as both organs of hearing and seed-boxes or containers (Shakespeare, *All's Well* 19n54). These lines imply that the planting of seeds in seed-boxes is a rudimentary horticultural technique, unlike grafting, which is innovative and requires the gardener to use care. The King's statement that he will merely "plant" Bertram's honour provides no prospect of combination between the King and his ward, nor does it suggest anything other than regular growth. The model for inventive and caring parent-child relations is instead the Countess's relationship with Helena.

Like her adoptive mother, Helena is a horticulturalist of sorts: she attaches herself to Bertram's family tree through marriage. When she chooses a husband at court, she uses the image of a grafted family tree to express her wishes to the King. Acknowledging her difference from members of the royal family, Helena states that she will not select a husband of royal status from among the King's wards:

> Exempted be from me the arrogance
> To choose from forth the royal blood of France
> My low and humble name to propagate
> With any branch or image of thy state. (2.1.194–7)

Helena has seemingly absorbed the Countess's horticultural view of familial formation. Her use of the grafting metaphor signals a typical familial bond; her language implies that a woman, when she marries, is grafted onto her husband's family tree.[47] In this case, however, Helena is the grafter and not the graft: she adds her own name to the Rossillion family tree despite Bertram's objections.[48] Helena extends the Rossillion line, fastening herself to the family not only as the Countess's ward and adopted daughter, but also as Bertram's wife.

Helena is also involved in a form of female-exclusive breeding. Although Helena eventually becomes pregnant with Bertram's child, it appears that the female characters control reproduction. By plotting with the Widow and Diana to arrange that Bertram be sent to her bed unknowingly, Helena manages to fulfill her husband's order that she show him "a child begotten of thy body that I am father to" (3.2.57–8). In doing so, she all but physically removes Bertram from the reproductive equation.[49] Erotic love and procreation in the play are embedded within what Asp terms "the larger sphere of female affectivity" (188). Helena employs motherhood to regain her husband; she controls her pregnancy and uses it to her own ends. As Gary Waller notes, *All's Well* "is remarkable for its affirmation of the heart of women to embody literally, that continuity and 'right' ordering of life" ("From" 48). The female characters assume responsibility for reproduction and familial formation: at the beginning of the play, the Countess creates an adoptive mother-daughter bond, and at the end of the play Helena becomes pregnant by manipulating Bertram.

In the final scene, Helena is reunited with Bertram, but her affective bond with the Countess overshadows her relationship with her husband. Helena's final line perhaps suggests, as Sheldon Zitner observes, that she has come to see the Countess as a fusion of a birth mother and an adoptive mother (137).[50] Asking, "O my dear mother, do I see you living?" (5.3.313), she turns her attention from Bertram to her surrogate parent. Helena has no reason to think the Countess dead, and the line thus appears with "unexpected suddenness" (Zitner 137). John V. Robinson argues that the first half of the line – "O my dear mother" – is spoken to the Countess by Helena and fulfills "the Countess's desire to be called 'mother'" (426). The second half of the line, he suggests, should be ascribed to the Countess and spoken to Helena. It is the Countess who believes Helena dead, according to Robinson, and who would therefore express surprise at seeing her alive (426). The line could, however, be spoken entirely by Helena and interpreted as her final acknowledgment of the Countess as a "living" mother, one whom she views as truly her own.

In three of Shakespeare's romances, the identities of the heroes or heroines are masked by their ties to their temporary adoptive families. Helena, however, knows exactly who she is: a physician's daughter. She is not, like Guiderius and Arviragus in *Cymbeline* or Perdita in *The Winter's Tale*, the long-lost child of a king, nor is she, like Marina in *Pericles*, only temporarily separated from the royal parents she knows to be hers. The romances dramatize reunions of lost children with their noble or royal birth families; *All's Well*, a comedy, depicts the adoption of a base child into a family of higher standing. In other words, the comedy allows for a permanent improvement to an adopted child's status. When the Countess accepts her, Helena acquires a new familial context: a bond is created not only by Helena's marriage to Bertram, but also by the Countess's emotional and maternal attachment to her.

The grafting metaphor is fundamentally an expression of female authority. It suggests that the actions of Helena and the Countess are socially progressive: each character adds to the family tree where she sees fit. While the play concludes with the patriarchy seemingly restored, and Helena an obedient wife and mother, the grafting metaphor continues to assert the ability of women to work within and outside patriarchal norms of familial formation. The association of Helena and the Countess with grafting not only establishes them as the play's most powerful creators, but also aligns them with the playwright himself, marking them as surrogate dramatists. Shakespeare often puns on the etymological link between writing and grafting. As I mentioned earlier, the sharp point of a graft links it visually to a quill. And "graft" itself is derived from the Greek *graphion*, meaning a stylus or writing instrument; the Greek word for writing is *graphesis*. In Sonnet 15, the speaker mentions both writing and grafting as techniques of creation, and seeks to revitalize his addressee with his words: "And, all in war with Time for love of you / As he takes from you, I engraft you new" (ll. 13–14). The poet's words give new life to the beloved. Like writers, horticulturalists seek to shape the world. The grafting metaphor in *All's Well* signals the power of the Countess and Helena to fashion and refashion their own destinies within patriarchal hierarchies – that is, their capacity, like that of the poet or dramatist, for invention.

Chapter Two

Animal Parenting in Shakespeare's *Titus Andronicus*

Given that *Titus Andronicus* is Shakespeare's most brutal and bloody tragedy, it might seem unexpected that it includes a conversation about adoption – about creating families instead of destroying them. In a critical moment, Lavinia begs to be spared from Chiron and Demetrius, who seek to rape her. She insists to Tamora, the men's mother, that "ravens foster forlorn children" (2.2.153),[1] by which she means that ravens, although commonly thought to be ill omens, care for distressed young people. Lavinia's implication is clear: Tamora, in the role of the compassionate raven, should treat Lavinia as her child and take pity on her. The word *foster* links the social practice of adoption to the animal world – or more precisely, to the avian realm – and suggests that the birds can teach their observers virtue.[2] Lavinia's plea, and her particular turn of phrase, emphasize the fickleness of the family: kin may be selected, and kind disregarded.

In *The Winter's Tale, Cymbeline,* and *All's Well That Ends Well,* social ties bind families together as tightly as blood relations, at least for a time. Moreover, Shakespeare's various comparisons of adoption to grafting suggest that biological families can even be improved by the intervention of a guiding human hand in matters of genetic fate or chance. In *Titus,* however, it is the natural world, ostensibly beyond culture, that illustrates the changeability of the family structure – a changeability that can be emulated by human observers. Lavinia's appeal to Tamora depends on the belief that ravens have the capacity to create new families when the occasion arises; as natural adoptive parents, the birds cross the species boundary to forge new bonds based not on blood ties but on compassion. Avian exemplars, ravens belong to the early modern convention of seeing in animal behaviour guides to human political and social life.[3] It is in the context of this convention, or discourse, that I examine *Titus,* which by alluding to corvine adoption suggests its broader concern with the matter of how people understand themselves in relation to others: as the ravens might show Tamora how to act, so animals more generally might show us how to be more humane. In *Titus*, as in other plays, Shakespeare envisions a human world characterized by potential individual and social fluidity; adoption and fostering provide the language with which he depicts the instability of the human subject.

Although editors of *Titus* often note the provenance of Lavinia's proverbs and sometimes cite the affinity between her ravens and the biblical story of Elijah, her plea has received little attention from critics. Several scholars, in fact, have dismissed it as ineffectual.[4] I believe, however, that the passage is significant even if Lavinia's request is denied. Lavinia asserts the role of human agency in the construction of the family in the specific terms of animal caregiving.[5] She figures Tamora as a bird, and herself as the forlorn child, to suggest that whatever gulf separates the two women could be bridged, just as the species divide between bird and human can be spanned by the considerate ravens.[6] Although she has been reduced to begging, Lavinia retains the power to reimagine her fate. In a play that concerns warring families, such power – and in particular the ability to redefine kinship and the boundaries separating individuals and describing families – is of signal importance.

In what follows, I trace the play's specific references to adoption, including both Tamora's and Lavinia's perspectives on the practice. As I noted in the introduction, in the Roman world of *Titus*, adoption has political and ideological resonances that contextualize Lavinia's appeal. Adoption was a fundamental aspect of Rome's founding myth and had important ramifications in the matter of Roman citizenship; it emerges in *Titus* as a mark of successful civic conduct. I subsequently examine classical, biblical, and early modern narratives in which animals care for vulnerable human children. Lavinia's reference to adoptive ravens belongs to an enduring fascination with human children raised in nature by beasts. Her statement, however, is qualified by the quotative phrase "they say," which implies that her raven story is not fact but folklore. Indeed, the elements of the natural world to which she alludes are so overdetermined by cultural meanings that they are hardly natural at all. Her entreaty involves a comparison of animal behaviour to human comportment, but it equally suggests the importance of storytelling: it is perhaps not the lesson from nature that could save her, but human art.

Titus foregrounds the question of choice in the composition of the family; characters are faced with the opportunity to select and transform their own relations. Central to the concept of choice and change is Aaron, the play's most reviled figure. His conversion from a loath-some villain to a dedicated parent is radical. Aaron's blackness is typ-ically taken as a sign of his race and his morality, but it also aligns him with the raven, as Titus notes when he asks in relation to Aaron, "Did ever raven sing so like a lark?" (3.1.159).[7] Titus' statement is ironic: Aaron's "song" is a message from the emperor asking for Ti-tus' dismembered hand in exchange for the lives of his sons, a bargain that the emperor does not intend to uphold. But Aaron's association with the bird nevertheless recalls Lavinia's adoptive ravens and links Aaron to them. Like the raven, Aaron defies expectation. He does not have the opportunity to adopt someone else's child, but he is unex-pectedly willing first to take in his own child and then to see the boy adopted.

"A Roman Now Adopted": Adoptive Practices in Rome

From its opening scene the play foregrounds figurative familial relation and its importance in Rome. Once Titus selects Saturninus as emperor and surrenders his prisoners to him, Saturninus acknowledges his debt to the Roman general by using familial language:

> Thanks, noble Titus, father of my life.
> How proud I am of thee and of thy gifts
> Rome shall record, and when I do forget
> The least of these unspeakable deserts,
> Romans forget your fealty to me. (1.1.257–61)

In calling him "father," Saturninus recognizes that Titus is the genitor of his appointment as emperor, of his new "life" as the leader of Rome.[8] He also indicates that Titus is set to become his father-in-law upon his marriage to Lavinia. Fewer than fifty lines later, however, Saturninus rejects Titus and "any of [his] stock" (1.1.305) for refusing him Lavinia, thus dissolving any pretence of familial feeling between them. But Sat-urninus is not without a symbolic parent for long. When he proposes to Tamora, she answers by suggesting that she will take on a maternal role in his life. She states that if she becomes his wife, she "will a handmaid be to his desires, / A loving nurse, a mother to his youth" (1.1.336–7). Although most obviously and literally Tamora would become a nurse and mother to the future children ("youth") that she and Saturninus will conceive, her phrasing implies that she will also be a surrogate mother to Saturninus in *his* youth since she is considerably older than him. Tamora replaces Titus as his figurative parent and influential political ally. Titus is called "father" by Saturninus, but Tamora calls *herself* Saturninus' mother.[9]

Once she is empress, Tamora announces that she is "a Roman now adopted happily" (1.1.468). She is adopted in two ways: as a married woman she becomes her husband's dependant, and as a foreigner married to a Roman citizen she too becomes a citizen of Rome. Roman marriages fell into one of two categories: *cum manu* and *sine manu*. In its *cum manu* form, marriage meant that a bride "left the agnatic family of birth just as fully as if she had undergone adoption" (Lindsay 97). A wife in a *cum manu* marriage was the rough legal equivalent of her husband's child: she was regarded as being *filiae loco* – in the situation of a daughter – and her inheritance rights were only equivalent to those of her own children (Gardner, *Women* 11). However, a husband did not hold the same power over his wife that he did over his daughter. As Gardner notes, "He did not have the right of life or death over her, nor of noxal surrender or sale (other than the fictitious one in a fiduciary *coemptio*)" (*Women* 11).[10] Any property that a wife owned prior to the marriage was placed under the control of her husband or his *paterfamilias*. If the woman had been legally independent (*sui iuris*) before marriage, she lost that independence (Lindsay 97). In a *sine manu* marriage, by contrast, the wife remained under the control of her own father or *paterfamilias*. This allowed a woman's property to stay in her natal family (Grubbs 21). Tamora's claim that she has been "adopted" could suggest that hers is a *cum manu* marriage, and that she must now defer to Saturninus as though she were his child – at least to flatter her new husband.

In addition to implying that she is now an obedient wife, Tamora's use of the term "adopted" indicates her rebirth as a Roman and her detachment from her Gothic roots and past grievances against Titus. As Julia Reinhard Lupton proposes, adoption is "a key model and metaphor of civic naturalization"; she explains that "in the rites of adoption and naturalization, a new nativity is artificially born through a legal process supplemented by psychosocial forces of reinvestment and reinvention in the face of exile and exposure, banishment and abandon" (127).[11] Through marriage, Tamora is the symbolic child-citizen of her new state and describes herself as being part of the wider family of Romans to which Titus also belongs; Tamora and Titus are now figurative siblings who stem from a new but common lineage conferred through citizenship. Her complementary assertion that she is "incorporate in Rome" also serves to place her among the Roman citizenry (1.1.467).[12] To "incorporate" in the early modern period (as today) could mean "to combine or form into a society or organization;

esp. to constitute as a legal corporation" (*OED*, V.3.a). But "incorporate" also meant "to combine or unite into one body ... to mix or blend thoroughly together" (*OED*, V.1). Tamora's statement implies that she now belongs to the Roman political body. Her figuration echoes the notion that family members are literally incorporate in one another by virtue of their shared blood. Tamora's adoption allows her to imagine herself – sincerely or not – as part of a civic and almost familial body. Her sanguine view of the body here is ironic in light of the bodily dismemberment that is the hallmark of the later scenes of the play.

Tamora's emphasis on Roman citizenry and familial attachment is a strategic reiteration of Titus' own views. When Titus thanks "kind Rome" for ensuring Lavinia's safety while he is away at war, he suggests that Rome both has acted kindly and is his kind, or his kindred (1.1.168).[13] As Jean E. Feerick observes, in this moment Titus "invokes a more expansive definition of family" ("Botanical" 88).[14] Tamora's reference to adoptive citizenship thus appeals to Titus' civic sense. But she uses the term "adopted," of course, to imply that she plans to forge a peaceful, familiar relationship with the Andronici when really she intends to "raze their faction and their family" (1.1.456). Tamora's Roman adoption does not fundamentally alter her kind, or her sense of familial allegiance; she merely pretends to forgive Titus so that she may reinforce her own biological family ties by avenging the death of her son Alarbus.

After her political adoption, Tamora denies Lavinia her request to be adopted personally, thus demonstrating the multi-faceted nature of adoption and accentuating the potentially strategic uses to which it might be put. Whereas Tamora insists, albeit deceptively, that she is adopted by Rome and by her husband, Lavinia envisions a distinctly female, animal-inspired adoptive world. Adoption was widespread in ancient Rome, but it was controlled by men: Roman men had "a recognized right ... to reshape [their] relationships" (Gardner, "Status" 77). Women could not adopt because they lacked *patria potestas*, or paternal power (Lindsay 218).[15] The particularly male ability to determine the contours of the family also extended to the cases of biological children: fathers had to recognize their children in order for those children to be accepted as legitimate. Children who were not duly recognized – often because they were ill or deformed – were abandoned or killed (Dupont 220). Lavinia's use of the term *foster* suggests a possible connection to Tamora that is a radical alteration of typical Roman adoption; it presents both women with the opportunity to remodel their families. In proposing that a Gothic woman might adopt a Roman girl, Lavinia also suggests that kind can be negated. Like does not only have to adopt like.

Kinds and Kindness: Adoptive Animals

In the early modern period, connections and likenesses among living things – including humans and animals – took precedence over the differences that became the focus of Linnaean taxonomy.[16] Jean E. Feerick and Vin Nardizzi note "humankind's complex embeddedness among creaturely life on earth, his tendency to be marked by a kind of limping distinction in only potentially occupying a step up from his creaturely kin and yet necessarily trailing a few steps behind them in the activities of sensation, strength, and growth" (2–3).[17] Humans had the capacity to be superior to other creatures, but they were not always their betters. Animals were figured frequently as teachers and exemplars who could shape human behaviour. Bees, for example, provided a model for political organization in the manner of Virgil's *Georgics*.[18] The child-rearing abilities of animals were also venerated. Pierre Viret states in the epistle to *The Schoole of Beastes, Intituled, the good Householder, or the Oeconomickes* (trans. 1585) that "I Have intituled this Dialogue, the good Householder, or the Oeconomickes, because I make comparison in the same, of the good and euil householders with beastes, which knowe best to prouide for their nourishment and conseruation as well of them as of their yong" (A2r). Animals, according to Viret, can demonstrate to humans how best to run their households and care for their children.[19] In particular, he admires animals that display "affection towardes their litle ones, and the care they haue of them" (A3r). Viret believes that the foundation of a functional household is familial affection, a quality that animals possess in abundance: "al the beastes generally (as *Plutark* wittnesseth) do loue entirely that which they ingender and bring forthe, and cherish them carefully" (C8r). Edward Topsell maintains that the animals on Noah's ark were saved so "than man might gain out of them much devine knowledge" (*Foure-Footed Beastes* A4r). Topsell reports in *The History of Foure-Footed Beastes* (1607) that birds care for their elders: "young storkes and Wood-peckers do in their parents olde age feed and nourish them" (A5r). "Who," he asks, "is so vnnaturall and vnthankeful to his parents, but ... will not repent, amend his folly, and bee more naturall" upon learning such information (A5r)? "Naturall" familial behaviour is that of animals and it is this conduct to which humans should aspire.[20]

Titus suggests the didactic potential of animals, as well as affinities among humans and animals. The play's concern with types, familial ties, and kindness relates to its interest in animal behaviour and the lessons that animals can teach humans. Lavinia presents two cases of exemplary animal conduct, both of which provide her with the language to suggest to Tamora that identity and allegiance need not be fixed, and both of which involve interspecies contact. The first casts a lion as a model: "The lion, moved with pity, did endure / To have his princely paws pared all away" (2.2.151–2). Lavinia alludes to the story of Androcles or Andronicus, a Roman slave, who is made to fight a lion for the emperor's entertainment with the expectation that the beast will behave savagely (Tilley H311). Surprisingly, however, the lion embraces Androcles rather than tear him to pieces. It is then revealed that Androcles had earlier helped the lion: when he came across the animal in the wild with a thorn lodged in its paw, he removed the source of its pain. The lion therefore chooses to follow a human example by showing mercy (Bate 93). Conversely, Tamora is asked to act like an animal. Other early modern accounts of the tale, such as that of Topsell in *The History of Foure-Footed Beasts*, take the idea of the lion's kindness even further and depict the creature caring for and feeding Androcles. The lion does not merely spare the slave's life: in tending to him it also treats him as a parent might treat a child. Lavinia desires just such care and flexibility from Tamora, whom she suggests could, like the lion, choose not to be brutal. Her plea demonstrates respect for and appreciation of the actions of other creatures; it positions the natural world in the role of educator, especially when it comes to adoptive behaviour.

   Lavinia's second animal example is remarkable because the gentle conduct that she describes is perhaps even more unexpected than that of the lion. In the same scene we hear of both the "fatal raven" (2.2.97) and the fostering raven. Ravens in Shakespeare often presage calamity. In *Othello*, for instance, the raven is "boding to all" (4.1.21), and in *Macbeth* a human messenger becomes a figurative bird whose breathlessness foretells ill doing: "the raven himself is hoarse / That croaks the fatal entrance of Duncan / Under [Macbeth's] battlements" (1.5.37–9). The birds are also sometimes described as being in search of victims, scavenging for food where they can: "Ravens … / Fly o'er our heads, and downward look on us, / As we were sickly prey" (*Julius Caesar* 5.1.84–6). In *Henry V* carrion crows – birds closely related to ravens – stalk the English army, waiting for corpses to drop, "impatient for their hour" (4.2.52). But Lavinia's mention of ravens recalls both Christian and classical stories of the propensity of birds to nurture human children. In giving the example of a helpful raven, Lavinia perhaps alludes to the biblical story of Elijah.[21] After Elijah announces to Ahab that there will be a terrible drought as punishment for Ahab's construction of an altar to Baal, God instructs Elijah to hide by a brook in the forest. Elijah is sustained by ravens that bring him "bread and flesh in the morning, and bread and flesh in the evening" (1 Kings 17:6). Other Christian figures who are fed by ravens include St. Benedict and Paul of Thebes.[22] In all of these stories, ravens follow divine instruction to offer protection to those in need. Like Lavinia's ravens, they are startlingly kind.

Less obviously, Lavinia's remark about fostering ravens also alludes to the mythological tale of Rome's founding, in which a bird sustains human infants. The story of the upbringing of Romulus and Remus was most familiar in early modern England from Thomas North's 1579 translation of Plutarch's *Lives*, which contains several versions of the brothers' origins. The tale that "carieth best credit of all, and is allowed of by many writers" (21) is that of Amulius and Numitor, brothers who are the joint inheritors of their father's kingdom and who are at odds with each other over who should control the land and wealth of the realm. Amulius is victorious and, in order to ensure that his brother has no grandchildren who might eventually succeed him, decides to send Numitor's daughter Rhea to a "nunne of the goddess Vesta" so that she will remain a virgin (21). The young woman soon becomes pregnant, however, and when her twin sons Romulus and Remus are born, Amulius commands his servant to "throwe them away, and destroye them" (22). The servant places the infants in a "trough" and takes them to the river, where they are carried downstream. When they eventually wash up on shore, a "shee woulfe" gives the twins "sucke" (22). But the wolf does not care for the babies on her own: a "hitwaw" – a woodpecker – "dyd helpe to norishe and keepe them" (22).[23] Remus later states that he and his brother were "fostered and geuen sucke more straungely, and in our tender yeres were fedd by birdes and wilde beasts, to whom we were cast out as a praye" (24).[24] While the wolf suckled them with her "teates," he says, the hitwaw "brought [them] litle crommes, and put them in [their] mouthes" (24). As Plutarch explains (in North's rendition), both the wolf and the hitwaw "are thought to be consecrated to the god *Mars*, & the LATINES doe singularly honour & reuerence the hitwaw" (22). That it is these two creatures that care for Romulus and Remus, Plutarch states, later convinces many people of the veracity of Rhea's claim that she was impregnated by Mars himself (22).[25]

Lavinia of course mentions a raven rather than a woodpecker, but her focus on the vital behaviour of a bird is in keeping with the legend of Rome's founding.[26] While today the role of the wolf in the story tends to eclipse that of the woodpecker – due in part, perhaps, to the most famous artistic representation of the tale, the Capitoline Wolf statue in Rome, which depicts the "shee-woulfe" suckling Romulus and Remus with no avian assistance[27] – it is clear in Plutarch's account that the bird plays an equal role in the twins' survival. And in fact, birds go on to be important to the boys throughout their lives. When they are older and disagree about where to found a city, the twins turn to birds to settle the matter: to choose a location, they rely on "the flying of birds, which doe geue a happy diuination of things to come" (25). Twelve vultures appear at Romulus' preferred site while only six visit the location chosen by Remus, thus determining the future site of Rome in Romulus' favour. As Plutarch states, this is why Romans in his own time continued to believe the "soothesayings of the flying birds" (26).[28]

Plutarch's account of the upbringing of Romulus and Remus by two different kinds of animals underscores the effects of particular forms of nourishment on children, a topic of interest to Lavinia as she considers how children's identities are shaped. A distinction is made between the ways in which Romulus and Remus are fed by each of their animal caregivers. Whereas the twins suck directly from the wolf's breast, they are given "crommes" from the beak of the woodpecker. Plutarch implies that the boys acquire vicious, lupine characteristics from the wolf's milk (27). These traits lead ultimately to fratricide. The woodpecker, however, does not impart any animal traits to Romulus and Remus, and has no such adverse effect on them. By emphasizing avian rather than mammalian care in her request to Tamora, Lavinia avoids an example of interspecies caregiving that involves suckling. She is keenly aware of the potentially negative power of breastmilk. In the moments before her adoptive plea, Lavinia discusses with Chiron and Demetrius the significance of Tamora's having nursed them: "The milk thou suck'st from her did turn to marble; / Even at thy teat thou hadst thy tyranny" (2.2.144–5). The men are doomed to act like their mother because they were breastfed; it is Tamora's milk that forms their natures. Such a statement echoes the opinions of some early modern medical writers who believed that breastmilk was composed of the mother's blood. In *Child-Birth or, The Happy Delivery of Women* (1612), Jacques Guillemeau advises that "it were fit that every mother should nurse her owne child: because her milke which is nothing else, but the bloud whitened (of which he was made, and wherewith hee had beene nourished the time hee staide in his Mothers wombe) will bee always more naturall, and familiar unto him, than that of a stranger" (1).[29] The belief that breastmilk was made of the same substance as the woman herself fuelled concerns that wet nurses could pass on their characteristics through their milk, confusing a suckling child's identity (Fildes, *Breasts* 188–95).[30] Lavinia is of course not about to nurse at Tamora's breast, but her unease about the effect of milk on Tamora's sons suggests the play's more general concern with nourishment, a subject that extends back to the story of Rome's establishment and that I also examine in relation to Aaron's baby below.

Lavinia's anxiety about the influence of milk stems from its supposed ability to alter permanently the behaviour of a child. But despite her concern that Tamora's milk has moulded Chiron and Demetrius irrevocably, Lavinia allows briefly that "every mother breeds not sons alike," and that it is possible for a child to act differently from its mother (2.2.146). To Chiron, however, like breeds like. He observes that if he were to "entreat [Tamora to] show a woman's pity," he would "prove [himself] a bastard" by behaving entirely unlike his parent (2.2.147–8). Lavinia agrees that a child cannot be wholly unlike its mother by stating that "the raven doth not hatch a lark" (2.2.149). It is notable that this comment is made before her plea for adoption. The idea that children were necessarily like their parents dates to the classical period. Aristotle claims in *Generation of Animals* (c. 320 BC), a zoological and philosophical treatise, that all human progeny should look like those who begot them, lest they risk bordering on the grotesque: "For even he who does not resemble his parents is already in a certain sense a monstrosity; for in these cases nature has in a way departed from the type" (1187). If a child is born unlike its parents, in other words, it must be somehow a monster. The conversation between Lavinia and Chiron confirms their mutual belief that it is impossible for one species to "hatch" another. But Lavinia effectively distinguishes fostering from hatching when she presents the prospect of ravens caring for human children. The raven may not birth a lark, but it can adopt one.

Like Tamora's statement of adoption – for which Lavinia was present – Lavinia's request that Tamora foster her implies that the differences between the Goths and the Andronici might be overcome; her animal example can teach humans about their own capacity for change. Her wish that Tamora be "nothing so kind, but something [so] pitiful" as a raven towards her links the quality of kindness to kind or type (2.2.156). Like Hamlet's "a little more than kin, and less than kind" (*Hamlet* 1.2.65), the statement should remind us that kinship and bloodlines play a central role in the play's tragic outcome.[31] Lavinia acknowledges that Tamora's "hard heart [may] say no" (2.2.155) to behaving like a raven, but hopes that if Tamora cannot be "so kind" – as compassionate as, or of the same type as, the bird – then she can at least express some measure of pity towards Lavinia.[32] The play's Ovidian source envisions repeatedly the mixing of kinds and the possibility of change with its many narratives of animal-human-plant transformations. The comparisons in *Titus* between Lavinia and Philomel align Lavinia herself with human-avian metamorphosis (2.3.38; 2.3.43; 5.2.194). Although Lavinia does not actually ask Tamora to become a bird, she does suggest that Tamora should emulate the behaviour of the raven by ignoring kind and caring for a member of another family. In Lavinia's model of cross-species parenting, a parent of one type can care for the offspring of another; she thus appeals to Tamora in terms that suggest a distinction between the seemingly inflexible nature of biology and the possibilities afforded by adoption. Of course, the compassion that Lavinia requests eventually becomes a plea for death: she asks that Tamora kill her "with thine own hands" (2.2.169).

Her adoptive plea and its focus on animal caregiving also express Lavinia's desire to defy generic convention, at least in the moments before she asks Tamora to kill her: she indicates that she wants to find herself in a romance rather than a tragedy. She is plainly not an abandoned or lost infant who will be rescued by an animal and raised by shepherds, but the generous, adoptive nature of such a romantic upbringing lies at the heart of her appeal. In *The Winter's Tale*, the mention of potential animal-human fostering heralds an instance of human-human fostering. Antigonus is instructed by Leontes to leave the baby Perdita in "some remote or desert place" (2.3.175). He hopes that wild creatures will behave less viciously towards her than has her own father:

> Come on, poor babe:
> Some powerful spirit instruct the kites and ravens
> To be thy nurses! Wolves and bears, they say,
> Casting their savageness aside, have done
> Like offices of pity. (2.3.184–8)

Unlike Leontes, Antigonus claims, animals can feel compassion for defenceless children despite their own "savageness."[33] As with the story of Elijah and the ravens, such sympathy is taken to be divine in origin: the tutelage of a "powerful spirit" allows these creatures to alter their behaviour. Antigonus' vision for Perdita's future does not come true: in fact, a bear eats him rather than caring for the baby that he places on the shores of Bohemia. But this episode draws the attention of the shepherd, who raises Perdita as his own daughter. Although in this instance nature does not demonstrate compassion for humans, it does inadvertently ensure an abandoned child's safety.

Shakespeare was many years away from writing romances when he composed *Titus*, but Lavinia's appeal to Tamora in romantic terms echoes the didactic possibilities of cross-species encounters in early modern prose romances.[34] Perhaps the best known of these narratives is *Valentine and Orson*, which is medieval in origin and was first translated from the French by Henry Watson. It appeared in print in at least sixteen editions between 1510 and 1700 (Dickson ix–xvi).[35] The romance begins with the marriage of King Pepyn's sister Bellysant to the Emperor of Greece. Not long after the wedding, Bellysant refuses the advances of a licentious archbishop who then seeks revenge by telling her husband that she has been unfaithful. When the Emperor hears of his wife's alleged adultery and learns that she is pregnant, he casts her out of his court.[36] Bellysant flees to France, where she gives birth to twin boys under a tree while alone in a wood. But Bellysant gets very little time with her babies: just after the birth "ther came vnto her a beer, the which was maruelously great and horrible, & toke one of her children in his mouthe, and wente his way into the thycke of the forest also faste as he might" (*The hystory* D4r).[37] Bellysant leaves her other child by the tree and chases after the bear, but she can find no trace of the animal. When she returns to the tree, the baby she left behind is also missing; unbeknownst to Bellysant, he has been taken by King Pepyn, who, unaware that the baby is his nephew, names him Valentine. The rest of the story involves the differing fates of the twin brothers, who are raised by either animals or humans, but focuses on the ursine twin Orson. Although the bear at first "caste[s] the chylde amonge hys whelpes to be eaten," "the younge Beeres dyd it no harme" (E3r). Instead, they show Orson compassion: "with theyr roughe pawes [they] strooked it softelye" (E3r). Seeing that her cubs accept the baby as one of their own, the mother bear becomes "right amerous of the chylde (so muche) that she kepte it and gaue it souke a hole yeare" (E3r). In stealing a human child to feed its own young, the bear acts as ferociously as might be expected and is mindful of her own kind. But in their compassion, both the mother bear and her cubs ignore kind and prove themselves to be less savage than the Emperor himself, who cast out his expectant wife.

The story of Valentine and Orson also serves a religious purpose: not only does the mother bear demonstrate kindness that is absent from the human realm, but she also allows Orson to be a better Christian. As in *The Winter's Tale*, the surprising sensitivity of animals is linked to a watchful heavenly eye. The bear's adoption of the boy is so virtuous that it is described as an act of God, who "neuer forgeteth his frendes" and so ensures that Orson is treated gently (E3r). The boy's diet of bear's milk and the companionship of his sibling bears influence his behaviour as he becomes "rough as a beere" and does "muche harme in the forest" (E3r). And yet when Valentine returns to the wood to recover him, Orson quickly becomes a fervent Christian. His time in the forest prepares him to be what Susan Wiseman terms a "kind of Christian berserker – a wild man for God" (169); exposure to the wilderness and to the behaviour of animals gives him an animal-like energy for the pursuit of religion. At the story's close it is revealed that after his death Orson becomes a "saynt cannonyzed" (c5v).

Lavinia idealizes animal generosity towards human children, but she also appears to venerate cruelty: as they foster human foundlings, the ravens leave "their own birds [to] famish in their nests" (2.2.154). Her avian model for adoption involves the rejection of birth children and makes leaving those children to starve a sign of virtue. Lavinia thus appears to conflate the biblical story of Elijah with other biblical accounts of ravens who desert their newly hatched chicks, leaving them to waste away unless nourished by God, as in the Book of Job: "Who provideth for the raven his food? when his young ones cry unto God, they wander for lack of meat" (Job 38:41). A similar question is probed in Psalms: "Who feedeth the young ravens when they cry?" (Psalms 147:9). Shakespeare refers to such heavenly intervention in the nourishment of abandoned birds in *As You Like It* when Adam notes that "he that doth the ravens feed / Yea, providently caters for the sparrow" (2.3.43–4). Lavinia does not appear to wish that, once deserted by their mother, Chiron and Demetrius be left to God's care. Instead, her amalgamation of two biblical stories emphasizes her flair for storytelling.[38] Although she indicates that it is the natural behaviour of animals that is most impressive, her combination of a story about adoption with one of abandonment perhaps suggests instead the power of art over nature. Lavinia's attempt to change Tamora's mind depends upon her ability to weave a narrative about adoptive ravens and forsaken chicks.

Shakespeare's other possible source texts do not show parental desertion: the bird that succoured Romulus and Remus did not do so while neglecting its own offspring, for example. But the behaviour that Lavinia recommends is somewhat similar to that of a goat in Angel Day's 1587 English translation of Longus' Greek romance *Daphnis and Chloe*.[39] Lamon, a goatherd, "keep[s] his charge" of his animals when he finds a baby boy, Daphnis, who has been "preserued by the sucke it receiued from one of his shee-goates" (3). "Against nature," the goat feeds the human baby and leaves "hir young kiddes vncherished" (3). The goat neglects her kids out of a seemingly innate recognition of the importance of sustaining an abandoned human baby of high birth. In Lavinia's proposition to Tamora, all of the biological and non-biological "children" in question are people of high birth, whether of Goth or Roman origin. Because they are roughly equivalent in social status, the choice as to which children should be privileged is less related to class than it is to virtue. Lavinia asks Tamora to act unusually by abandoning her "own birds," or sons, because of the evil that they plan to commit. Rather than being cruel, Lavinia suggests, Tamora's rejection of her biological children would act as a corrective to nature: honourable but adopted Lavinia would be nurtured while dishonourable but biological Chiron and Demetrius would be neglected. Lavinia thus imagines the undoing of Tamora's biological relatives in a way that is similar to and yet distinct from Tamora's desire to "raze" Titus' family (1.1.456). By proposing that she disregard her own children, Lavinia also recommends that Tamora behave in a way that is comparable to Titus, who has killed his own son.

Lavinia's appeal is, however, fruitless, and the queen of the Goths sanctions the girl's rape and mutilation. Tamora's curt response to Lavinia's reference to fostering ravens is "I know not what it means" (2.2.157). The reply suggests that she either does not understand Lavinia's proposal, or does not comprehend the concept of pity. Lavinia's plea also has the effect of reminding Tamora of her own earlier incompetent pleading: "Remember, boys, I poured forth tears in vain / To save your brother from the sacrifice" (2.2.163–4). Tamora's refusal to be swayed by the parallel between humans and animals indicates Lavinia's failure to change the play's narrative and, more broadly, her failure with language.[40] Although she has no success with Tamora, Lavinia does for a brief moment bring to the fore the potential for adoptive thinking to alter the play's outcome. And her vision for changing the family is realized in an admittedly different way at the play's close with Aaron's baby.

Aaron's Forlorn Child

The notion of adding to or subtracting from a family line is revisited later in the play with the birth of the son of Tamora and Aaron. Tamora rejects her baby and orders him "christen[ed]" – or rather, murdered – with a "dagger's point" (4.2.72) because of his revealing dark skin, but the child is saved by his father. In Lavinia's words, Aaron is Tamora's "raven-coloured love" (2.2.83); the blackness of his Moorish skin associates him with the moral blackness of the usually menacing raven. As I noted previously, Titus confirms the association when he listens to Aaron speak and asks, "Did ever raven sing so like a lark?" (3.1.159). Lavinia's talk of fostering ravens suggests, however, that even the most unexpected figures can exhibit kindness towards desperate children. Aaron does not act precisely like Lavinia's ravens: he neither adopts a child nor shirks his responsibility for his own. Yet he does become a surprisingly devoted parent who thinks adoptively in that he is willing to see his son raised by others for the child's own benefit. That is, he is an attentive father who thinks flexibly about the composition of his family. Aaron plans to have his friend Muliteus and his wife bring up the boy in place of their own baby, whose light skin enables them to pass him off as Saturninus' child. As a result, Muliteus' "child shall be advanced / And be received for the emperor's heir" (4.2.159–60) while Aaron's baby will be raised as a commoner but in the anonymous safety of the countryside. Aaron thus acts unlike Lavinia's ravens and yet is associated with them by his willingness to alter his family. He does not "foster forlorn children," but he creates the conditions for protective fosterage of his own son.

Aaron's plans for his child's adoptive upbringing soon change, however – or perhaps his story about Muliteus was only ever a pretence – and he is suddenly intent on caring for his boy himself. Like Lavinia, Aaron uses the terms of pastoral romance as he envisions an ideal new life for the boy; his dream for raising his son is in some ways reminiscent of Lavinia's earlier entreaty for cross-species pity:[41]

> Come on, you thick-lipped slave, I'll bear you hence,
> For it is you that puts us to our shifts.
> I'll make you feed on berries and on roots,
> And fat on curds and whey, and suck the goat,
> And cabin in a cave, and bring you up
> To be a warrior and command a camp. (4.2.177–82)

The rustic life that Aaron describes might be found in a typical early modern romance in which a forsaken child is protected by nature. The boy will live off the land and a goat will act as his wet nurse in the absence of his human mother. He will not be abandoned or exposed, and although he will not strictly be raised by animals, he will live among animals and be sustained by them. The goat's milk perhaps even stands as a corrective to the milk that the baby would have received from Tamora, milk that Lavinia earlier established as responsible for the depraved personalities of Tamora's sons. But Aaron's fantasy may in fact concern bare survival: it would be impossible for him to rear the child in the city with a human wet nurse without raising suspicion. And he pictures a belligerent future for his son, not one of bucolic peace.

Aaron remains concerned for his son's well-being until the end of the play. Although he is a prisoner, he is in control of his child's life, negotiating for the boy's survival through a series of commands. He first tells Lucius to "touch not the boy" (5.1.49) and to "save the child, / And bear it from me to the empress" (5.1.53–4), demanding that the baby be returned to its mother. When Lucius does not agree to do as he wishes, Aaron threatens to take information about the "complots of mischief" performed throughout the play with him to his grave (5.1.65).

The warning forces Lucius to swear that Aaron's "child shall live," and that he "will see it nourished" (5.1.60). Lucius may mean simply that he will guarantee that the child is given to a wet nurse, but his mention of nourishment recalls Lavinia's insistence that one species can feed and care for the child of another. Lucius agrees to bridge the divisions between Goths and Romans in the same way that Lavinia envisions a breaking down of barriers between species. The line also echoes the emphasis on the kind of nourishment received by fictional lost or abandoned infants from Romulus and Remus to Daphnis. Lucius' promise and Aaron's subsequent directive to him to "save my boy, to nurse and bring him up" (5.1.84) place Lucius in the role of adoptive parent. The baby is thus in a way, to borrow Tamora's phrasing, "a Roman newly adopted" by Lucius. Compelling this adoption is Aaron's final act. The care that Aaron demands from Lucius ensures the continuation of Aaron's family line because it safeguards the survival of his child. Exactly what kind of treatment the baby will receive is beyond the scope of the play, but Aaron's son holds the potential to demonstrate the mutability of the divisions between Moor, Goth, and Roman. And by insisting upon his son's adoption, Aaron maintains the power that was once Lavinia's to reimagine his own fate – in this case a fate tied to that of his offspring – through the use of adoption. Productions, of course, may differ markedly in how they stage the baby's future.

Whereas Shakespeare's plays that use grafting as a metaphor for adoption are concerned with the distinction between nature and culture, in *Titus* the animal parenting metaphor suggests that innate adoptive tendencies in the animal world might be emulated by humans. Such exemplary behaviour implies that adoption is a practice linked to the natural world. But to some degree the play is also concerned with the relations between nature and art: it is the story about the ravens that is the source of Lavinia's possible salvation. The pastoral future that Aaron briefly envisions for his son depends similarly on tales that romanticize animal-human contact. His plea to see his son cared for by others, even his enemies, idealizes adaptability and the possibility of changing the narrative.

Chapter Three

Middleton's *A Chaste Maid in Cheapside* and Adopted Bastards

Like many early modern comedies, Middleton's *A Chaste Maid in Cheapside* (1613) is preoccupied with marriage, inheritance, and the extension of the family line through procreation. In a culture obsessed by familial continuity, biological heirs (almost always male children)[1] ensured not only that a family's property would be passed on, but also that children would maintain their family names and, in a figurative sense, extend their parents' lives.[2] In *The Glasse of Godly Loue* (1569), a tract on virtuous behaviour, John Rogers describes children as "the highest guift" because "in their children do the Parents liue (in a manner) after their death" (85); he suggests that "they dye not all togethers, that leaue collops of their owne flesh aliue behind them" (85). The conceptualization of children as extensions of their parents' bodies had a counterpart in the medical world. Helkiah Crooke's landmark medical treatise *Mikrokosmographia* (1615), for example, posits children as a source of everlasting youth:

> For so euery individuum, extending itself as it were, in the procreation of another like unto it selfe, groweth young again and becommeth after a sort eternall. The father liveth in the sonne, and dyeth not as long as his express and living Image stands upon the earth. (200)

Comedic resolution, as many critics including Northrop Frye and Alexander Leggatt have noted, depends upon sexual reproduction and the creation of the next generation.[3] But reproduction and futurity in Middleton's play are far from straightforward. While couples in *A Chaste Maid in Cheapside* come to have heirs, the play suggests that heirship does not necessarily derive directly from procreation, and that sexual reproduction can be improved upon as the basis for familial continuity. Middleton depicts the failings of fertility and the ways in which too much or too little thereof can be corrected to ensure economic and familial stability. In the play, a particular level of fecundity is not assumed – the production of offspring can be encouraged or discouraged – and reproduction often occurs outside the sanctioned family structure. The problem of fecundity involves interaction between, and in some cases collaboration among, families. Save the Yellowhammers and the Touchwoods, no family produces children independently, and children, who are not necessarily tied biologically to a single family, circulate among several families. The family line does not depend upon "collops of [parents'] owne flesh."

A *Chaste Maid in Cheapside* is highly concerned with material and social advancement, as well as with the particular moral and physical conditions of its urban setting. A city comedy, it is aligned with the commercial growth of London and the emergence of the middle class; its characters aspire to financial success and increased social status.[4] Despite its emphasis on mercantile activity, however, considerable time is devoted to family life: the households of the Yellowhammers, the Allwits, the Touchwoods, and the Kixes are portrayed in great detail. As Samuel Schoenbaum suggests, by focusing simultaneously on marriage, family, and commerce, Middleton "conveys, perhaps more adequately than any of his contemporaries, the breakdown or corruption of traditional values in the wake of the new materialistic order" (293). Such a "breakdown" is exemplified by the frequency with which characters violate social conventions, including the expectation that reproduction take place only within marriage. Some interpretations have proposed that the characters' immoral conduct is affected by environmental change as well as by financial considerations. Bruce Boehrer suggests that Middleton "likens urban behavior to environmentally conditioned illnesses": the corruption associated with city life "arises from changes in Londoners' lived relation to the natural world" (*Environmental* 42). As London's population increased dramatically – "by Middleton's day, there were more people per square mile in London than almost anywhere else in Europe" (42) – Londoners' experience and knowledge of the natural world were changed.[5] Not all behaviour can be explained by environmental circumstances – Middleton's characters also have intrinsic qualities – but the abundance of bastard children in Cheapside and the fertility problems that plague some characters are linked to city living. The play's vision of urban life assumes that families will be composed in manifold ways.

Francis Bacon observes that through human intervention, "nature, like *Proteus*, is forced by art to do what would not have been done without it: and it does not matter whether you call this forcing and enchaining, or assisting and perfecting" (*Descriptio* 101). The "art" in question in *A Chaste Maid in Cheapside* is the alteration of the natural world and the consanguineous family. In three of the play's families, children are the biological descendants of only one parent or neither parent at all. Infertility takes on a critical role in familial formation; the play suggests that physical failings might be circumvented and that husbands and wives can control reproduction. Infertility is not the only cause of families of mixed biological origin, however. Some families also struggle with excess fertility and the production of bastards, who share certain characteristics with adoptees. But whether such familial formations allow nature to be "perfected" is questionable.

In the play's postlapsarian setting, adoptive practices are common. As Michelle M. Dowd observes, urban relocation provided the city's residents with the ability to develop relationships that were based in London itself rather than in kin networks. The city thus "became a place in which various forms of voluntary, extrafamilial social relationships could emerge as alternative pathways to patrilineal stability" (215). In the play's densely populated Cheapside neighbourhood, where bastards proliferate and are redistributed among families, children are thought of in economic terms. The promoters calculate that the child left to them will cost them half their profits (2.2.199); Sir Oliver and Lady Kix are willing to pay four hundred pounds to conceive a child (3.3.147–9); Touchwood Sr. and his wife determine that additional children will ruin them financially (2.1.7–14); and Allwit manages to earn his living by keeping the children of another man (1.2.15–57).[6] In each of the play's families, children represent an essential part of the "oeconomie," the financial management of the household.[7] As Brian Gibbons observes, Middleton's satire focuses "on those characters for whom all human relationships are conceived of in terms of financial contract" (167). Economic necessity dictates the composition of the family; social and familial relation is closely linked to financial need. Adoption permits families to be changed for financial purposes and the unnatural space of Cheapside is aligned with apparently unnatural familial practices. The play does not necessarily endorse adoption, which it associates with immoral urban life, but it depicts adoption as a customary, if not pervasive, aspect of contemporary society. It suggests a divide between the ideal of socially sanctioned, "natural" patrilineality and a reality in which lineage is routinely contrived.

The Kixes' barrenness and resulting social status cause them to alter – whether knowingly or not – the biological makeup of their family. Sir Oliver's role as a cuckold links him to other fathers in the play who raise bastard children who are not theirs by blood. For entirely different reasons, Allwit and the promoters also form makeshift families in which the role of parent is given to men who have not procreated. In portraying these families, the play links cuckolds, bastards, and adoptees. Like adoptees, bastards could reveal divisions between nature and culture. Although "bastard" was a cultural designation that marked a child as diverging from the norm of legitimate birth in marriage, it was also interchangeable with the term "natural child." As Alison Findlay notes, "the adjective 'natural' denotes a bastard's metaphorical exclusion from culture, from divine spirit and human law" (129).[8] According to Michael Neill, a bastard is "an 'out of joint' member of a hybrid genus, he is defined as neither one thing nor the other ... [his] mixed nature is expressed in an idiom that systematically subverts the 'natural' decorums of kind" (129–30). *A Chaste Maid in Cheapside* challenges "decorums of kind" by suggesting that paternity and biology need not coexist, particularly in the face of economic instability.

The Economics of Procreation

Even the Yellowhammer family – the only family not formed, at least in part, by a surrogate parent or child, and not involving any bastard children – is unable to escape the corrupting influence of the city and its effect on familial proliferation. I introduce the Yellowhammers here as a counter-example to the play's other families, and as the primary instance of the use of children as financial instruments that are easily substitutable; they establish the concept of children as currency that permeates the rest of the play. Moll, the daughter of the Yellowhammers, is of marriageable age and her parents conspire to make her a financially and socially advantageous match. Although Moll is clearly not inclined to marry Sir Walter, her parents are charmed by the prospect of having a rich, influential son-in-law. As they fuss over Sir Walter's arrival, the Yellowhammers subordinate Moll's personal interests to those of the family; they privilege a socially and economically valuable marriage over their daughter's happiness. Maudeline, Moll's mother, insists that Moll act politely to Sir Walter (1.1.41–2). She informs Moll that in order to attract the knight's attention, she must "instruct her hand thus" (1.1.43), or behave and move in a particular way in an effort to charm him. Maudeline educates her daughter in the art of seduction in order to see her married for financial and social gain.

Early modern linguistic practice shows how children and the process of procreation were conceptualized in terms of the contemporary financial system. As Elizabeth Sacks observes, the English Renaissance was "a particularly auspicious time for the metaphor of generation"

(4). Henry VIII's trouble producing a male heir and Elizabeth's childless reign brought matters of succession and inheritance to the forefront
of political thought (4). Metaphors for breeding were frequently economic, equating reproduction with financial dealings. Children, for
example, were often said to be "coined," "stamped," or "minted" by
their parents.[9] To stamp, or to "strike an impression" on something
(*OED*, V.III), indicated that item's genuineness. Shakespeare's mention
of "stamp" in relation to birth appears to be one of the first figurative
uses of the term:

> And that most venerable man, which I
> Did call my father was I know not where
> When I was stamped. Some coiner with his tools
> Made me a counterfeit. (*Cymbeline* 2.5.3–6)

The same image is found in Robert Burton's *The Anatomy of Melancholy*
(1621):

> Severus the Emperor in his time made laws for the restraint of this vice:
> and as Dion Niceus relates in his life, *tri millia moechorum*, three-thousand
> cuckhold-makers, or *naturae monetam adulterantes*, as Philo calls them, *false
> coiners* and clippers of nature's money, were summoned into the court at
> once. (3: 308)

Both Shakespeare and Burton suggest that illegitimacy interferes with
the process of coining and stamping. Adultery forges an illegitimate
child just as a coin might be counterfeited. To be falsely coined or to be
a bastard was to lack authenticity and value.

Such monetary metaphors conveyed the parents' sense of ownership:
in producing children, parents marked them as their own and "stamped"
them, or asserted the children's origins, presumably through familial
likeness. Children were created in their parents' images, these financial metaphors imply, just as currency bore the likeness of the reigning monarch. Coins and stamps, like seals, stood in for the monarch;
their worth was derived not only from the intrinsic value of the raw
material, but from their symbolic value as well. Economic metaphors
of reproduction also emphasized the fact that children had genitors.
The royal mint produced currency on royal authority; to state that children were "stamped" or "coined" implied that they were a type of currency issued by their genitors. The equation of children with currency
aligned them with a system of exchange, and acknowledged the possibility that they might be circulated, replaced, or substituted. Parallels

between children and economics pointed both to a sense of ownership of children by their biological genitors, and to the prospect that such ownership might be transferable. Just as procreation was described in financial terms, economics were understood in terms of procreation; the two concepts were to some degree interdependent. The perceived connection between human relationships and the market was evident in the use of procreation as a metaphor for financial transactions. Money was said to be "bred" as it accumulated. Usury was commonly thought of as a kind of reproduction; the accrual of interest was envisioned in terms of propagation. Money that was lent was believed to proliferate, in a sense, because it multiplied itself as it collected interest.[10]

When Moll lies on the brink of apparent death, she is described by her brother in monetary terms. Asked how his sister looks and whether she has changed as a result of her illness, Tim replies: "Changed? Gold into white money was never so changed, / As is my sister's colour into paleness" (5.2.20–1). This economic simile suggests the financial value assigned to Moll by her parents; her appearance is devalued as from gold to silver. In death, she is worthless to her family: she can no longer supply the wealth and status that an advantageous marriage produces. Tim's simile is particularly notable when viewed alongside a metaphor that Sir Walter uses earlier in the play. In claiming that he will raise the value of the Welsh gentlewoman (in the dramatis personae, "Sir Walter's whore" [3]) by marrying her to an unsuspecting citizen, Sir Walter states that he will "bring [her] up to turn [her] into gold ... and make [her] fortune shine" (1.1.98–9). As the Welsh gentlewoman's monetary and social worth rises, she is imagined to be transformed to gold; as Moll's value falls, she becomes associated with a less precious metal. Moll is as much a financial resource to her parents – and, by extension, to her brother – as gold itself. Although the Yellowhammers claim to "spare no cost" (5.2.30) for her care and provide her with a drink made of "dissolved pearl and amber" when she is ill (5.2.29), it is clear that they only invest in Moll in the hope that they will gain a return on this investment when she recovers and is subsequently married.

The Yellowhammers think of their son and daughter as interchangeable financial opportunities. Upon learning of Moll's supposed death, Mr. Yellowhammer immediately embarks upon another financial scheme that involves the replacement of one of his children with the other: if he cannot see his daughter married to Sir Walter, then he will see his son, Tim, gainfully matched with the supposed Welsh gentlewoman. This new marriage is scheduled to take place even before the Yellowhammers bury Moll (5.3.107–12). Tim thus becomes as much a marketable commodity in his parents' eyes as Moll had been.

Maudeline reacts to her husband's plan by celebrating the fact that they will not, in the end, forfeit the financial opportunity afforded by their children: "Mass, a match! / We'll not lose all at once, somewhat we'll catch" (5.3.114–15). The Yellowhammer family is not unique in the drama of the period; many plays include parents who scheme to see their children profitably married.[11] The Yellowhammers stand as an example of the typical, almost clichéd depiction of children as social and economic tools. They illustrate the equation of children with financial wealth through marriage. Mr. and Mrs. Yellowhammer seek to alter the social and economic status of their children by the most available means: in a class-based society, new ties forged through marriage could change a person's social status significantly.

Fertility and Its Failings

Whereas the Yellowhammers have children with which to fulfill their economic and social ambitions, the Kixes are unable to procreate: after seven years of marriage, they have failed to produce a child (2.1.136). While the cause of the Kixes' childlessness is not explained, the early modern belief that the city could diminish reproductive effectiveness may explain their situation, although there are numerous other illegitimate children in the play.[12] The Kixes appear to suffer from sterility or, at the very least, a lack of virility. The family name hints at a possible source of the problem. As Alan Brissenden notes in his edition of the play, a kix is a "dry, hollow plant stem, figuratively a sapless person" (3). Sir Oliver Kix has no sap, or viable sperm, with which to impregnate his wife. "Whorehound," the family name of the virile Sir Walter, by contrast, is close to "water hound," a plant that "grows in moist, low places," is used to induce childbirth, and thus signals fruitfulness (3). Lady Kix eventually accuses Sir Oliver of willfully hindering generation (3.3.121). It is not immediately apparent, however, that Sir Oliver is to blame. Davy observes that "Lady Kix is dry, and hath no child," locating the cause of the couple's barrenness in the aridity of her womb (3.2.244). Touchwood Jr. similarly suggests that the tears that Lady Kix spills over her childlessness will only compound the problem, causing her to "weep herself to a dry ground" and lose her fecundity permanently (3.3.12). Both husband and wife are associated with dehydration as an impediment to their ability to reproduce.[13]

The Kixes' economic concerns are as dominant as their desires to perform their respective roles in social and civic life. Sterility is an obvious barrier to succession. In the absence of an heir, property will not remain within the immediate family; Sir Walter, their distant relative, will inherit everything they own. Lady Kix notes that their "goodly lands and livings" are "kept back" (2.1.155–6) and that their "dry barrenness puffs up Sir Walter" (2.1.159). "Puff[ing]" implies that Sir Walter prospers and is figuratively pregnant while Lady Kix remains deflated. Because the Kixes are unable to reproduce, Sir Walter's wealth is increased: he "gets by [their] not-getting" (2.1.160). Many early modern families lacked heirs; primogeniture, the ideal model of inheritance, was difficult to sustain in the face of infertility. The desire, verging on obligation, to leave estates to relatives often led childless couples to strengthen ties to their relations.[14] If a couple did not reproduce, property was not always left to the Church (as Church officials expected), but could be kept within a family through the renegotiation of kinship roles. Economic necessity in some cases required familial relations to be re-examined and manipulated. The Kixes, however, do not want a distant relative to inherit their wealth. They do not want Sir Walter to be, in any sense, their adopted heir; they want desperately to find a way to conceive so that their estate remains within their immediate family.

There were social repercussions for childlessness in the early modern period. Although barrenness was relatively common, it was often seen as a social failing.[15] The imperative to pass on wealth and titles made infertility especially problematic for members of the gentry. Lady Kix's social status and personal contentment depend on her ability to produce a child.[16] When asked by her husband if she will attend the gossiping (i.e., christening) of Mistress Allwit's child, Lady Kix laments the fact that other women conceive more easily:

> Everyone gets before me – there's my sister
> Was married but at Bartholomew eve last,
> And she can have two children at a birth;
> O one of them, one of them would ha' served my turn. (2.1.171–4)

Her sister became pregnant even before she was married: "Bartholomew eve" (23 August) is scarcely six or seven months before mid-Lent (the setting of the play) and the children have already been born (Brissenden 30). Yet the birth of the sister's twins trumps her scandalous behaviour. Producing children matters to Lady Kix more than the circumstances of their conception.

Like motherhood, fatherhood affected social standing. Sir Oliver seeks to be recognized as a father, which would ensure his respectability.[17] In light of his apparent infertility, he devises a means of reproduction that prioritizes the public over the personal and that affords him another way to become a father figure: he will perform charitable works and "make good deeds [his] children" (2.1.148). In "Of Parents and Children," Francis Bacon makes a similar recommendation, claiming that men can reproduce themselves through their works: "The perpetuity by generation is common to beasts; but memory, merit, and noble works, are proper to men. And surely a man shall see the noblest works and foundations have proceeded from childless men; which have sought to express the images of their minds, where those of their bodies have failed" (742). Childless men, Bacon contends, prove themselves honourable by fathering significant intellectual achievements. He also suggests, in "On Marriage and the Single Life," that unmarried men can create great works precisely because they are not burdened by familial responsibilities. He maintains that "certainly the best works, and of greatest merit for the public, have proceeded from the unmarried or childless men; which both in affection (love) and means (generosity) have married and endowed the public" (743). Lady Kix, however, will not equate philanthropy with reproduction. "Give me but those good deeds," she says, "and I'll find children" (2.1.149). In other words, she will gladly take the money that her husband is prepared to spend on the public and use it somehow to acquire heirs on her own. Her solution to infertility is indeed to "find children" outside her marriage.

In the early modern period, it was not only expected that wedded couples produce children, but virtually required; a childless marriage was viewed with suspicion. Christian teachings emphasized the enormous significance of reproduction within marriage and took the birth of a healthy child to indicate divine blessing. In Deuteronomy, for example, Moses explains to the Israelites that if God's commandments, statutes, and judgments are upheld, fertility will follow: "Thou shalt be blessed above all people: there shall not be male or female barren among you, or among your cattle" (7:14). Religious writers of the period condoned sexual activity and conception so long as they took place within marriage (Cressy, *Birth* 17). Whereas Protestant ministers recognized the value of companionship in marriage as well as the importance of having children, therefore suggesting that barrenness was no calamity, Puritans considered infertility to be divine punishment for ungodly behaviour – a kind of "supernatural justice" (Berry 165).[18] Unfruitfulness signalled a failure to find favour with God, and those who wished to avoid having children were thought to be defying God's will. In *The Child-birth or Womans Lecture* (1590), a Puritan treatise, Christopher Hooke states that some people thought "children to be a charge; and therefore if they might have their choice, had rather be without them than have them" (C3). The intentionally childless come to this conclusion, Hooke believes, "by reason of their ignorant hearts, which never were instructed in Gods schools" (C3). To be deliberately without children was to be a heathen.

Despite the importance of reproduction, infertility was not uncommon. As historian Chris Wilson observes, "in any population of reasonable size at least a small proportion of couples are unable to bear any children because of physiological impairments to either or both spouses" (209). Lawrence Stone estimates that from 1540 to 1660, 19 per cent of first marriages among the nobility were childless, and that the sterility rate for all couples was between 5 and 13 per cent (*Crisis* 168).[19] Infertility was thought to be caused by incompatibility between spouses. For instance, it was accepted that if husband and wife were not of "generally complementary stature," then they may not physically have been able to produce a child (A. McLaren 43–4). Living conditions were also thought to affect reproductive rates. Burton notes in *The Anatomy of Melancholy* that youthfulness, lustiness, and being "free from cares, like cattle in a rank pasture," helped with reproduction (3: 67) – a comment that attests the belief that the country was more conducive to conception than the city. Although London's population surged in the sixteenth and seventeenth centuries – primarily because of migration from the country – some medical practitioners imagined city dwellers to have low rates of fertility.[20] Urbanites lacked the daily physical exertion thought to be beneficial for country men and women; insufficient activity could render the seed of the men (in the language of the time) less potent (Berry and Foyster 174).

Fertility was seen not as an innate condition but instead as something that could be obtained. As historian Angus McLaren observes, fertility was not natural, but "part of [women's] social and cultural creation" (32). "Upon investigation," he remarks, "one finds that the birth process was not left to fate, but marked at each stage by social rituals" (32). Fecundity preoccupied early modern English women, who tried to avoid leaving conception to chance by seeking out remedies for any hint of infertility. Common prescriptions for barrenness included changes in diet or carrying lodestones for their allegedly curative magnetic qualities (Berry and Foyster 176–7). Treatments made from sea holly and nutmeg were typical suggestions, as were hot baths (A. McLaren 38). Potential cures proliferated for men as well. Male sterility was treated with foods that were assumed to be highly nutritious but that also caused flatulence; artichokes, dates, garlic, and scallions were among the recommended therapies (A. McLaren 35). For men as for women, the ability to reproduce was not inevitable or even fixed, but instead required attention and care.

The Kixes depend neither on nature nor on God alone, but instead take fertility into their own hands. Following their "doctor's advice" (2.1.141) and then that of Touchwood Sr., they try a variety of fertility treatments. They are also willing to pay for fertility. Arguing with his wife over the price of the apothecary's treatment, Sir Oliver insists that he will "be at more cost yet" to obtain a child because they "are rich enough" (2.1.133–4). He informs Lady Kix that he would "give a thousand pound to purchase fruitfulness" (2.1.144). Although he is prepared to pay an incredible sum, fertility is finally assigned a specific price: the Kixes buy Touchwood Sr.'s fertility potion – a "little vial of almond-milk" for which he originally paid three pence – for four hundred pounds (3.3.103; 3.3.147–9). Sir Oliver considers Touchwood's fee "a bargain" and observes that Touchwood should be paid lest they "prove ungrateful multipliers" (5.3.14–16). For the Kixes, fertility is a commodity.

The eventual solution to the Kixes' fertility problem does not involve medical intervention; the fertility potion that Touchwood sells them does nothing. Instead, the substitution of one sexual partner for another, and the resulting introduction of a different biological contributor into the Kixes' marriage, solves their reproductive dilemma. Touchwood Sr. insists that his fertility cure "must be taken lying" (3.3.167). He means, of course, as the audience understands, that he will lie with her and impregnate her himself. While Sir Oliver is sent off "a-horseback" (3.3.141) in a supposed effort to enhance the useless potion, Touchwood goes about his work with Lady Kix. Touchwood Sr. and Lady Kix improve upon the ineffective attempts at sexual reproduction that had been taking place within the Kix marriage. The child produced by the extramarital union belongs biologically to Lady Kix but not to Sir Oliver: it is a bastard conceived by an ostensibly anonymous father who sells his services as reproductive therapy. Because he is (presumably) unaware that Touchwood is the child's biological father, Sir Oliver considers the child his own. Although the child is not born during the play, Sir Oliver will raise it, the audience can assume, as though he had fathered it, and will never know that it is not his offspring. A Chaste Maid in Cheapside thus points to a distinction between sexual reproduction and social parenthood. Touchwood stands in as genitor for Sir Oliver, but Sir Oliver will play the role of father. What matters most to Lady Kix is not how she conceives a child but that she conceives at all.

The Kixes' ability to procreate depends directly upon Touchwood's own fertility. The Touchwoods are characterized by their fecundity: they produce a child every year, "some years two" (2.1.15), rendering them "too fruitful for [their] barren fortunes" (2.1.9).[21] In order to curb this growth, the Touchwoods must live apart (2.1.7–8).[22] Birth control in the early modern period typically involved determining various ways of increasing the number of pregnancies a woman might have, not preventing them (A. McLaren 31).[23] The Touchwoods' deliberate interference with reproduction therefore stands out in a time when people were continually reminded by the Church that a marriage could be judged by the number of children that it produced. Yet the financial cost of child-rearing also made fertility something to be feared.[24] While it was necessary to give birth to some children in order to ensure familial continuity, the birth of too many children threatened to overwhelm a poor or middle-class family.

The Touchwoods underscore the intertwining of children and finances: each is required to support the other. Touchwood Sr. remarks that while "some only can get riches and no children, / We only can get children and no riches" (2.1.11–12). Both children and wealth are necessary for financial security; without them, a family cannot be guaranteed stability and permanence. The Touchwood family is not merely a biological unit, but also a financial entity: as Touchwood explains, "The feast of marriage is not lust but love, / And care of the estate" (2.1.50–1). Touchwood's statement is ironic, however, because while he manages to control his sexual urges for his wife – and thus to stabilize his household economy – he acts out such urges with other women; as a result, he produces bastards for whom he at least sometimes has to offer financial support, as with the Wench (2.1.98). Although Touchwood Sr. ensures that his own family's procreation is restricted, his tendency to populate other families is uncurbed.

Touchwood's unusual solution to the Kixes' infertility leads to a blending of families. When Sir Oliver invites Touchwood and his wife "to live no more asunder" (5.4.80) and instead to use his "purse, and bed, and board" (5.4.81), it is unclear whether he is offering to support them as they live in their own home or to house them with his own family. Regardless, Sir Oliver becomes the Touchwood family's patron, and he announces that Touchwood can once again produce children with his estranged wife and that the Kixes will "keep them" (5.4.83). Sir Oliver likely ensures, unwittingly, that his wife will again become pregnant by Touchwood and that he will "keep" their bastard children. Sir Oliver's infertility leads to a comical familial interaction, in which the ties that bind are not always biological. Moreover, Sir Oliver is oblivious to Touchwood's meddling: familial relation, the play suggests, can be disguised and misconstrued. The result of Lady Kix's infidelity is a form of unintended adoption – a result, the play could be taken to imply, of the infidelity that could occur, and perhaps go undetected, in any marriage. Such a scheme was only possible for women to implement.[25]

Attuned to the possibility that elements of genealogy can be covert or invisible, Middleton, for the purposes of satire, reveals to his audience genealogical secrets, lampooning the assumption that genealogy and biological reproduction are intrinsically connected. Sir Oliver's fortune will not follow what he presumes to be his bloodline, but will instead be inherited by Touchwood's progeny.

Bastards, Cuckolds, and Adoptees

The disruption of patrilineal inheritance links the figures of the adoptee and the bastard. Adoption inserts into a family line a previously unrelated child, the new heir, as a means of ensuring familial and financial continuity. Bastards, too, existed outside the conventional pattern of inheritance.[26] Because children were only absolutely identifiable as their mothers' children and not their fathers', bastards could pose a challenge to the social fiction of the legitimate genealogical line.[27] If an illegitimate child was not known by his or her father or by society generally to be a bastard, a form of counterfeiting took place in which the ostensible purity of the family line was sullied. In the system of primogeniture, the designation "bastard" separated those who were able to inherit from those who were not (Neill 130).[28] But bastards were also, in some cases, recognized by their families as such and accounted for legally. Although bastards were not permitted all of the rights of inheritance conferred upon legitimate children, English law did allow them to be named in their parents' wills.[29]

Under common law, the child of a married woman was presumed to be her husband's legitimate child; the law was unconcerned by any fatherly or public uncertainty about a child's origins. Legal paternity was essentially distinct from genetic fatherhood. As early as the time of Henry Bracton, the English jurist who wrote *On the Laws and Customs of England* (c. 1220), lawyers argued that if a child was recognized as a legitimate heir by both husband and wife, then it must be considered as such under the law, even if its paternity was questionable (Bracton 3.311). Bracton states that "if he [the husband] has avowed it, and there is some presumption that the child could be his, though in truth it is not, as where husband and wife have been together, he will then be adjudged heir though he is not" (3.311). The only exception to this principle was if "the husband's avowal and admission cannot be reconciled with nature, that is, if he has been absent for a year or two" or "has been in fact castrated or is so infirm that he cannot beget" (3.311). As long as the child could plausibly be understood to be the husband's natural offspring, then the assumption of legitimate fatherhood was upheld.

This legal view was maintained well into the early modern period, as in the 1617 case of *Done and Egerton v. Hinton and Starkey*, in which the judges ruled that only "if the wife of a man who had been beyond the sea for such time, before the birth of the issue which the wife had in his absence, that the issue could not be his, it is a bastard" (qtd. in Cormack 296). Unless the husband was away when his wife conceived, he was to be regarded as the child's father.[30]

Because of this legal consensus, bastards could be transformed into adoptees. Bracton notes that "illegitimates born of unlawful inter-course, of persons between whom there could be no marriage, are com-pletely excluded from every benefit," but also that they are "sometimes legitimized, by a sort of adoption" (2.186). He explains:

> as where a wife has had a child by someone other than her husband, and where, though this is in fact true, the husband has taken the child into his house, avowed him and raised him as his son, or if he has not avowed him expressly has not turned him away; he will be adjudged legitimate and his father's heir, whether the husband does not know that the child is not his or knows or is in doubt, because he is born of the wife, [that is], pro-vided it can be presumed that he could have fathered him. The same may be said of a supposititious child, and thus common opinion sometimes is preferred to truth. (2.186)

Biological fact could be deemed secondary to illusory legitimacy in the interest of alleviating concerns about the diffusion of property and wealth. As Bracton also observes, however, the taking in of an illegit-imate child could occur with or without the husband's knowledge. In any case, once it had been accepted, a known or unknown bastard be-came an adopted child. A husband's bastard – his child with another woman – could also be named his heir if no legitimate children were produced within the marriage.

The link between illegitimacy and adoption can also be witnessed in the early modern discourse of marital infidelity. *Cuckold*, the English term for a husband whose wife has committed adultery, derives from the cuckoo, whose habit of abandoning its young has been recognized since ancient times. In *History of Animals*, Aristotle states that the cuckoo laid its eggs in the nests of other birds (1: 962), a claim that has been con-firmed by modern science.[31] Leaving its eggs to be hatched by another bird, the deceptive cuckoo secretly renders that bird a surrogate parent. In *The Fowles of Heaven; or History of Birdes* (1613–14), Edward Topsell notes that "the Cuckoe preserueth her race in other birds neasts without so much as thankes for all their labour and paynes. Vnto this part also belongeth their singuler ingratitude to their fosterers or Nurses" (243). The cuckoo relieves itself of all responsibility for its offspring while ensuring that its parental duties will be fulfilled by another bird: "She neuer layeth them in an emptie neast but therein where shee findeth eggs ... because shee knoweth that the birde will not forsake her oune eggs" (236). A kind of parenting collaboration ensues, even if the foster bird is unaware of its role. As Topsell asks about the cuckoo's lack of interest in being a parent, "must not the weaknes of one birdes nature be supported by the streingth of an other?" (236). Topsell points to the specious reasoning of naming the wronged husband after the cuckoo given that he is the one who takes in a bastard child rather than the one who deserts it.[32] While country peasants "call them Cuckolds which father the adulterous bratts of their wyves," Topsell writes, "daily experience teacheth the contrary. For not Cuckoes but other birds doe hatche Cuckoes and straingers to their kinde" (238).[33] Although he finds it illogical to associate the deceived husband with the cuckoo, Topsell nevertheless explains the bird's child-rearing habits in relation to bastardy. Citing the medieval Italian author Alciatus, he observes that the cuckoo "leaues her younge in neasts of forreyne breede / like a false spouse defilde with strangers seede" (243).

The ornithological analogy was common. As Pompey observes in Shakespeare's *Antony and Cleopatra*, the cuckoo "builds not for himself" (2.6.28). And according to the final song in *Love's Labour's Lost*, "a cuckoo then on every tree / Mocks married men" (5.2.891–2); husbands, perhaps saddled with bastard children, are taunted by the bachelor bird. Implicit in the avian origins of the term *cuckold* is the idea that a cuckolded father must provide for his wife's bastard child. The notion of the cuckolded husband thus presumed, to some degree, the inadvertent adoption of illegitimate children by married men. In *A Chaste Maid in Cheapside*, Allwit and Sir Walter form a joint illegitimate family for mutual benefit. Unlike the cuckoo, Sir Walter does not leave his own offspring to be secretly adopted. Instead, he does so openly and with the cuckolded husband's consent. Allwit is enthusiastic, ready to fill his home with children not of his kind. His name, a pun on "wittol," or "willing cuckold," signals his readiness to have his wife commit adultery and bear bastards. For Allwit, these children are part of a financial plan that equates procreation with profit: he sells Sir Walter exclusive sexual access to his wife (1.2.16). Sir Walter "not only keeps [Allwit's] wife, but a keeps [Allwit], / And all [his] family" (1.2.17–18). With household labour "all out of [his] hands" (1.2.52), Allwit is free to do as he pleases. Proud of this arrangement, he notes that he profits not only financially, but also emotionally. Because he knows who is sleeping with his wife, and because he has arranged the affair himself, he does not need to be envious or resentful; whereas doubting husbands are "eaten with jealousy to the inmost bone" (1.2.46), Allwit is already privy to his wife's extramarital activities, from which he profits. He is a cuckolded husband who is not mocked by the cuckoo.

Critics often note that although he believes that he assumes Sir Walter's wealth and masculinity, Allwit is in fact feminized by his cuckolding.[34] The price that he pays for this fantasy is, according to Boehrer, "the abdication of his own manhood as figured through the exercise of domestic authority in general and sexual authority in particular" (*Shakespeare* 93). Yet Allwit in fact has invented a new version of fatherhood. Allwit the wittol forgoes the possibility of biological fatherhood in favour of the financially secure option of adopting bastards: he calls his wife and Sir Walter's children his own, and they know him as their father. He allows genealogical relation to be forged – the children's genteel origin is concealed by Allwit's name – and he accepts the children of another man as his own. He is therefore the father of bastard children in one of the senses that Bracton outlines: he knowingly adopts children although they are not related to him by blood. Allwit might be feminized, but he has also circumvented the patriarchal imperative to reproduce. He understands lineage in terms of financial gain, not genealogical veracity. The Allwits thus resemble the Kixes and the Yellowhammers in their fixation on the ties between offspring and wealth, and on the practical solutions landed upon in order to maintain both.

Although Allwit raises Sir Walter's bastard sons as his own, and although he refers to them as his own children – Sir Walter, he says, gets "me all my children" (1.2.19) – the nature of his attachment to them is not entirely clear. The sons, Wat and Nick, believe that Allwit is their father, but Allwit refers to them as illegitimate when they are in the company of Sir Walter. When the first boy enters the room during Sir Walter's visit and calls Allwit "father," Allwit implores him to stop talking (1.2.118). The second boy who greets Allwit is also entreated to be silent and is called a "bastard" (1.2.119–20). Allwit is perhaps afraid that Sir Walter will be offended if the boys address Allwit as their father. To emphasize the paternal-filial relationship between Sir Walter and Wat and Nick, Allwit calls the boys "whoresons" and instructs them to kneel before Sir Walter, who is, although the boys do not know it, their biological father (1.2.124–5). Their genuflection, which signals respect for one's parents, is employed by Allwit to reassure Sir Walter of his role as provider and patriarch.[35]

Whereas Allwit is willing to incorporate his wife's illegitimate children into his family, Sir Walter is unwilling to integrate the same children into the legitimate family that he anticipates forming. Sir Walter appears to have no interest in his biological children. Upon seeing the boys with Mistress Allwit, he wonders how he will "dispose of these two brats" when he is married (1.2.127) and insists that they "must not mingle / Amongst my children that I get in wedlock" (1.2.128–9). To be rid of them, he will see them apprenticed: "I'll bind Wat prentice to a goldsmith, my father Yellowhammer; / As fit as can be. Nick with some vintner; good, goldsmith / And vintner; there will be wine in bowls, i'faith" (1.2.131–4). Sir Walter evidently does not accept these children as his own in terms of social standing; he will provide them with middle-class apprenticeships rather than with genteel lives befitting their biological pedigree.[36] The distinction between the views of Allwit and Sir Walter emphasizes the mutability of familial formation, which in this case does not depend on biology. Although Allwit is a caricature of the cuckolded husband and an obviously comical figure, the Allwits emerge triumphant.[37] They plan to use the material goods that they receive from Sir Walter to begin a new life as brothel owners in the Strand (5.1.168–76): their family is apparently stable and financially successful. They thrive by exploiting the conventions of adoption and child-rearing.

While Allwit knowingly becomes the custodian of bastard children, the promoters are unwitting new fathers. In one of the defining scenes of the play, a country wench, anxious to divest herself of her bastard infant, devises a plan to trick the promoters. Approaching them while they patrol the streets during Lent, she uncovers a piece of mutton in her basket to attract the attention of the officials who are supposed to confiscate meat during the period of fasting. Pretending that the mutton is for her mistress who is ill and therefore exempt from the restrictions of the religious holiday, the Wench insists that the promoters swear to keep her basket until she can return with her master to prove her innocence (2.2.157–72). Pleased to have caught another citizen with contraband that they can keep for themselves, the promoters celebrate their luck and tally the results of their windfall – until they discover the baby hidden beneath the cuts of meat. Newly burdened with the baby, their "unlucky breakfast," the promoters instantly become surrogate fathers, while the biological mother abandons her parental role (2.2.192).

The Wench understands bastard children to have economic value. She relies upon reproduction and adoption to make her way in the world, and her fecundity is ultimately profitable. When she first appears in the play, she has given birth to a child out of wedlock and is thus in financial need. She confronts Touchwood Sr., shows him the baby, which she considers his "workmanship" (2.1.65), and threatens to spread the truth of its parentage "through the streets" (2.1.67), using the threat of public embarrassment to gain his financial support. Although he denies that he is the father and asks to be "excused" from responsibility for it by claiming that it lacks fingernails (meaning that it is the child of a syphilitic, and therefore of another man), Touchwood is assured that the baby is his (2.1.82–5). To compensate the Wench and to provide for the child's rearing, he gives her everything he has, "purse and all" (2.1.98). As the scene progresses it becomes clear that the Wench is well-practised in the business of producing children for economic gain. Although she claims that she was "a maid before" her encounter with Touchwood and that she can prove her virginity with a certificate from both of the churchwardens (2.1.70), she reveals that she is experienced in childbirth. In an aside, she states that her child with Touchwood is her fifth bastard (2.1.104). Middleton's depiction of the Wench's fertility echoes his observation in *The Witch* (c. 1609–16) that "bastards come upon poor venturing gentlewomen / Ten to one faster than your legitimate children" (2.1.43–4). Promiscuous women, that is, are said to conceive at a greater rate than the virtuous. Because she never mentions the need to support her other children, and because she is believed by the other characters to be a childless maid, the clear implication is that the Wench has left those children in the care of other unsuspecting strangers. With no children to raise she does not need help from the babies' fathers, but it is apparent that she has been living off money that she has solicited from men like Touchwood.

The Wench is skilled at taking advantage of the urban setting to perform immoral actions; although she is from the country, she visits London to dispose of her bastard children. In this particular instance, the city is not the cause of debauched behaviour but it does accommodate illicit activity. As the Wench herself observes, she "hath wit" to "shift anywhere," or is clever enough to deal with any situation (2.2.148). The promoters likewise make the most of the corrupt city. Allwit identifies the promoters as self-interested: "This Lent will fat the whoresons up with sweetbreads, / And lard their whores with lamb-stones" (2.2.68–9). The city affords them the opportunity to exploit their fellow citizens and to ignore religious laws for their own profit. The trick that Allwit plays on the promoters demonstrates that they exploit new immigrants to the city. Pretending to be "a stranger both unto the city / And to her carnal strictness" (2.2.76–7) – that is, a country bumpkin in search of meat during Lent – Allwit allows the promoters to think that he will lead them unwittingly to a butcher who is operating in secret during the holiday. The promoters' greed is exposed, however, when Allwit reveals that he is in fact a citizen of London and that his wife is exempt from Lenten dietary restrictions because she is lying in after childbirth (2.2.103). Allwit's scheme thus exposes that of the promoters. The effect is to suggest that trickery and dishonesty are pervasive.[38]

Like the play's other men saddled with bastards, the promoters become the baby's parents. Angry that they have been tricked when they are "but poor promoters / That watch hard for a living" (2.3.197–8), the men tally the price of raising the baby:

Half our getting must run in sugar-sops
And nurses' wages now, besides many a pound of soap,
And tallow; we have need to get loins of mutton still,
To save suet to change for candles. (2.2.199–202)

They soon realize that the cost of caring for the infant will outstrip any profit to be gained from selling the mutton that they find with it. Whereas the baby is a possible financial burden but eventual financial benefit to its mother, it represents only a loss to the promoters. Their determination to care for the child is therefore remarkable. The Wench "made [them] swear to keep" the baby (2.2.194); otherwise they "might leave it else" (2.2.195). It may seem surprising that they are so committed to keeping their word when their business is to profit from a religious holiday, but they stake their souls by swearing that they will take care of the basket until the Wench's return, and they are obviously unwilling to risk eternal damnation. They have not sought to adopt a baby, nor are they happy with their acquisition; their bond with the child is financial, not emotional. Nonetheless, the promoters have formed a family unit and they are obliged to take on new social roles. At first they resign themselves to their new duties and plan to work through the rest of Lent to "get it up" (2.2.206), or to make up for the money that they have lost in acquiring a dependant. The second promoter soon suggests, however, that they wait for the tide to rise so that they can "send the child to Branford" (2.2.213), a suburb of London notorious for prostitutes and horse racing (5.4.97), and where children were frequently sent to wet nurses. It seems unlikely that the promoters will ever retrieve the child. Instead, it will presumably become a foundling and be taken in by yet another family, so long as it survives the voyage up the Thames. A series of potential adoptive familial relationships, started by the Wench and continued by the promoters, is thus set in motion.

John Fletcher's *The Chances* (c. 1617; pub. 1647), a play staged not long after *A Chaste Maid in Cheapside* (1613), also depicts a baby's surreptitious abandonment. The similarities between the baby-as-package scenes in each play are striking, but Fletcher's play amplifies the indignation that Middleton's promoters feel at having been tricked into caring for a child. Don John, a Spanish gallant, accepts a package from a woman who, he assumes, is in some kind of trouble. Sure that he has obtained "some pack of worth" from her, he declares that he will "never refuse a fortune" (1.3). When he opens the package, however, Don John discovers a baby inside and realizes that he is now responsible for it. Disappointed, he complains:

> ... why, it would never grieve me,
> If I had got this Ginger-bread; never stirr'd me,
> So I had had a stroak for't: 't had been Justice
> Then to have kept it; but to raise a dayrie,
> For other mens adulteries, consume my self in candles,
> And scowring works, in Nurses Bells and Babies,
> Onely for charity, for meere I thank you,
> A little troubles me: the least touch for it,
> Had but my breeches got it, had contented me. (1.6)

Like the promoters, Don John tallies the cost of the abandoned child; for merely a "thank you," he must devote his time and resources to its upbringing. He also imagines an unpaid debt of pleasure. Had he received "a stroak for't" – had he enjoyed the sexual act by which the child was produced – he would shoulder his new financial burden. As it stands, he is now at a financial loss because other men have chosen to practise adultery. Don John has obtained a baby passively, through chance instead of procreation, in much the same way as Middleton's promoters are thrust by happenstance into the role of fathers and placed in financial distress as a result.

As my examples have indicated, Middleton's characters take ostensibly natural matters into their own hands by attempting to control their fertility and the composition of their families. By definition, city comedies take place in urban environments and make the experience of city life a primary theme. In *A Chaste Maid in Cheapside*, the city is depicted as an unnatural space from which evidence of rural life has been banished. In counter-pastoral London there are no bucolic sheep – there is only mutton. Allwit describes the citizenry as lifeless animals when he claims that the promoters plan "to arrest the dead corps of poor calves and sheep" (2.2.63). The promoters intend to arrest people, not animals, but the effect is to suggest that the city cannot sustain animal life. The city's only animals are humans, who are repeatedly compared to beasts. To Allwit, the promoters sniff out their prey like "rich men's dogs" (2.2.60) and are "sheep-biting mongrels" (2.2.102). For their part, the promoters view Allwit as a "green-goose" that they will "sauce" (2.2.83).[39] These animals belong to a rural environment. The play's setting is a parody of country life in which unflattering depictions of the human characters take the place of animals. Implicit in the genre of the city comedy is the disappearance, or at least alteration, of rustic ways. Touchwood himself effects change upon the countryside. By his own admission, he "hinder[s] hay-making": he interferes with hay-making in nearby villages because he impregnates so many of the young rural women who would normally work in the fields (2.1.61). His excessive virility disrupts country life and the patterns of the harvest. When it comes to reproduction, expected patterns and modes of generation are banished from Cheapside, leaving instead a world in which the alteration of the biological family is the norm. Middleton reveals rather than conceals the indeterminacy of genealogy.

Chapter Four

Adoptive Names in Middleton's
Women Beware Women

Thomas Middleton's *Women Beware Women* (c. 1621) suggests, for a time, the possibility that familial lineage could be changed at will, and that names and relations were not fixed determinants of identity but instead mere verbal conventions that could be dispensed with to suit a character's ambitions. At a time when blood-based kinship was a perpetual concern that affected matters royal and common alike, faith in the reliability of genealogy was paramount: heirs had to be identified correctly for honour and inheritance to hold. Middleton's play offers a surprising view of lineage in flux; Isabella's calculating use of verbal markers of familial relation appears to demonstrate the fragility of the family structure itself. Yet the conclusion of *Women Beware Women* provides a more conservative account, and, as order is restored, it suggests that the conventions of lineage are necessary to avoid social calamity: Middleton portrays the consequences of fictionalizing lineage.

The play's two convoluted plots revolve around the characters' intricate connections and their conflicting desires. At the centre is the widow Livia. Aware that Hippolito, her brother, is in love with their niece, Isabella, and aware too that Isabella is resistant to his incestuous desire, Livia lies to the girl: she tells Isabella that although she has been raised by Fabritio, her supposed father, she is not related to him – nor thus to any member of his family – by blood. Livia claims that the Marquis of Coria, a Spaniard, is Isabella's biological father, and emphasizes the distance between supposed niece and aunt:

> LIVIA: Then know, how ever custom has made good,
>   For reputation's sake, the names of niece
>   And aunt 'twixt you and I, w'are nothing less.
> ISABELLA: How's that?
> LIVIA: I told you I should start your blood.

> You are no more allied to any of us,
> Save what the courtesy of opinion casts
> Upon your mother's memory and your name
> Than the merest stranger is, or one begot
> At Naples when the husband lies at Rome:
> There's so much odds betwixt us. (2.1.131–40)[1]

The passage suggests that Isabella's name and her position as Fabritio's daughter and Livia's niece have been granted through social convention alone. Insisting that Isabella's usual familial markers are no longer applicable, Livia compares her to a "stranger" and compels her to begin an allegedly non-incestuous sexual relationship with her uncle. With the terms and ties of relation fictitiously removed, Isabella loses all aversion to Hippolito and now believes him to be a potential romantic partner. But Isabella's attraction to Hippolito is in fact incestuous, and Livia's machinations therefore override any aversion to incest that might be expected between uncle and niece.

Opinion on the grounds for incest avoidance in the period was established in large part by Henry VIII's divorce from Catherine of Aragon. Henry's supporters argued that incest is unnatural and that its prevention is fundamental to human nature. Endogamous marriage is "incest, beastly, and unkynde" (Surtz and Murphy 198), or "not in accordance with the natural or normal course of things" ("unkind," *OED*, Adj.1.a). As Bruce Boehrer notes, early modern thinkers who believed that aversion to incest is innate often represented human nature as "coextensive with animal instinct," providing examples of animals who were devastated to learn that they had been tricked into committing incest, and insisting that this feeling of distress was natural (*Monarchy* 24). Henry's followers, in advancing the view that "the law of nature and reasone, moued by the lawe and the worde of god, dothe commaunde and teache vs, that [incestuous] conjunction muste be utterly abhorred / as a wicked sinne ageynst nature" (Surtz and Murphy 205), dismissed any possible cultural reasons for avoiding incest and instead relied on the authority of nature (Boehrer, *Monarchy* 33).[2] By inventing an adoptive relationship where none truly exists, Livia compels her niece to behave in a way that was typically thought to be unnatural, and to demonstrate that incest aversion – and by extension nature – can be superseded by a lie.

The play's critics tend to focus on its commodification of women and its portrayal of Bianca's rape, while Livia's management of familial relation is often overlooked.[3] Isabella's fictional status as a child not raised by her biological father has been noted in passing as a convenient lie – a plot device that permits Livia to procure her niece for her favourite brother.[4] Livia is often mentioned in light of her role as bawd; she is adept at coaxing young women into illicit sexual relationships, supplying the Duke with Bianca and Hippolito with Isabella. Other scholars interpret Livia's manipulation of women as evidence of her empowerment. Ann C. Christensen, for instance, proposes in a study of improper modes of settling house that Livia takes any available opportunity to free female characters from patriarchal control and "to grant other women a certain mobility," even if that mobility leads to adultery (499). Lisa Hopkins notes some aspects of Livia's interest in familial relation, suggesting that she is a "substitute mother" to Isabella, and that she uses imagined motherhood both to dupe and to help her niece (30). By emphasizing her alleged role as confidante to Isabella's mother, Hopkins argues, Livia gains the young woman's trust: her "repeated invocation of [Isabella's] dead mother ... guarantees Livia's psychological ascendancy over her niece" (33).[5] Although Livia starts by using the guise of motherhood to influence Isabella, Hopkins understands her to think of herself in time as a genuine mother despite her literal childlessness. She becomes a "self-sacrificing," "toiling" mother who will do anything to "gratify others" (36). In this respect, Hopkins's assessment of Livia resembles that of Christensen: both critics perceive Livia to believe that she is working in Isabella's best interest.

I suggest, in contrast, that it is not Livia's possible role as an adoptive mother that most defines her, but instead her interest in the definition of Isabella's role as niece and daughter. My argument follows from those of Christensen and Hopkins in that I propose that Livia's manipulative behaviour offers Isabella some independence, but I see this independence as temporary and do not interpret Livia's actions as benevolent. Although Hopkins suggests that Livia comes to believe her verbal creations, it is my contention that her modification of familial relation is essentially tactical. Livia influences other characters by discounting existing familial relations rather than by forging them. Her ability to unmake her family grants her a power that otherwise she would not have. Livia's fictional account of Isabella's parentage emphasizes the expression of familial relation as strategy, performance, and source of linguistic capital. *Women Beware Women* draws attention to the ways in which the complexities of familial relations establish one's place in the world; familial markers create and transform identities, and alter social and emotional ties. Livia is aware that a woman is identified first by her father's and then by her husband's family name. She therefore attempts to free her niece from the imposition of such names. As Hopkins puts it, Livia "usurps the traditional force of the *nom-du-père* by inventing and naming an alternative father for Isabella" (35). But Livia's alteration of Isabella's familial markers is, in the end, for her own benefit. Boehrer suggests that the play promotes "a devaluation of kinship ties both through its rhetoric and its action" and that "in the end its language militates against the very institution of the affective nuclear family" (*Monarchy* 109). While the play at first appears to propose that it is the interpretation of lineage that determines kinship rather than lineage itself, it ultimately points to the absolute nature of blood-based relations by staging the gory aftermath of treating lineage as mutable. Adoptive familial relationships never truly exist in the play, and the tragic conclusion indicates the dangers of attempting to alter the structure of the family.

In the following pages I use Pierre Bourdieu's models of negotiable familial relation and speaking power, and focus on Livia's transformation of Isabella in Act 2, Scene 2, in order to chart the complex and seemingly changeable nature of the family in *Women Beware Women*. First, I compare Bourdieu's models to Erasmus's theory of adoptive naming and examine how the fictionalization of familial relation in the early modern period could be used to amass social capital. I then investigate ways in which the reshaping of familial relations in Middleton's play establishes not only familial roles but also the speaking power and positions of various family members. Finally, I argue that Livia's lie about Isabella's parentage allows Isabella provisionally to remake her life. As William C. Carroll notes in the introduction to his edition of *Women Beware Women*, Livia is a character of Middleton's own invention (xv).[6] Her presence foregrounds the potential instability of familial relation, and her aspiration to restructure her family also demonstrates her ability to construe the world as she sees fit. Such an ability proves fatal.

The Fictionalization of the Family

The scholarship of Pierre Bourdieu, work that is devoted to tracing the maintenance and manipulation of social order and power, is useful in considering early modern strategies for social and familial interaction. In *Outline of a Theory of Practice* (1977), his study of kinship, matrimonial strategies, and the reproduction of social formations, Bourdieu traces the symbolic capital inherent in familial relationships. With less genealogical distance between relatives comes increased capital: "the descriptive value of the genealogical criterion is greater when the common origin is nearer and the social unit is more limited" (39). Genealogical exclusivity or proximity is valuable to those who seek to benefit from familial ties. Conversely, genealogical inclusivity, or the "*assimilative* power" gained by "push[ing] back the boundaries of the lineage" and acknowledging extended family members, comes at the expense of those who possess "*distinctive* power" as the result of their positions "nearer the point of common origin" (38). The recognition of distant relatives diminishes the capital of more immediate family members.

In Bourdieu's estimation, familial relationships are neither innate nor natural but are instead constructed and changeable: they are "something people *make*, and with which they *do* something" (*Outline* 35). And what can be made can of course be remade or undone. To Bourdieu, genealogy is strategic, supple, and at least partly notional; genealogical fact matters less than genealogical fiction. Suggesting the social necessity of such fictions, he observes that "the genealogical relationship is never strong enough on its own to provide a complete determination of the relationship between the individuals which it unites" (39). Familial relations must instead be cultivated. Kinship is "practical" in his view in the sense that it must be "continuously practiced, kept up" (37). The symbolic capital implicit in familial distance and hierarchy is increased or decreased as kinship ties are maintained or neglected.

Bourdieu's notion of fluid familial relations establishes the importance of the management of kinship to the accumulation of social value. When this concept is combined with his notion of linguistic capital, familial relation can be understood to decide the verbal authority of the various members of a particular family. Bourdieu proposes an economic analogy in "The Economics of Linguistic Exchanges" (1977) to delineate ways in which discourse has value in particular contexts. The social worth of an utterance and the degree to which it is received depend on the perceived worth of the person speaking. The success or failure of linguistic exchanges is established by the social positions of the interlocutors: "to give an account of discourse," Bourdieu claims, "we need to know the conditions governing the constitution of the group within which it functions" (650). In his account of linguistic capital there is a "legitimate language," a language of authority and competence – "the condition and sign of the right to speech, the right to power through speech" (649). The extent to which various speakers command authority determines the structure of linguistic production. Language is "an instrument of power" and "a person speaks not only to be understood, but also to be believed, obeyed, respected, distinguished" (684). Bourdieu does not include familial status among the attributes that grant linguistic authority, but the symbolic capital associated with such status can surely influence the power to speak. A boy's words, for instance, may hold more sway with his father than with his uncle, while a nephew's words may influence an uncle to a greater extent than those of a stranger. But because familial relation is not, in Bourdieu's estimation, a static entity, linguistic capital is always subject to circumstance.

Bourdieu's views have a distant antecedent in Erasmus, who was intrigued by the epistolary power of fictional familial naming. Erasmus's teachings on letter-writing, Lynne Magnusson suggests, allow his students to navigate a complex social world through language. He urges his pupils to "conceive of friendships and same-sex intimacies," she asserts, as "performative and strategic" (70).[7] In "On the Writing of Letters" (1522), Erasmus examines proper forms of salutation. He values the simplicity with which the ancients greeted one another by the "mere mention of names": "Pliny gives his Calvus greeting!" is cited as a model form of address (51). As he observes in a humorous statement, "there is something particularly attractive in being called by one's proper name, the hearing of which seems to please even dumb animals" (51). But he allows that other forms of address might be used to gain favour or to acknowledge a debt. In a section on epithets and adoptive names, he contends that "sometimes it is a matter of politeness and courtesy to add honorary or adoptive names" when addressing a letter (57).[8] "Adoptive names" – familial signifiers that do not depend upon strictly biological relationships – permit an author to establish intimacy with an addressee by amplifying or even fabricating the degree to which they are related. Such terms, in Erasmus's estimation, are socially useful because they are performative and persuasive: "an example ... is calling an old man to whom we are indebted 'father,' a young man who is dear to us 'son,' a step-mother 'mother,' a sister's husband 'brother'" (57).[9] In each case, familial terms of address intensify the importance of the addressee to the writer and transform mentor, friend, or relation by affinity to figurative blood relative. In short, Erasmus's adoptive names bridge the genealogical distance between those who are not related by blood, creating familial connections where none exist otherwise.

Erasmus believes that correspondence will be received more favourably if its author exploits particular terms of address. The relationships upon which adoptive names often draw reflect conventional familial hierarchy: the names convey social status in a recognizable way. As Erasmus explains, "names of adoption are effective in the same contexts, as when we call the powerful, by whose influence we are supported and by whose kindness assisted, 'patrons,' 'fathers,' and 'instructors'; the women 'patronesses' and 'mothers'; our close friends 'brother and sisters'; our companions in the same study or professors of the same subject 'fellow-soldiers'; young men 'sons'; pupils 'nurslings'" (60). "The powerful" can be termed "fathers" and "mothers" (or "patrons" and "patronesses," from the Latin *pater* for "father"), designations of authority; friends become "brother and sisters" (or classmates and colleagues "fellow-soldiers" in a military example of brotherhood), designations of parity; and youths and pupils are referred to as "sons" or "nurslings," designations of inferior age, lower standing, and need of training and care. Whereas an address by the "mere mention of names" encodes no social standing, adoptive names indicate deference, equality, or authority. By recommending adoptive names as appropriate and strategic forms of address for written communication, Erasmus casts kinship as an elastic type of relation, the manipulation of which may gain the correspondent favour.

In addition to elucidating the social value of familial terms of address, Erasmus anticipates, across a gulf of time, the model of politeness and familial honorifics advanced by anthropological linguists Penelope Brown and Stephen C. Levinson in *Politeness: Some Universals in Language Usage*. As Magnusson argues, "On the Writing of Letters" provides Erasmus's students with "strategies for ingratiation" (68) that are "all recognizable as positive politeness strategies, which Brown and Levinson consider the building blocks of friendship and intimacy" (69). Their model asserts that, from a pragmatic linguistic perspective, there is often a great disparity between what is said and what is implied, much of which can be attributed to strategies of politeness. Speakers are polite in order to shape their interactions with other speakers; politeness serves an intended social function. "There are very general social motivations for using various techniques of positive politeness and negative politeness," Brown and Levinson note, which "operate, respectively, as a kind of social accelerator and social brake for decreasing or increasing social distance in relationships" (93). They identify the use of in-group identity markers, such as fictive kinship terms, as a positive politeness strategy by which a speaker can "implicitly claim the common ground with [the hearer or addressee] that is carried by that definition of the group" (107). Kinship terms, according to Brown and Levinson, promote in-group identification, convey intimacy, and create a social bond. They also, however, function as addressee honorifics, or "direct grammatical encodings of relative social status between participants, or between participants and persons or things referred to in the communicative event" (276). Brown and Levinson observe that honorifics are not "automatic reflexes or signals of predetermined social standing" but are instead "typically *strategically* used to soften [face-threatening actions], by indicating the absence of risk to the addressee" (182). Honorific kinship terms – Erasmus's "adoptive names" – create familial bonds and smooth social relations among speakers.

The early modern term *cousin* provides a particularly useful example of adoptive naming. Rather than indicating a specific familial relationship such as *mother*, *brother*, or *uncle*, the term was often employed to describe any biological link between two people. Shortened to *coz*, it also implied familiarity. As such, it could be used by a speaker to convey both deference and social proximity to an unrelated person. In an important discussion of in-group identity markers in Shakespeare's *As You Like It*, Clara Calvo observes that Celia uses such markers calculatingly when she addresses Rosalind as "sweet my coz" and when she uses the familiar pronoun of address *thou* (109). Although Celia and Rosalind are related, Celia is above Rosalind in social rank and certainly in favour at court. Celia's use of *coz* is thus tactical: "With this strategy," Calvo argues, "Celia is claiming the existence of some 'common ground' between Rosalind and herself; she is also indicating that she disregards the slight difference in social status existing between them ... and that she considers herself Rosalind's equal" (109). At times *cousin* was used even in the absence of familial connection. In Webster, Heywood, and Rowley's *A Cure for a Cuckold*, for example, Rochfield admits that *cousin* is a "word of courtesie" of which he and the bride both take advantage (5.1.95). They are "foreign as two strangers" save for their use of the kinship term that binds them together (5.1.97).

The letters between Queen Elizabeth and King James offer an illuminating historical instance of "adoptive naming" and fictitious kinship. The English queen and Scottish king were by blood only second cousins, but they refer to one another in correspondence as "brother" and "sister." Their use of horizontal terms of kinship can be explained by their equal status as sovereigns; they conceive of themselves as siblings in monarchy. More noteworthy, perhaps, is James's occasional use of vertical kinship terms – those of parent and child – to address Elizabeth in a strategic show of deference to the far more powerful figure. Elizabeth had recently discovered William Parry's plot to assassinate her and, believing that Mary, Queen of Scots, was involved, placed her under more watchful custody. Elizabeth wrote to James in 1585 in a cryptic letter to assert her power and to assess his mood concerning his mother, Mary:

> I might condemn you as unworthy of such as I mind to show myself toward you; and therefore I am well pleased to take any color to defend your honor, and hope that you will remember that who seeketh two strings to one bow, they may shoot strong but never straight. And if you suppose that princes' causes be veiled so covertly that no intelligence may bewray them, deceive not yourself: we old foxes can find shifts to save ourselves by others' malice, and come by knowledge of greatest secret, specially if it touch our freehold ... I write not this, my dear brother, for doubt but for remembrances. (Marcus et al. 262)

After Elizabeth aims these thinly veiled threats at her "brother," James begins to address her not only as his "cousin" and "sister," but also as his "mother." The adoptive name signals, as Erasmus might have it, increased reverence for Elizabeth as a representative of "the powerful, by whose influence we are supported and by whose kindness assisted" (60). James, the son of Elizabeth's enemy, attempts to increase his linguistic and social capital by addressing the queen in deferential familial terms. His letter to Elizabeth of 31 July 1585, for example, is addressed to "Madame and mother" and signed "Your most loving and devoted brother and son" (Marcus et al. 263). James's simultaneous use of several kinship terms suggests his ardent desire to placate the queen and to earn her trust. Moreover, James uses "adoptive names" not only to flatter Elizabeth but also to facilitate political adoption. By referring to himself metaphorically as Elizabeth's adoptive son, he seeks to identify himself as her heir. Jonathan Goldberg observes that James begins to call Elizabeth "mother" just as he abandons Mary (12–17). He deserts his birth mother for a political matriarch: close familial relation to the powerful Elizabeth is far more valuable than his close relationship to the traitorous Mary. He appears to write himself into the English royal family as the successor to the throne even if Elizabeth has not adopted him as her child. Writing on 1 August 1588, James states that he is moved to tell Elizabeth of his "zeal to the religion [Protestantism], and how near a kinsman and neighbor I find myself to you and your country" (Marcus et al. 356). He promises that he will behave himself "not as a stranger and foreign prince, but as your natural son and compatriot of your country in all respects" (357).[10] The term *stranger*, as I show below, has a particular sense that Middleton exploits in *Women Beware Women*.

Livia and the Manipulation of Relation

Elizabethan and Jacobean dramatists who sought to convey the fluidity and strategic possibilities of familial relation echoed in their dramatic inventions Erasmus's advice about adoptive naming as well as the machinations of Elizabeth and James. But in *Women Beware Women* the variability of kinship terms does not always lead to unambiguous resolutions. Middleton depicts the manipulation of familial relation as both liberating and dangerous; he dramatizes the rewards and risks of fictionalizing the family.

Women Beware Women draws attention from the outset to kinship terms as unfixed markers of social relation. Leantio, having married without his mother's knowledge, brings home Bianca, his bride. Before she learns that Bianca is her new daughter-in-law, Leantio's mother expresses her happiness to see her son, welcoming him "with all the affection of a mother / That comfort can express from natural love" (1.1.2–3).[11] This profession of "natural love" springs from the "birth-joy" that followed "her curse of sorrows," the labour pains that she suffered (1.1.4–5). She links her affectionate verbal acknowledgment of Leantio as her son to their biological ties. As Christensen puts it, Mother's "speech roots hospitality in maternity ... and likens the event of a child's departure from the womb and arrival into the world to his coming home again as an adult" (504). When Leantio introduces her to Bianca, however, Mother suggests that the acquisition of a child by means other than birth requires the new mother-in-law and daughter-in-law to envision the terms of their kinship.[12] Mother is unhappy with her son's choice to marry a wealthy woman; she believes that Bianca will not be satisfied to live within their means. Mother is careful, however, to show that she now considers Bianca her daughter. She does so by changing her terms of address. First acknowledging Bianca as "gentlewoman" and noting that "thus much is a debt of courtesy / Which fashionable strangers pay each other / At a kind meeting" (1.1.111–13), Mother then concedes that the formal term cannot convey their newfound social proximity. There is "more than one" (1.1.113) form of address, she maintains, that suits their relationship:

> Due to the knowledge I have of your nearness:
> I am bold to come again, and now salute you
> By th' name of daughter, which may challenge more
> Than ordinary respect. (1.1.114–17)

Erasmus's observation that out of "politeness and courtesy" a letter-writer might call "a step-mother 'mother,' a sister's husband 'brother'" (57) provides a useful explanation for Mother's calling Bianca "daughter" rather than "daughter-in-law." By exaggerating their familial relation, Mother welcomes Bianca as her child by nature rather than by law. The use of the term *daughter* to refer both to a biological child and to a daughter-in-law was not uncommon, but Mother's deliberate juxtaposition of the two forms of address – "gentlewoman" and "daughter" – confirms her willingness to embrace Bianca as a member of the family.[13] (She also erases class boundaries: Bianca is of higher social standing than Mother and Leantio.) The "nearness" that Mother and Bianca now share extends beyond a polite "debt of courtesy" (1.1.111). Mother, determined to please her son by accepting his wife, thus assures Bianca that she has a natural place within their home.

Bianca, for her part, follows Mother's example and underscores their newfound proximity. Addressing her deferentially as "kind Mother" (1.1.125) and "sweet Mother" (1.1.149), Bianca assures her that she (Bianca) considers Leantio's family her own. She even claims that she will reconceive her familial history to suggest that her married life is indeed her only life: "I'll call this place the place of my new birth now, / And rightly too: for here my love was born, / And that's the birth-day of a woman's joys" (1.1.139–41). In this second life, she will replace her own mother and place of origin with those of Leantio. She declares that it is now Mother's speech to which she will be most receptive: "The voice of her that bare me is not more pleasing" (1.1.150). Bianca courts Mother's favour with flattery and by equating motherhood acquired through marriage with biological motherhood. In so doing, she promises to disregard her own past in order to ease Mother's fears about her willingness to accept her new and inferior social situation.[14] Bianca and Mother both overstate their relatedness to assert their respective positions within the household.

Whereas Bianca and Mother amplify the bonds of kinship, Livia is eventually shown to diminish relation deliberately. Many contemporary editors have understood the sibling relationship between Livia and Hippolito to be a one-sided incestuous attraction. Roma Gill, for instance, observes that Livia's tenderness towards Hippolito suggests an unnatural affection (xxiii).[15] Some other commentators view Livia's procurement of Isabella as a game of substitution. As Richard Dutton writes, "It does not take a Freudian to see, in her supposed removal of the incest impediment between uncle and niece, a displaced removal of the same impediment between herself and her brother, Hippolito" (xxiv). But such interpretations do not attend to Livia's illustrations of ways in which kinship is made and unmade. Her intended effect on Isabella is therefore notable. By lying about Isabella's identity, Livia muddles familial markers, unfixing relation and demonstrating the influence that accompanies the capacity to alter or destroy familial identity, even if only in language.

As the play begins, Livia holds a position of authority, although it is clear that as a woman she is still subject to the repression inherent in a patriarchy.[16] As a wealthy widow, Livia is able to voice her opinion on several familial matters; her opinion is sought after. Bourdieu asserts that "one of the most important factors bearing on linguistic production is the anticipation of profit which is durably inscribed in the language habitus, in the form of an anticipatory adjustment (without conscious anticipation) to the objective value of one's discourse" ("Economics" 653). Each speaker has a "language habitus," a context of the history and reception of his or her past speech. The habitus is formed according to the history of the speaker's social connections and influences, as well as to previous successes or failures in conversation. Livia first appears as a privileged family member and speaker. Her brother Fabritio asks "What think you, Lady sister?" (1.2.21) when he argues with Guardiano about whether a woman should have any reason, beyond the command of her father, to love a man. Fabritio's question implies Livia's ability to speak freely; it suggests that she is often granted the right to state her mind. The self-assurance with which she delivers her answer is equally telling:

I must offend you then, if truth will do't,
And take my niece's part, and call't injustice
To force her love to one she never saw.
Maids should both see and like: all little enough;
If they love truly after that, 'tis well. (1.2.29–33)

Livia does not conform to the early modern stereotype of the quiet, complacent woman; instead, she asserts her right to offend others with her opinions. Although she is asked to speak and therefore does not in this case create her own opportunity for speech, she nonetheless establishes herself as a vocal and esteemed member of her family.

Livia further insists upon her skill as rhetorician, telling Hippolito that her words can overrule her niece's aversion to her brother:

Sir, I could give as shrewd a lift to chastity
As any she that wears a tongue in Florence:
Sh'ad need be a good horsewoman, and sit fast,
Whom my strong argument could not fling at last. (2.1.36–9)

Livia recognizes the power of forceful speech. Her influence lies in her understanding how language and familial relation function in various contexts. Rather than make a "strong argument" (2.1.39) and persuade her niece to enter into an incestuous union with her uncle, as she tells Hippolito she will do, Livia lies about Isabella's parentage in order to speak more effectively in favour of the union with Hippolito. Livia asks Isabella to "set by the name of niece awhile" (2.1.90), where "awhile" implies that familial names can be revoked or granted as best suits the occasion. Requesting that Isabella not take offence at this change, Livia indicates that the two women might speak as "strangers." *Stranger* meant not only an "unknown person" or a "foreigner," but also a "guest or visitor, in contradistinction to the members of the household" or "a person not of one's kin" (*OED*, N.4.a, 1.a, and 3.a). Speaking in a "stranger fashion" (2.2.91), Livia implies, allows for frank discussion without familial constraints. She gains linguistic capital as she establishes a trustworthy speaking position as someone who is apparently unrelated to Isabella.[17]

Familial signifiers as Livia envisions them are not obliged to reflect genealogical reality. To make the case for speaking in a "stranger fashion," Livia suggests that to adopt this manner of speech is no mere preference but instead an obligation, for the "stranger fashion" is truthful. She informs Isabella that "the names of niece / And aunt" (2.1.132–3) as they have used them are merely customary terms (2.1.131) and not markers of true familial bonds. Telling Isabella that she is "no more allied to any of us [the family], / Save what the courtesy of opinion casts" (2.1.135–6), Livia proposes that children are assumed to be biologically related to their parents out of "courtesy," a form of politeness that presupposes that children are not bastards: standard social practice takes Isabella to be the child of Fabritio and his deceased wife. In this sense, Livia suggests that the names *niece* and *aunt* are adoptive: they imply a familial connection between people where none exists. The family that may be perceived to be whole and biological might in actuality be the opposite.

Livia elaborates upon Isabella's fictional lineage, giving the girl further details of her ostensible parentage. Although she states that their long-standing familial signifiers have no genealogical validity, she proposes that they must continue to use them to uphold the semblance of an intact family line. While Livia in private refers to Isabella not as a "niece," but as "my wench," a term of endearment that does not convey familial relation (2.1.163), she asserts that in public Isabella should preserve the fiction of their relation: "I pray forget not but to call me aunt still" (2.1.167). Livia maintains that Isabella's use of the terms *niece* and *aunt* must be deliberate and for show – that is, a performance. Isabella now believes that she acts out the appearance of her relation to Fabritio, Livia, and Hippolito for strategic purposes: the names must disguise Isabella's mother's supposed indiscretion with the Marquis of Coria. But Livia's declaration also forces Isabella to misrecognize her relation to Fabritio as a performance, albeit one she did not know she was giving. Supposing that she is the daughter of the Marquis, Isabella begins to perform relation consciously as she calls Livia "aunt." It is of course an irony that Isabella believes herself to be acting when she calls her true aunt, Livia, by that name. Similarly, Hippolito is now a "good gentleman" to Isabella, rather than a relative, but for the sake of appearances she continues to address the man whom she believed to be her uncle as "uncle." What Isabella believes to be a performance in fact reflects the truth.

Livia understands that familial status and markers yield linguistic capital and can be exploited to particular effect. As she remarks, Fabritio "may compel out of the power of father" (1.2.131); his words will be well received and his desires met because of his parental position and title. He is characterized by his incessant desire to command his daughter to obey him; his dialogue in the first act consists of little but declarations. By insisting that Isabella marry Guardiano's ward, Fabritio establishes his parental power. Isabella, he presumes, owes him obedience because she is his child – her duty outweighs her own wishes. Fabritio repeatedly uses the modal verb "shall" to convey what he believes to be her absolute obligation to follow his word: "No matter, she shall love him" (1.2.2); "you shall have him, / And you shall love him" (1.2.128); "Marry him she shall, then" (1.2.137). Isabella enters the play bound to honour her father's commands. She cannot escape his control nor assert her reluctance to fulfill the marital destiny that he envisions for her. Isabella assures her aunt that, "being born with that obedience / That must submit unto a father's will," she "must of force consent" to her father's wishes (2.1.86–8). She believes that she is by birth obligated to occupy a position of subservience that leaves her powerless against her father's word and that places her at a linguistic disadvantage.

Livia associates her removal of Isabella's familial title with a decrease in Fabritio's speaking power in relation to his daughter – a decline that increases Livia's own rhetorical capital. Coppélia Kahn observes that, as "a widow subject to no man, Livia is free to speak her mind" (165), but also notes that Livia's "words have no power to sway a father's will" (165). While I agree that Livia's words do not change Fabritio's view of his own authority, I believe that they do convince Isabella, his auditor, that his speech is powerless. Livia teasingly pretends to be reluctant to tell the secret of Isabella's true parentage. She claims that Fabritio's word does not, in fact, convey a father's power: "That which you call your father's command's nothing; / Then your obedience must needs be as little. / If you can make shift here to taste your happiness" (2.1.119–21). Isabella only "call[s]" Fabritio "father": the name is artificial, adoptive. Livia convinces her niece that she is now free to do and think as she likes, and is no longer required to obey Fabritio:

How weak his commands now, whom you call father?
How vain all his enforcements, your obedience?
And what a largeness in your will and liberty,
To take, or to reject, or to do both? (2.1.158–61)[18]

Livia's protestations thus seem ironic in light of her previous assertion of the strength of a "stranger fashion" (2.1.91). (And of course underlying her conversation with Isabella is the doubly ironic fact that the women are actually aunt and niece.) Livia simultaneously values and devalues kinship in order to ensure that her words, and not Fabritio's, are received by Isabella. She also knows that Isabella will be most receptive to what she wants to hear. As Christensen notes, "In recasting Isabella's origin in order to eliminate (nominally) the threat of incest, Livia necessarily resorts to a cuckold story, which produces in her auditor the desired relief ('this blest hour' [2.1.183]) rather than shock or shame for the mother who putatively played her father false" (501). Livia, having refashioned Isabella's family in precisely the way that Isabella desired, usurps Fabritio's command of his daughter, who now appears to be an illegitimate child. Isabella believes that her identity has changed because she thinks that she is the daughter of the Marquis, which occasions an epiphany:

> Have I passed so much time in ignorance,
> And never had the means to know myself
> Till this blest hour? Thanks to her virtuous pity
> That brought it now to light. (2.1.181–4)

Of course, Isabella's self-knowledge is prompted by a lie and therefore is not an epiphany at all; she does not know her true self, but is merely distanced from her genealogical identity.

Isabella's new sense of identity underscores the close association between fictional relation and incest. Livia's destabilization of Isabella's kinship directs Isabella to think that she can safely enter into a sexual relationship with her biological uncle. The excitement that Isabella feels once her aunt informs her that she is unrelated to Hippolito is not necessarily alarming by the standards of the day. Although, as Marc Shell observes, adoption was an impediment to marriage in classical and medieval times, in early modern England adoption was not viewed as a legal obstacle to involvement in a sexual relationship.[19] Because adoption itself had no official legal status and was not founded in biological genealogy, it existed outside of statutes prohibiting incest. The Church of England's "Table of Kindred and Affinity" (1560) did not specify that adopted siblings were unable to marry. Affine relations such as brothers- and sisters-in-law were included in the table, but adoptive relations were not.[20] Not until 1986 was the "Table of Kindred and Affinity" amended to forbid adopted children from marrying their adoptive parents, and there is still no entry that disallows marriage between adopted siblings. If Isabella were to involve herself with an adopted relative rather than a consanguineous one, she would break no civil or canon law because none existed. But because Isabella is not, in fact, biologically unrelated to Hippolito, the sudden shift in her attitude towards him is somewhat startling. Isabella's socio-emotional ties to the people she once deemed her relatives are negated and changed by Livia through the lie of her adoption, as are those ties that are supposedly "natural" or innate.[21] The play does not present adoptive relation as a barrier to sexual desire. On the contrary, adoptive relation is used to legitimate a sexual pairing.

Although sex between non-consanguineous people who thought of themselves as relatives was not prohibited, it was not necessarily viewed as acceptable. John Fletcher's comedy *Monsieur Thomas* (c. 1610–16; pub. 1639), also known as *Father's Own Son*, depicts Valentine, a guardian who is engaged to Cellide, his ward.[22] Although Cellide initially appears content to marry Valentine, it gradually becomes clear that she is distressed by the prospect. Theirs is not a typical case of wardship, in which the guardian is concerned with his ward's finances above all else, but is instead an adoptive relationship founded on great care and feeling.[23] Valentine is, as far as the play reveals, the only father Cellide has ever known. Valentine's sister observes that, as adoptive father, Valentine has managed his ward well and has "won [Cellide's] minde, / Even from her houres of childehood" (1.1.16–17). Valentine lost his wife and son at sea, and his ward is obviously intended to replace both his spouse and his child (1.1.30–42).

Cellide loves her adoptive father – she weeps with joy upon his return from a voyage – but she also appears to hesitate when others insist upon making the arrangements for their marriage (2.1.7–13). And while she is initially upset when Valentine breaks off their engagement, she later chides him for having presented himself to her as both parent and potential husband:

> O fond and ignorant,
> Why didst thou foster my affection
> Till it grew up, to know no other father,
> And then betray it?" (5.7.14–17)

While Valentine is sexually attracted to a daughter who is not his by blood, and therefore ignores his adoptive fatherly ties to her, Cellide is mindful of his social role as her parent. Although he is her father only in name, she recognizes that he should occupy only one familial role in her life. As Valentine's supposed friend Francis notes, Valentine's eventual termination of their engagement causes Cellide to lose "Father, Friend, herselfe" (3.1.148). Valentine is at once parent and lover ("friend" here is meant in the romantic sense) and this confusion of roles confuses Cellide's own identity. She eventually seeks refuge from this perplexing tangle of familial relation in a convent, where the Abbess includes her in a system of universal spiritual kinship that is far more straightforward than the kinship offered in her adoptive home.

Unlike *Monsieur Thomas*, Middleton's *Women Beware Women* does not portray a character's shock at being treated first as a relative and then as a lover. Instead, the play initially depicts the ease with which familial relation might change. It also emphasizes the possible similarities between adoption and incest. Livia's use of the lie about Isabella's adoption fuels the familial confusion that both adoption and incest have the potential to enact. Just as adoption might blur the outline of the family, incest casts family members in multiple and simultaneous familial roles, thereby obscuring the limits of relation. Both practices redefine relation. By renaming Isabella, Livia assumes a position of privilege. She revokes markers of familial identity and alters other characters' sense of self. Livia is thus aligned with Middleton himself. Referred to throughout the play as a magician, she wields the influence of a dramatist. Hippolito notes her power to transform Isabella:

What has she done to her, can any tell?
'Tis beyond sorcery this, drugs, or love-powders.
Some art that has no name, sure, strange to me
Of all the wonders I e'er met withal
Throughout my ten years' of travels. (2.1.231–5)

By "some art that has no name," Livia rewrites her niece's life; her lie to Isabella also makes Livia the instigator of the play's subsequent action. In fact, by reshaping Isabella's sense of family, Livia usurps the role of patriarch, although she must do so covertly. But for all of her apparent control, Livia of course does not change any fundamental ties: Isabella's biological relationship to Hippolito is fixed and Livia's attempt to "set by" familial terms cannot undo the fact of blood relation.

Livia also conceives of herself as a physician, a comparison that emphasizes her role in influencing her family. Although early modern English women were allowed to practise home remedies and lay medicine, they could not become licensed doctors; their supposed resistance to medical theory is often cited as cause for their banishment from the profession (Pettigrew 44).[24] Livia's self-depiction as a physician is remarkable because she envisions herself in a position of male authority.

Drawing attention to her capacity to influence others verbally, she imagines that her words are "ministered / By truth and zeal" (2.1.28–9), or with religious fervour, and playing the part of his caring physician, she tells Hippolito that she "minister[s] all cordials" (2.1.48) to cure his lovesickness. Others also see her in this role. Guardiano, having heard Livia assess Fabritio's overenthusiastic approach to fatherhood as "foolish," praises her and states that she has "let [Fabritio's] folly blood in the right vein" (2.2.74), or properly diagnosed him. The reference to bloodletting indicates Livia's ability to identify problems and administer cures, and also recalls her distancing of Isabella from her blood family. That is, Livia metaphorically "lets," or drains, her family's blood from her niece's veins in order to shape for her a new social existence.

But Livia's actions do not necessarily heal. By altering the story of her niece's lineage, Livia liberates Isabella from patriarchal rule, but only for a time. Not only does Isabella no longer have to obey her father's word, but she is also free to form new attachments. Livia therefore serves her well, in a sense, when she lies: Isabella is seemingly released from the patriarchal order only so that Livia can help the brother whom she loves "so well" (2.1.63), but she is released nonetheless. Isabella is freed from her father's authority, however, only to fall under it again. Livia's lie and the need to conceal her supposed illegitimacy cause Isabella to decide that "this marriage shall go forward" (2.1.206) and that she will obey her father's command to wed the Ward. Certain that she is not committing incest with her uncle but that she must still act in secret, Isabella sees the marriage as advantageous.[25] She believes that her actions are insubordinate when in fact she plays the stereotypical part of the well-behaved daughter. Livia does not truly free her niece from anything: as Fabritio remarks in reaction to his daughter's absolute compliance, "My will goes not so fast as [Isabella's] consent now / Her duty gets before my command still" (2.2.52–3). Livia's duplicitous assertions of familial relation in this instance maintain the status quo.

Although in some ways Livia's machinations effect no tangible change, her position as pseudo-dramatist and doctor finally leads to the total destruction of the family that she influences: familial relation cannot withstand the flexibility with which she attempts to treat it. *Women Beware Women* envisions a society in which familial markers might be mere coinages; they are imagined to be the fluid and sometimes counterfeit currency of familial relationships. But such markers have fatal consequences, suggesting that familial structures are not malleable. Hippolito murders Livia's lover, Leantio, spurring Livia to reveal Hippolito's incestuous affair. Disorderly kinship is to blame above all for the play's tragic outcome. Upon learning that she has committed incest, Isabella comments on the "confusion of life, soul, and honour" that her aunt has caused (4.2.126). Livia's lie leads to a loss of identity for Isabella, first through a removal of kinship ties and then through a blurring of kinship roles in an incestuous relationship. The play thus combines a somewhat progressive vision of the family as a changeable entity with the more conservative view that fluidity leads to chaos: Middleton is critical both of patriarchal order and of its potential destruction. The muddled, re-defined nature of Isabella's lineage leads to familial, and by extension social, destruction. Kinship becomes hazardous because the markers of familial relation are readily manipulated and can be used to any end. Isabella's reaction to her aunt's fictionalization of her kinship, and the Ward's and Guardiano's reactions to Isabella's incestuous affair, prompt Isabella, the Ward, and Guardiano to mount a theatrical performance in which everyone but the Cardinal is murdered. Following the path of apparent familial liberation results in death. Livia's daring, albeit self-interested, distortion of kinship roles suggests the lasting strength of familial bonds and the futility of trying to break them.

Women Beware Women's deadly ending owes much to the play's genre. Middleton and Rowley's *A Fair Quarrel* (c. 1615–17) also deals with a lie about parentage, but the tragicomedy's conclusion avoids the destruction caused by the dissolution of identity that *Women Beware Women* cannot escape.[26] In the interim, however, the play considers the challenge to identity posed by the alteration of familial relation. *A Fair Quarrel* begins by establishing that titles are potentially insignificant. As Captain Ager tells the Colonel, *colonel* is a mere epithet. He encourages his friend and superior to disregard titles and to instead "throw[] by those titular shadows, / Which add no substance to the men themselves" (1.1.80–1) so that they might assess one another "uncompounded, man and man" (1.1.82). It is the "men themselves" who matter, rather than the names that they are called. When the Colonel becomes agitated and calls Ager "the son of a whore" (1.1.347), however, the younger man cannot disregard the label as the typical, ritual insult of the duelling field and instead takes the charge literally: he obsesses over the idea that he might truly be the son of an unchaste woman. Ager cannot dis-regard the "titular shadows" that he so recently deemed unimportant to a man's worth; the name that he is called suddenly becomes significant.

In doubting his mother's honesty, Ager questions his own identity. Asking "who lives / That can assure the truth of his conception / More than a mother's carriage makes it hopeful?" (2.1.14–16), he expresses a generalized concern that any woman's outward "carriage," or her read-ily apparent conduct, might not actually reflect the truth of her child's birth. Ager begins to lose all sense of himself as he doubts his mother.

If "blood flows through forty generations," bestowing common characteristics upon family members (2.1.56), why is he not then more like the father whom his mother describes as "hasty" (2.1.52)? His fear that his mother has told him "a lie to birth" (2.1.231), however, is actually unfounded: Lady Ager is chaste. But the idea that she is a dissembler is only groundless until Ager beings to doubt her and forces her to become untruthful. Although Lady Ager refutes the charge that she is a whore, she reverses course when she thinks that her son, now assured of the legitimacy of his birth, will duel with the Colonel to defend his family honour. Like Lady Twilight in Middleton's *No Wit, No Help Like a Woman's*, Lady Ager lies in order to protect her son. As Suzanne Gossett observes in her introduction to *A Fair Quarrel*, Ager's "lack of faith ... corrupts his mother's sincerity" (1209). From this point onward, the story of Ager's birth is indeed fabricated.

Lady Ager's falsehood causes Ager to renegotiate his identity based on what he now believes to be his biological parentage. He shifts his responses to being called particular names given his new sense of lineage. When the Colonel cannot prompt him to fight by calling him a bastard, he instead labels Ager a "coward" (3.1.112). Because Ager now believes himself to be illegitimate, he feels that he has the right to react only to this second, typically less hurtful name. As Ager's friend marvels, "coward [can] do more than bastard" (3.1.119). Lady Ager's lie is therefore ineffective because it does not stop her son from duelling: he finds another name against which to fight. But in reacting to being called a coward, Ager proves that his mother is chaste and thus reinstates his own identity. His swift response to *coward* marks him as Sir Ager's hasty son. And in behaving bravely and duelling successfully, he further proves himself to be neither a coward nor a bastard, but instead his father's legitimate heir. Despite his own beliefs that titles are flexible, and despite his mother's attempts to alter his sense of lineage, Ager's behaviour demonstrates that his identity as his parents' biological son is fixed. This identity is later confirmed by Lady Ager's announcement that she was lying about his origins, and by the Colonel's withdrawal of the accusation that he is a bastard.

Like Isabella in *Women Beware Women*, Ager's sense of self is influenced by a lie about his parentage. But unlike its tragic counterpart, *A Fair Quarrel* aims to amend error. Lady Ager's lie does not prompt Ager to behave as though he is not his father's son in the way that Livia's lie allows Isabella to disregard her kinship with Hippolito and begin an incestuous relationship. Her lie instead ensures that he behaves in an honourable, if misguided, fashion that guarantees – once the Colonel has recovered from his duelling injuries – that a disastrous ending is averted.

Seemingly negotiable identity is ultimately inflexible in both plays, but the outcome of the negotiations is markedly different. Ambiguous paternity prompts Ager to behave in a different and yet not entirely new way: he continues to find excuses to carry on his original behaviour. But for Isabella the breakdown of kinship delineation is imagined to result in the collapse of purportedly natural, blood-based deterrents to incest; the lack of familial demarcation, made evident by Isabella's fictional adoption and by her very real act of incest, leads to chaos.

In loco parentis

In 1977, Patrick Steptoe and Robert Edwards carried out the first instance of in vitro fertilization (IVF) that led to a live birth: Louise Brown was born to Lesley and John Brown on 25 July 1978 in Manchester. Despite its success, the procedure was viewed by some as an example of human arrogance. The soon to be elected Pope John Paul I worried that the scientists responsible were, like the novice in Goethe's "Sorcerer's Apprentice," in danger of being unable to control the outcome of their actions (Sommerlad).[1] An otherwise celebratory article in *The Guardian* warned of the long-term political and moral implications of embryology: "You do not need the still distant possibility of human cloning to begin to get worried" (Tucker). *Time* magazine opined that "man will never be happy until he has proved that he is at least as smart as nature" ("Science" 74). As research advanced and embryos were transplanted from woman to woman, an article in the *New York Times* questioned "the ethics of manufacturing human life" (Fleming 14). IVF has been framed as being in competition with nature since at least 1944, when John Rock and Miriam Menkin first fertilized an ovum outside of the human body. Conceived in Petri dishes rather than in their mothers' wombs, "test tube babies" are not the result of a conjugal act and they blur the lines between genetic and gestational parenthood. Although widely accepted as a means of producing a child today, IVF remains controversial given the possibility that it presents for genetic editing – that is, not only for manufacturing human life but also for tailoring it to precise specifications.[2]

The contemporary family faces continual redefinition: its characterization and borders are always in question. New reproductive technologies inevitably change perceptions of what is natural and what is artificial, as well as what is a violation of accepted practice. In *Undoing Gender* (2004), Judith Butler writes that

> debates about the distinction between nature and culture, which are clearly heightened when the distinctions between animal, human, machine, hybrid, and cyborg are no longer settled, become figured at the site of kinship, for even a theory of kinship that is radically culturalist frames itself against a discredited "nature" and so remains in a constitutive and definitional relation to that which it claims to transcend. One can see how quickly kinship loses its specificity in terms of the global economy, for instance, when one considers the politics of international adoption and donor insemination. For new "families" where relations of filiation are not based on biology are sometimes conditioned by innovations in biotechnology or international commodity relations and the trade in children. And now there is the question of control over genetic resources, conceived of as a new set of property relations to be negotiated by legislation and court decisions. (126–7)

Although it appears to contravene nature, non-biological relation is always measured against nature. But families can today be constituted in so many ways as to make defining familial relation virtually impossible. Technology and innovation have opened even kinship up to a global economy, to market forces, and to international trade.[3] As new ways to create offspring and families are developed, societies will be obliged to question their values regarding kinship and nature.

Concerns about the alteration of nature in relation to the family existed well before the intervention of modern science. As I have shown, anomalous methods of familial formation have long occasioned unease about what constitutes familial relation. The possibility for altered familial forms that Butler sees in the biotechnological innovations of the twenty-first century were imagined in a less technical form in the literature of the early modern period, where adoption was viewed frequently as a kind of meddling with nature that might lead to both positive and negative outcomes. Early modern conceptions of the family were often grounded in ideas of difference and omission. Such exclusion was premised in notions of consanguinity and likeness and was, to some degree, institutionalized by the English legal system. There was, however, continuous popular opposition to the official discourse concerning the family; adoption was one of several alternative, less visible modes of familial formation that were outside the law, and that therefore challenged the sanctioned categorization of the family. Adoption displaced any presumption that sexual and biological relations were the sole basis of kinship. The ties of kinship that bind family members to one another in early modern English drama are not necessarily based in biological reproduction, but instead in emotional or even financial bonds. Adoption thus gives fictional families the means to alter nature's forms or to establish their own, non-blood-based ties. Plays such as those by Shakespeare and Middleton offer a historical precedent for envisioning "new" familial formations of the sort that Butler describes, including non-procreative and non-heteronormative formations.

Adoption has long been a familiar trope for representing issues of difference and the amalgamation of unrelated entities. It allows the adoptive family and the adoptee opportunities for self-making. Adoption challenges the element of chance in family life; it provides choice in the composition of the family whereas the particular children who result from procreation within the family cannot be anticipated. The Second Suitor in Middleton's *The Widow* draws attention to this fact when he calls his protégé Ricardo "my adoption, / My chosen child" (4.1.20).[4] In *Strangers and Kin: The American Way of Adoption*, Barbara Melosh claims that adoption is "a quintessentially American institution, embodying the reckless optimistic faith in self-construction and social engineering that characterizes much of [that country's] history" (10). The practice of course long predates the existence of the United States, but Melosh recognizes the link between adoption and the construction of a new life, one that involves "dreams of upward mobility and self-invention" (106). In its most hopeful form, adoption confirms the strength of affection over biological difference. As Melosh suggests, "if we trust that strangers can become kin, then maybe we can also forge families, communities, and nations that welcome the stranger" (11).

Shakespeare and Middleton both portray the family in terms of the modification of nature and also depict aspects of self-control and self-making in adoptive practices. Their approaches to these topics differ greatly in many respects, however, with Middleton living up to his reputation as a playwright with a bleak outlook on the world. Gary Taylor, continuing a long-standing tradition of referring to literary works as orphaned or abandoned children, sees Middleton's works themselves as forlorn infants in the twenty-first century, and links this condition to the playwright's own worldview. Taylor argues that one major distinction between Shakespeare and Middleton is the fact that Shakespeare's long association with the Lord Chamberlain's Men and the King's Men meant that he and his plays always had a home. In contrast to Shakespeare, Middleton "was born into a mobile, brutal, uncertain world, and suffered as a result" (Taylor). He had no consistent publisher or theatre company. As Bruce Boehrer suggests, however, this point of view "risks depicting Middleton as a deviation from the Shakespearean norm when, if anything, the reverse is true" and it was Shakespeare's professional and personal circumstances that were anomalous (*Environmental* 46–7). Taylor also notes that Middleton's biography was such that he understood non-biological families: his father died when he was young, and his stepfather famously sought to control his inheritance. As a result, Middleton's view of the family was likely dim, as was his stance on so many topics. By contrast, Taylor asserts, "Shakespeare has never been an orphan. He has always belonged. He began life in a landed rural family, in a small town where his father was mayor. He worked for the same theatre company for at least 20 years. In this regard, Shakespeare and Middleton have nothing in common." And yet each playwright was capable of imagining in particularly vivid terms what it meant to question and complicate the natural, biological family.

With the advent of genetic testing, modern science has changed the family even for adoptees: biological kinship is now eminently knowable. For the first time in history, people can determine conclusively from whom they are biologically descended. Motherhood has always been the more intelligible quantity because women carry and then give birth to children; paternity could previously only be assumed. Genetic tests can now give people a sense of belonging and identity that may have been missing – or even assigned mistakenly – throughout their lives. Whereas paternity was once based primarily in social interactions, or in the assumption of particular rights and responsibilities that came with presumed fatherhood, it can now be aligned more closely with procreation. As Nara Milanich declares in her study on paternity, "Science has definitively vanquished social and legal (mis)understandings of paternity, kinship, and identity. Commercialization has provided unfettered access to testing. The will to biological truth has displaced other social values once and for all" (260).

However, social aspects of parenthood persist. In a ruling of the Superior Court of Justice in Ontario (2008), a judge found that a Toronto-area man had to continue to pay his ex-wife child support despite a DNA test proving that he was not the biological father of her twin girls. The man raised the girls as his own, unaware of their biological parentage, until they were sixteen years old. Madam Justice Katherine van Rensburg used an expansive definition of parenthood to reach her decision:

The respondent's obligation to pay child support for the children would arise if he is a "parent" within the extended definition of that term under s. 2(2) of the *Divorce Act*. The issue is whether the respondent "stood in the place of a parent" toward them. This phrase and the extended definition of "parent" in s. 1(1) of the *Family Law Act*, to include "a person who has demonstrated a settled intention to treat a child as a child of his or her family," have been interpreted by a number of court cases. ("Cornelio v. Cornelio" Sec. 2)

While the mother's evident infidelity and her failure to disclose to her husband the possible parentage of the twins were ruled "a moral wrong against [her ex-husband]," the judge noted that "it is a wrong that does not afford [the ex-husband] a legal remedy to recover child support he has already paid, and that does not permit him to stop paying child support" ("Cornelio v. Cornelio" Sec. 22). The ex-husband's assumption of the role of father – his position as adoptive rather than birth parent – trumped his lack of biological connection to the girls. Despite the existence of a definitive test to determine paternity, social parenthood was in this case deemed of paramount importance.

The judge's decision has something in common with Henry Bracton's characterization of fatherhood (c. 1220) as based in presumption or appearances, where "common opinion ... sometimes is preferred to truth" (2.186). Under the law as interpreted by Justice van Rensburg, as in the early modern period, the family is not determined solely by biology but is instead a social creation – a paradox that playwrights such as Shakespeare and Middleton put at the centre of their works. In early modern English drama, adoption is variously material for romance, comedy, and tragedy. The practice is both empowering and potentially anxiety-inducing for characters and audiences alike, and its frequent occurrence in early modern literature suggests a profound uncertainty about what lies at the heart of familial relationships. I hope that the present study provides literary scholars interested in pre-genetic notions of kinship and procreation with a valuable record of early modern concepts of familial possibility.

Notes

Introduction: Shaping the Family

1 On the early modern management of nature, see Charlotte Scott, *Shakespeare's Nature*, esp. 3–7; Bruce Boehrer, *Environmental Degradation in Jacobean Drama*, esp. 7–27; and Vin Nardizzi, *Wooden Os*, esp. 6–31.

2 See Rebecca Bushnell, *Green Desire*, esp. 47–8.

3 Although the link between grafting and adoption may not have been prevalent, as Scott observes, "Shakespeare's lifetime ... witnessed an extraordinary growth in the discourses of cultivation" (32).

4 The adoption statute that was passed in Parliament in 1926 is generally believed to have come about as the result of the abundance of orphaned children in England after the First World War and the Spanish influenza pandemic. However, many had agitated for legalized adoption well before 1926. For a detailed description of the circumstances of the creation of the statute, see Peter Conn, *Adoption* 49.

5 Adoption was absent from English law from the medieval period onwards, as well as from the legal codes of other Western European countries. Jack Goody notes that "there is no entry for adoption in the whole thirteen volumes of Sir William Holdsworth's *The History of English Law* (1909 etc.)" (73). Conn observes that adoption is mentioned only once in *History of English Law* (1895), which cites a medieval case in which an unrelated child was treated by a husband and wife as their legitimate daughter, "permitting something that was very like adoption" (qtd. in Conn 61n69).

6 Although I am drawing a modern distinction between adoption and fosterage, Marianne Novy observes that in the early modern period "the terms *foster* and *adoptive* could be used interchangeably" (*Reading* 59).

7 Further complicating matters, however, is the fact that in the early modern period, the term *natural* often denoted an illegitimate bastard child who existed outside marriage and therefore apart from legally sanctioned society.

8 For further resistance to Philippe Ariès and Lawrence Stone, see in particular Alan Macfarlane, *The Family Life of Ralph Josselin, a Seventeenth-Century
Clergyman* and *Marriage and Love in England*; Linda Pollock, *Forgotten
Children*; and Steven Ozment, *When Fathers Ruled*. But as Su Fang Ng and
Fred B. Tromly have both warned, scholars should be "wary of replacing
the stereotype of the despotic father with the equally misleading stereotype of a kinder, gentler patriarch devoted to the tender nurture of his
domestic flock" (Tromly 16). Familial emotional detachment or intimacy
is likely to have varied according to class, gender, and birth order (16). See
Ng, *Literature and the Politics of the Family in Seventeenth-Century England*
4–5 and Tromly, *Fathers and Sons in Shakespeare* 15–17 for further discussion
of affective familial bonds.

9 Novy proposes that Brabantio's words "convey the sense that because
parents identify more closely with children of their own blood, it is easier
to disown an adoptee" (*Reading* 78–9) and "suggest[] that the adopted
child could be a second-class child, of whom not much was expected, who
could be easily disowned" (79). I read the passage as instead privileging
adoption as a way of constructing a desirable family. Novy's reading applies more closely, in my opinion, to *Much Ado About Nothing*, in which
Leonato declares that rather than having had a child by birth he wishes
he had "took up a beggar's issue at my gates" (4.1.132). Had he adopted
a child rather than created one, Leonato could at least distance himself
from that child's wrongdoing by stating that "No part of it is mine; / This
shame derives itself from unknown loins" (4.1.134–5).

10 As Novy observes, children were often raised by multiple sets of parents,
whether because of the death of one or both parents, remarriage, or involvement with institutions outside the family home ("Multiple Parenting
in Shakespeare's Romances" 188).

11 Stone calls the practice of fostering out "peculiar to England," and notes
that children "left home between ten and seventeen to begin work as
domestic servants, labourers or apprentices, but in all cases living in their
masters' houses rather than at home or in lodgings": "What one sees at
these middle- and lower middle-class levels is a vast system of exchange
by which parents sent their own children away from home – usually
not very far – and the richer families took in the children of others as
servants and labourers" (*Family* 84). For further discussion of the practices of apprenticeship and fostering, see Macfarlane, *The Family Life of
Ralph Josselin, a Seventeeth-Century Clergyman* 206–10; Beatrice Gottlieb,
The Family in the Western World from the Black Death to the Industrial Age
8–14, 171, 175; Ilana Krausman Ben-Amos, *Adolescence and Youth in Early
Modern England* 84–131; Paul Griffith, *Youth and Authority* 161–9; and Patrick Wallis, "Apprenticeship and Training in Premodern England." On

servants as the equivalent of family members, see, for example, Susan Dwyer Amussen, *An Ordered Society* 40.

12 See, for example, William Perkins, *Christian Oeconomy* 152–6.

13 As Alan Bray notes of sworn brotherhood, "its companions were the bonds created by adoption and fostering, and the friendship that could be created between families by the practice of adolescents leaving their parents' home to act as servants in households higher in the social scale, often with their parents receiving children in similar circumstances from below: a gift across social divisions that curiously echoes the communal eating and drinking in the hall of a great house or in the Eucharist, creating bonds of social cohesion at precisely the points at which the symbolic system emphasized social division" (214).

14 For further details of James's involvement with wardship, see Wallace Notestein, *The House of Commons* 85–96. An overview of the practice of wardship is presented in Joel Hurstfield, *The Queen's Wards*.

15 While some families employed live-in wet nurses, most sent their infants to live in the homes of the wet nurses themselves, frequently in the countryside (Fildes, *Wet* 91). Linda Campbell notes that the use of wet nurses among the upper classes may have been traditional, with breastfeeding associated only with the lower orders (368). For a discussion of the various medical arguments for and against wet nurses, see Valerie Fildes, *Wet Nursing* 68–78. Jack Goody observes that "although the practice was … condemned by the Church, it continued for very much longer, in England until the end of the nineteenth century when it retreated before the spread of feeding bottles and baby formulae" (40). For an account of wet-nursing in early modern English drama, see Gail Kern Paster, *The Body Embarrassed* 197–201.

16 See Fildes, *Breasts, Bottles, and Babies* 188–95. For a detailed description of the ideal qualities that wet nurses were thought to require in order not to negatively affect the children for whom they cared, see Fildes, *Breasts, Bottles, and Babies* 168–83.

17 Wet nurses were not always strangers to the families by whom they were employed. Campbell, for instance, observes that wet nurses were sometimes former servants (369).

18 According to Fildes, wet nursing was "practiced on such a scale that it can be classed as a cottage industry" ("English" 169).

19 Although the many poor law statutes of the Elizabethan era prioritized kinship care whenever possible, in cases where children had no means of support, parishes were required to provide for them. The Poor Law Act of 1536 is the first to mention the care of parentless infants by families within the parish (Fildes, *Breasts* 281). The most important incarnation of the Poor Laws for abandoned children was Elizabeth's *An Act for the*

Relief of the Poor, passed by Parliament in 1598. It stated that every parish was responsible for finding work for its parishioners, including neglected children. The parish was tasked with raising the fees necessary to care for the poor and indigent (Forbes 184). In 1601, a supplementary law was introduced to confirm that children had to be supported by their parents. If parental support was unavailable, responsibility for the child fell to its grandparents (185). Brothers, sisters, aunts, and uncles bore no legal responsibility to care for a relation in need. For more on early modern kinship networks and responsibilities, see Bernard Capp, *The Ties That Bind*, esp. 3–5; Keith Wrightson, "Household and Kinship in Sixteenth-Century England"; David Cressy, "Kinship and Kin Interaction in Early Modern England"; and Naomi Tadmore, *Family and Friends in Eighteenth-Century England* 110–14.

20 Fildes notes that poor women who were employed as wet nurses by London parishes sometimes took in as many as forty infants. Many of these women "were not proper *wet* nurses but fed the babies on bread and water pap or other unsuitable cereal foods and gruels and, in many cases, buried most of the infants they took in" (Fildes, *Wet* 97).

21 For examples of the charges billed to the parish of St. Botolph without Aldgate for such children, see Thomas Rogers Forbes, *Chronicle from Aldgate* 195–7. Writing about St. Botolph without Aldgate, Forbes notes that "it probably was not unusual for the parish to be faced with the care of a dozen youngsters at one time," which was no small burden given that the parish was also responsible for the adult poor (200).

22 For a brief summary of the history of infant care at Christ's Hospital, see Fildes, *Wet Nursing* 74 and *Breasts, Bottles, and Babies* 287.

23 As Fildes demonstrates, the babies and the women who cared for them came from varied social backgrounds ("English" 149).

24 Fildes notes that "by the late-sixteenth century, fewer suckling infants were accepted by the hospital, and by June 1624, the only children accepted under four years of age were children of Freemen of London and born within the city. By 1640, no children under three years were accepted, and the charity became an educational institution only" ("English" 153). For information on infant and child mortality rates at Christ's Hospital, as well as the average rates of pay for wet nurses there, see Carole Cunningham, "Christ's Hospital" 37–40.

25 The hospital was founded by Thomas Coram, who opposed "the Inhumane Custom of exposing New born children to Perish in the Streets" (qtd. in Zunshine 103).

26 For Novy's work on adoption in Shakespeare's romances, see "Adopted Children and Constructions of Heredity," "Multiple Parenting in *Pericles*," and "Multiple Parenting in Shakespeare's Romances." There is to date no

book-length study of adoption in early modern English literature; scholarship on literary instances of adoption focuses primarily on contemporary American literature. See, for example, Carol J. Singley's *Adopting America*, Cynthia Callahan's *Kin of Another Kind*, Mark Shackleton's *International Adoption in North American Literature and Culture*, and John McLeod's *Life Lines*. Novy's *Reading Adoption* – a study of adoption plots from Sophocles to Barbara Kingsolver – is exceptional in considering adoption in literature from a historical perspective. *Imagining Adoption*, an earlier collection edited by Novy, brings together several essays on nineteenth- and twentieth-century British and American adoption plots.

27 See, for example, Barbara L. Estrin, *The Raven and the Lark* and *Shakespeare and Contemporary Fiction*; Heather Dubrow, *Shakespeare and Domestic Loss*; Pollock, *Forgotten Children*; and Alison Findlay, *Illegitimate Power*. Estrin makes several important observations about adoption. She notes, for instance, that lost-child plots typically "predicate that the biological parents are superior to the adoptive ones" (*Raven* 14).

28 Christine Coch argues that "by transforming motherhood into a self-descriptive metaphor, Elizabeth escaped practical and cultural constraints while retaining the political benefits of an emergent maternal authority. Her figurative motherhood naturalized the anomaly of female rule and defined the bonds joining subject to queen as those of loving mutual responsibility" (425). Elizabeth also feminized the long-standing concept of *pater patriae*, the idea of the king as the father of his people. James I, for instance, wrote that "by the Law of Nature the King becomes a naturall Father to all his Lieges at his Coronation: And as the Father of his fatherly duty is bound to care for the nourishing, education, and vertuous gouernment of his children; euen so is the king bound to care for all his subiects" (qtd. in McIlwain 55).

29 Mary I used adoption to similar effect before Elizabeth: "I cannot tell how naturally a mother loveth her children, for I was never the mother of anie; but certeinlie a prince and governor may as naturalie and as earnestly love subjects, as the mother dothe hir child" (qtd. in S. Frye 28).

30 All biblical citations are taken from *The Bible: Authorized King James Version with Apocrypha*, edited by Robert Carroll and Stephen Prickett.

31 For more on the Christian concept of universal siblinghood, see Marc Shell, *The End of Kinship*, esp. xi–xii, 10–20, and 184–99.

32 Jack Goody notes that "despite their heavy debt to Rome," the legal codes of the "German, Celtic, and Romanized peoples in the West" contain practically no mention of adoption (73).

33 Jack Goody suggests too that the Church looked favourably upon godparenthood, and that metaphorical forms of adoption flourished while the actual practice of adoption was not sanctioned (75). For more on the ties

of "spiritual kinship" or godparenthood, see Macfarlane, *The Family Life of Ralph Josselin, a Seventeenth-Century Clergyman* 144–5.

34 Mireille Corbier has recommended that Jack Goody's argument be moderated. As she observes, to place all of the blame for adoption's disappearance on the Church is to participate in a long-standing tradition of characterizing the Church as Machiavellian ("Introduction" 10–11).

35 I know of no existing evidence of informal adoption contracts in England.

36 For a discussion of the case with which Cicero was concerned, see Hugh Lindsay, *Adoption in the Roman World* 174–81.

37 On the legal differences between public and private adoptions in Rome, see Jane F. Gardner, *Family and Familia in Roman Law and Life* 124–35.

38 Gardner provides an example of the formula of the *rogatio*, the measure proposed to the legislative body, given in such instances:

> May it be your will and command that L. Valerius may be to L. Titius in right and in law his son, just as if he were born from his as *pater* and from his *materfamilias*, and that he (Titius) may have in relation to him (Valerius) the power of life and death, as there is to a father in the case of a son. (qtd. in *Family* 127)

39 For more on the legal intricacies of Roman adoption, see Corbier, "Divorce and Adoption"; John Crook, "Patria Potestas" 113–22; Alan Watson, *The Law of Persons in the Later Roman Republic* 49–62; John Boswell, *The Kindness of Strangers* 66; Cynthia Jordan Bannon, *The Brothers of Romulus* 132–45; and E.N. Goody, "Forms of Pro-Parenthood" 331–45.

40 Adoption allowed the adoptee "to assume many aspects of the social personality of the adopter on his death" and was thus undertaken frequently for purposes of succession (Lindsay 103).

41 Satirical literature, Boswell observes, suggests that the childless wealthy were sought out by fortune-hunters who hoped to gain wealth via their adoption into these affluent families (115).

42 Michael Peppard gives the example of the Trajan–Hadrian "ADOPTIO" coins in the High Empire (69).

43 Margaret Giggs (1508–70) was raised from early childhood with More's children. She is, like More's daughters, notable for having been exceptionally learned. Algebra was her apparent specialty. For more biographical information on Giggs, see the entry for "Clement, Margaret" in the *Oxford Dictionary of National Biography*.

44 Giggs was included in the portrait despite having already left the More household after her marriage (Guy 174). Although the painting was destroyed in an eighteenth-century fire, Holbein's sketches survive. For more on the history of the portrait, see John Guy, *A Daughter's Love* 172–7.

45 Giles Heron, whose father John, the king's Treasurer of the Chamber, died when he was a minor, married Cecily More (Ackroyd 257). Anne Cresacre,

an orphan who had inherited estates and income, married John More (Ackroyd 146). Anne was included in the Holbein portrait; Giles and Alice were not.

46 Until the discovery of East's will in 1975, Snodham's identity was unclear. He was at times taken to be the second husband of Lucretia East, or his name was thought to be Thomas East's alias (J. Smith 9).

47 For a detailed description of Snodham's negotiations with Lucretia East over her husband's estate, see Jeremy L. Smith, *Thomas East and Music Publishing in Renaissance England* 122–4.

48 It is important to note that in the case of an older child or adult, an adoption would have been practically impossible to hide. Conversely, the adopted status of a baby might conceivably have been concealed to all but the innermost family circle; the adoptees themselves may have remained ignorant of their biological origins.

49 Jonson oversaw gatherings at the Devil Tavern of a group of poets and wits who came to be known as "the Tribe of Ben." Although the exact composition of the group is unknown, Percy Simpson lists Thomas Randolph, Robert Herrick, Thomas Carew, Shackerley Marmion, William Cartwright, James Howell, and Lord Falkland among its members (367). For more on the Tribe of Ben, see Joe Lee Davis, *The Sons of Ben*, and Claude J. Summers and Ted-Larry Pebworth (eds.), *Classic and Cavalier*. C.H. Cooper also notes several examples of Jonson referring to the members of his group as his adopted sons (588–9).

50 William Winstanley cites the following tale of Randolph's adoption by Jonson:

> Mr. Randolph having been at London so long as that he might truly have had a parley with his Empty Purse, was resolved to go see Ben Johnson with his associates, which as he heard at a set-time kept a Club together at the Devil-Tavern near Temple Bar; accordingly at the time appointed he went thither, but, being unknown to them, and wanting Money, which to an ingenious spirit is the most daunting thing in the World, he peep'd into the Room where they were, which being espied by Ben Johnson, and seeing him in a scholar's threadbare habit, John Bo-peep, says he, come in, which accordingly he did, when immediately they began to rime upon the meanness of his Clothes, asking him, If he could not make a verse? and withal to call for his Quart of Sack; there being four of them, he immediately thus replied,
>
> > I John Bo-peep, to you four sheep,
> > Which each one his good fleece,
> > If that you are willing to give me five shilling,
> > 'Tis fifteen pence a piece.
>
> By Jesus, quoth Ben. Johnson, (his usual Oath) I believe this is my Son Randolph, which being made known to them, he was kindly entertained

into their company, and Ben. Jonson ever after called him Son. (qtd. in Winstanley 143–4)

51 Many poets and playwrights were self-described members of the Tribe of Ben. Randolph claims that Jonson adopted him deliberately, but this would not necessarily have been the case for all of Jonson's followers.

52 Early modern literature frequently associates adoption with linguistic and literary practice. Patrons, for instance, were often portrayed as surrogate parents to literary works. The etymological root of patron, the Latin *pater*, or father, bestows upon the patron an adoptive parental right to the author's creations. That is, what the author produces becomes the possession, or, in a sense, the offspring, of his patron. Such thinking is often evident in the dedicatory prefaces of early modern works. Thomas Dekker, for example, presents his *News from Hell* (1606) to "Mr. John Sturman, Gentleman" and describes the tract as a child in need of a parent:

> Sir, the begetting of Bookes, is as common as the begetting of Children; onely herein they differ, that Bookes speake so soone as they come into the world, and giue the best wordes they can to al men, yet are they driuen to seek abroad for a father. That hard fortune followes al & falls into, vpon THIS of mine. It gladly comes to you vpon that errand, and if you vouch safe to receiue it louingly, I shall account my self and It very happie. (A3r)

John Heminge and Henry Condell, the editors of the 1623 folio of Shakespeare's plays, similarly note in their "Epistle Dedicatorie" that patrons are the custodians of works of literature: "We have but collected them, and done an office to the dead, to procure his Orphanes, Guardians" (A2v). Shakespeare's plays, figured as his offspring and described as his "remaines," will find adoptive parents, his editors imply, in the patrons who will oversee their care (A2v). For a sustained discussion of the links between procreation, publication, and authorship, see Douglas A. Brooks (ed.), *Printing and Parenting in Early Modern England,* and esp. Margreta de Grazia, "Imprints, Shakespeare, Gutenberg, and Descartes" 29–58.

53 Claudia Nelson has explored the links between adoption and staging in Noel Streatfield's children's fiction. Streatfield, she argues, depicts children who perform – they act, dance, skate, etc. – and are thus moved from "domestic confinement into a more liberating public sphere" (188). The nineteenth-century trope of the performing orphan undergoes "changes that cast performance as a way to get beyond domesticity rather than as a way to achieve it" (189). The connection that Nelson notes between adoption and performance has also been treated by Jill R. Deans, who investigates the practice as part of a larger social performance in the plays of Edward Albee in "Albee's Substitute Children."

Margaret Homans analyses adoption novels and surmises that an "increased attentiveness to the subject of adoption might complicate narrative theory" (4).

54 Novy suggests that "the theme of multiple identity, which adoptees incarnate, is an inherently theatrical one" (*Reading* 85).

1. Shakespeare's Adopted Children and the Language of Horticulture

1 My translation, from *Des Hermaphrodits, accouchemens des femmes, et traitement qui est requis pour les relever ensanté, & bien élever leurs enfants* 168.

2 *All's Well That Ends Well*, edited by G.K. Hunter. All further citations from the play are taken from this edition.

3 Shakespeare's romances, in particular, include children who are removed from their families and sent to live with non-biological parents. For an analysis of characters in the romances who have both birth parents and adoptive parents, see Marianne Novy, "Multiple Parenting in Shakespeare's Romances" 188–208 and "Adoption and Shakespearean Families" 56–86.

4 Several scholars have examined grafting in relation to human reproductive sexuality. See in particular Claire Duncan, "'Nature's Bastards'"; Erin Ellerbeck, "'A Bett'ring of Nature'"; Jennifer Munroe, "It's all about the gillyvors"; Vin Nardizzi, "Shakespeare's Penknife"; and Miranda Wilson, "Bastard Grafts, Crafted Fruits."

5 For scholarship that considers the ties between grafting and writing, see Leah Knight, *Reading Green in Early Modern England* 81–108; Jessica Rosenberg, "The Point of the Couplet" 25–7; and Miriam Jacobson and Vin Nardizzi, "The Secrets of Grafting in Wroth's *Urania*" 176–8.

6 See W.L. Braekman, "Bollard's Middle English Book of Planting and Grafting and Its Background" 19–39.

7 Shakespeare's *Henry IV, Part 2* notably features Justice Shallow remarking to Falstaff, "Nay, you shall see my orchard, where, in an arbour, we will eat last year's pippin of mine own grafting" (5.3.1–3).

8 For an account of the growing importance of grafting in early modern horticulture, see Blanche Henrey, *British Botanical and Horticultural Literature before 1800* 1: 55–6.

9 In *Sylva Sylvarum*, Francis Bacon claims that "it is reported, that in the Low Countries they will graft an apple-scion upon the stock of a colewort, and it will bear a great flaggy apple, the kernel of which, if it be set, will be a colewort, and not an apple" (2: 487). He continues that "It were good to try whether an apple-scion will prosper if it be grafted upon a sallow, or upon a poplar," and notes that he has "heard that it hath been tried upon an elm, and succeeded" (2: 487).

10 See Thomas Hill, "Epistle" in *The Profitable Arte of Gardening*, and N.F., "The Epistle to the Reader" in *The Fruiterers Secrets*.

11 See Andrew Marvell's "The Mower against Gardens" for a literary example of the anxiety associated with grafting in the period. Noting that a tree's natural form has been altered, the speaker observes that humankind has "dealt between the bark and the tree" in order to create "forbidden mixtures" through grafting (ll. 21–2).

12 For a detailed account of Anaxagoras' views on the connections between plant and animal life and Aristotle's adoption of these views, see A.G. Morton, *History of Botanical Science* 24. Morton also offers a general account of the history of botany that describes the links the ancients imagined to exist between plants and other living things (19–57).

13 I have discussed plants and embryological development in *On the Nature of the Child* in "'A Bett'ring of Nature'" 87–8.

14 For more on how metaphor can be used to explain that which is occluded from human understanding, see Elizabeth D. Harvey, "Sensational Bodies, Consenting Organs" 299–300. Harvey posits that botanical analogies and metaphors were used to shed light on the hidden qualities of the reproductive system.

15 Ernest H. Wilkins discusses M. Conrat's study of the *arbor iuris* in relation to Book IV of the *Sententiae* of Julius Paulus. Conrat, Wilkins notes, suggests that the diagram may have been developed to illustrate the eleventh chapter of the book, which concerns consanguinity and inheritance. The diagram appeared in several treatises on civil law (Wilkins 63).

16 The term *arbor iuris* was used as early as AD 874. See Wilkins, "The Genealogy of the Genealogical Trees of the 'Genealogia Deorum'" 63.

17 Wilkins observes that the *arbor iuris* and the Jesse tree are apparently unrelated. His article explores the ways in which Boccaccio's genealogical trees, however, are derived from both templates. Wilkins also notes Boccaccio's familiarity with legal knowledge. Roman *stemmata* – collections of shrines or paintings representing deceased family members as connected by lines – preceded European genealogical charts, according to Wilkins, but appear to be distinct from them (62).

18 See in particular Harold S. Wilson, "'Nature and Art' in *The Winter's Tale* IV, iv, 86 ff" 114–20; G. Wilson Knight, *The Crown of Life* 105; and Robert Egan, "'The Art Itself Is Nature'" 56–89. For a consideration of Perdita as an adopted child, see Novy, "Multiple Parenting in Shakespeare's Romances," esp. 191–3 and 195–7, and *Reading Adoption* 67–86.

19 Novy notes that the defence that Polixenes "uses of the grafting that created these flowers [the gillyvors] is a defense that can also be made of adoption as itself natural" (*Reading* 83), but she stops short of identifying Perdita, as I do, as herself a "grafted" child who survives because of her attachment to

a stronger, safer stock. Novy does not analyse the play's horticultural focus or the analogous terms in which grafting and adoption are conceived.

20 Duncan also considers that Perdita might be the result of grafting, although she does so by viewing the girl as a presumed bastard: "Perdita and Polixenes's grafting discussion signals the alternate genealogical nightmare of Leontes's from the Sicilian half of the play that concerns both Perdita and Polixenes: their debate must be read through Leontes's misguided belief that Perdita is actually Polixenes's bastard daughter" (141). In this reading, Perdita is "the flowering product of grafting" (140).

21 As Duncan observes, the practice of grafting flowers was widespread, and "gillyvors seem to have been particularly known for grafting" (138).

22 For an analysis of the play's treatment of the friendship between the two kings, see Laurie Shannon, *Sovereign Amity* 199–222.

23 In *Pandosto*, Porrus debates whether he can afford to raise an abandoned child. He eventually discovers, however, that the baby girl comes with a purse of gold and that he can justify fostering her "with the sum to relieve his want" (Greene 200).

24 Not all critics agree that Polixenes goads Perdita. Simon C. Estok, for example, takes his words as genuine and does not consider his motivation (*Ecocriticism* 97).

25 Munroe examines the debate from an ecofeminist perspective and suggests that "if we see the questions raised by Perdita and Polixenes as engaging with the practices and gendered implications of art used to alter nature in husbandry and housewifery manuals, we might see new ways to read the art/nature debate and gendered power relations in the play at the same time" ("It's all" 140–1).

26 It should be noted that Hermione is, of course, a fit parent, and could likely have raised the child well. Leontes, however, is clearly branded as a dangerous father at the beginning of the play.

27 Novy suggests that the Shepherd's "pastoral world seems, emotionally, a better environment for child-rearing than the cold and suspicious world of the court" (*Reading* 68).

28 For a detailed description of the "influence of heredity" in the play, see Novy, *Reading Adoption* 69–72.

29 Novy observes that this disturbing, "fear-motivated virtual disowning brings about the happy ending, as Polixenes recognizes Perdita as Leontes' lost daughter and sends word to him" ("Multiple Parenting in Shakespeare's Romances" 193).

30 Patricia Parker considers Shakespeare's rhetoric of joints in *Shakespeare from the Margins* 88–102.

31 Belarius comments several times on the innate princely behaviour that he also observes in the boys: "How hard it is to hide the sparks of nature! ... their

thoughts do hit the roofs of palaces, and nature prompts them / In simple and low things to prince it much / Beyond the trick of others" (3.3.79, 83–6).

32 Posthumus also shares an attachment to his father, mother, and two brothers beyond the grave as they appear in a dream to call to the god Jupiter for help (5.3).

33 Novy notes that such episodes provide examples of "mysterious affinity stemming from 'blood'" ("Multiple Parenting in Shakespeare's Romances" 201).

34 For further discussion of biblical references and Christian revelation in *Cymbeline*, see Robin Moffet, "*Cymbeline* and the Nativity" 216.

35 "Thus saith the Lord GOD; I will also take of the highest branch of the high cedar, and will set it; I will crop off from the top of his young twigs a tender one, and will plant it upon an high mountain and eminent: / In the mountain of the height of Israel will I plant it: and it shall bring forth boughs, and bear fruit, and be a goodly cedar: and under it shall dwell all fowl of every wing; in the shadow of the branches thereof shall they dwell" (Ezekiel 17:22–3).

36 In the Book of Romans, Paul expresses man's dependence on his maker in agricultural terms. Explaining man's detachment and reattachment to God's "tree," he envisions the Jews as currently grafted out of God's chosen people, but sees the possibility for their return, or their re-grafting, at the same time as he wishes that the Gentile Romans would appreciate their own attachment to God:

> For if the firstfruit be holy, the lump is also holy: and if the root be holy, so are the branches. / And if some of the branches be broken off, and thou, being a wild olive tree, wert graffed in among them, and with them partakest of the root and fatness of the olive tree; / Boast not against the branches. But if thou boast, thou bearest not the root, but the root thee. / Thou wilt say then, The branches were broken off, that I might be graffed in. / Well; because of unbelief they were broken off, and thou standest by faith. Be not highminded, but fear: / For if God spared not the natural branches, take heed lest he also spare not thee. / Behold therefore the goodness and severity of God: on them which fell, severity; but toward thee, goodness, if thou continue in his goodness: otherwise thou also shalt be cut off. / And they also, if they abide not still in unbelief, shall be graffed in: for God is able to graff them in again. / For if thou wert cut out of the olive tree which is wild by nature, and wert graffed contrary to nature into a good olive tree: how much more shall these, which be the natural branches, be graffed into their own olive tree? (11:16–24)

Just as the scion relies upon the stock for support, so does man depend upon God to sustain him. As Paul notes, the branches do not bear the root, but the root bears and cares for them. God is able to lop off those "natural branches," or people, to whom he is connected as easily as he is able to graft in new dependants.

37 Examining images of birth, pregnancy, and conception in *Pericles* and *Cymbeline*, Novy notes that such imagery is "often used metaphorically, and sometimes the point of the metaphor is to make the reunion of parents and children into a rebirth or a reconception" (*Reading* 74).

38 Jean E. Feerick argues that the re-grafting of Guiderius and Arviragus onto Cymbeline's family tree is an image of British hybridity: "the emphasis on the act of rejoining these severed botanical parts works against notions of pure lineal identity by foregrounding an act of cultivation ... The princes, after all, have been transplanted to Wales and reared far from court, renaturing them over time and making them 'strange shoots' to the native tree of their father ... Their return to court smuggles back into Britain the savage tinge of that soil" ("Imperial" 225).

39 Novy cites George Bernard Shaw's rewriting of the play's last act to convey a similar point: "We three are fullgrown men and perfect strangers. / Can I change fathers as I'd change my shirt?" ("Multiple Parenting in Shakespeare's Romances" 203). She observes that in *The Winter's Tale* there is "little attention to how Perdita, Guiderius, and Arviragus feel about discovering a different set of parents or how they come to terms with those they earlier thought of as their only parents" (203).

40 For a similar line of argument, see Carolyn Asp, "Subjectivity, Desire, and Female Friendship in *All's Well That Ends Well*" 175–92.

41 For more on Helena as a physician, see Catherine Field, "'Sweet Practicer, thy Physic I will try'" and Terry Reilly, "'Doctor She.'"

42 Painter's text was reprinted in 1569 and 1575.

43 On the play's emphasis on childbirth, see Michele Osherow, "She Is in the Right." David M. Bergeron notes a hint of incest in the Countess's first lines that confuses the boundary between father and son (176). See also Parker, "*All's Well That Ends Well.*"

44 Helena has no legal or religious reason to fear that sharing an adoptive bond with Bertram would mark as incestuous any future sexual relationship between them. The Church of England's "Table of Kindred and Affinity" (1560), a document identifying which relations a person was prohibited from marrying, did not specify that adopted siblings were unable to marry. The table was amended in 1986 to forbid adopted children from marrying their adoptive parents, but there is still no rule in place that disallows marriage between adopted siblings.

45 For a discussion of how the term *daughter* could imply relation by marriage or birth, see Parker, "*All's Well That Ends Well*" 365–6.

46 Several critics have noted the connection between Shakespeare's King's treatment of his ward and abuse of the Elizabethan ward system. See in

particular Howard C. Cole, *The All's Well Story from Boccaccio to Shakespeare* 95–100 and Reilly, "*All's Well*." Margaret Loftus Ranald argues that although the King is allowed to "arrange a suitable marriage for his ward in terms of age, rank, and wealth," he is unable to force Bertram to marry someone of lower social status (79–80).

47 The comparison between marriage and grafting was not unusual. In Thomas Middleton and John Webster's *Anything for a Quiet Life*, for example, an old man is told that to "graft such a young blossom into [his] stock" by marrying a younger woman is foolhardy (1.1.23). In her 1665 diary, Katherine Austen provides a historical account of thinking of a woman's marriage as a kind of graft. Austen, a widow who was free to marry, rejected a suitor and never remarried because of her lasting love for her husband and "the respect she owed the 'name and Kindred' into which she had been 'grafteed'" (qtd. in Todd 76–7).

48 Parker emphasizes Bertram's family's grafting of Helena. She observes that "the plot is, finally, the story ... of the opening of an aristocratic family to a more expansive exogamy, an expansion that links it with the famous images of grafting from *The Winter's Tale*. Despite his best efforts to prevent it, Bertram's noble family expands just enough to graft onto itself a slip of lesser stock, an image used several times in this play for the 'breeding' that enables such 'increase'" ("*All's Well*" 388).

49 For a detailed account of Bertram's passive role in Helena's pregnancy, see Osherow, "She Is in the Right" 157–62.

50 Sheldon P. Zitner notes that although the line can be thrown away, "taken advantage of, it can stunningly qualify the import of the reconciliation. This is no warrant to cobble together a deep-analytical revision of the play in which Helena is seen as really searching for her female parent. Yet it does force a backward look, a recognition that the affectional centre of the play is the interview between Helena and the Countess in Act 1" (137).

2. Animal Parenting in Shakespeare's *Titus Andronicus*

1 *Titus Andronicus*, edited by Jonathan Bate. All further citations from the play are taken from this edition, unless otherwise noted.

2 Marianne Novy notes that the terms *foster* and *adoptive* were used interchangeably in the early modern period (*Reading* 59).

3 On the convention, see in particular Laurie Shannon, *The Accommodated Animal* 3 and Helen Smith, "Animal Families" 75–8. Smith "explore[s] how animal exemplars operated as ideals whose emotional and oeconomic behaviour was celebrated in terms which were often distinctly unflattering to the humans with whom they were compared" (77).

4 S. Clark Hulse calls it "babble," for instance, and claims that "it is the wrong argument, directed to the wrong audience" (109). Although she does not consider this passage in particular, Lynn Enterline similarly suggests that Lavinia is unpersuasive by noting that her language often "encourages what it tries to evade" (14). Mary L. Fawcett argues that Lavinia fails to find appropriate literary precedents to persuade Tamora to overcome their differences (267).

5 Two critics in particular observe the familial tone of the passage. Barbara L. Estrin acknowledges that Lavinia does not get what she wants, but sees her reference to fostering ravens as an attempt to make a familial connection with Tamora (*Raven* 15). She proposes that Lavinia's request "appeals to a notion of universal motherhood" and is an effort to "replace for Tamora the son Titus sacrificed" when he killed Alarbus (15). Lavinia promotes "a kinship based on caring rather than consanguinity" (15). Like Estrin, Marie Rutkoski points to the familial focus of the passage, but she considers the importance of the concept of childhood in relation to it. Rutkoski argues that Lavinia characterizes herself as a victim, and that her request reveals that she is "dependent on an adult effort to sustain her" (204). By repeatedly comparing Lavinia to an infant, she insists, the play frustrates the early modern tendency to think of children as "easily known quantities" who can be understood by their parents or others (204). In this respect, Rutkoski's assessment resembles Estrin's: both critics view Lavinia as using figurative parent-child relations in her own defence.

6 This chapter is aligned with ecocritical scholarship on *Titus*. Erica Fudge, for instance, examines the "uncertainty about animal-human difference" in the play ("Saying" 84). She notes that "*Titus Andronicus* is full of images of animals, images that, by their frequency, begin to upset the normal distinction made between human and animal" (83). Fudge observes that in the banquet scene the sons are "mere flesh, mistaken for animals" (85). Simon C. Estok also considers the blurring of animal-human boundaries in relation to eating in *Titus*, and sees the play as challenging "the acceptability of animals as food" ("Theory" 63). Writing about botany, blood, and race, Jean E. Feerick discerns "a larger pattern in the play whereby natural forms are made to carry complex social valences" ("Botanical" 87). Jennifer Munroe observes that men metaphorize women and non-human nature throughout the play, with Lavinia in particular presented as a doe ("Is It Really" 41). I propose that in this passage Lavinia herself does the metaphorizing.

7 See, for example, Ania Loomba, *Shakespeare, Race, and Colonialism* 75–90 and Francesca T. Royster, "White-Limed Walls" 432–55.

8 Feerick notes that in this moment Saturninus "momentarily concedes to" Titus' own interest in "a language of kinship" and his insistence that "their

two natures have become one" ("Botanical" 89). Katharine Rowe suggests that these lines are "fulsome and insincere" and that they instead "introduce the possibility of revenge" (290).

9 For a detailed discussion of "adoptive" names and familial honorifics, see chapter 4.

10 "Noxal surrender" involved a *paterfamilias* surrendering a dependant who had committed a wrong rather than paying a fine (Gardner, *Women* 7). *Coemptio* refers to the groom paying a token fee to marry his bride (Gardner, *Women* 17).

11 On the similarities between the practice of adoption and the conferring of citizenship, see Julia Reinhard Lupton, *Citizen-Saints* 127. In a discussion of Christopher Marlowe's *The Jew of Malta*, Lupton states that the adoption of Ithamore by Barabas is "of interest to the literature of citizenship, since it implies a *universitas circumcisorum* that would link disparate groups in common projects, provisional universals, without dissolving their unique jurisdictions" (66).

12 Heather James and Feerick both read this line as a statement of Tamora's knowledge of Roman values. See Heather James, *Shakespeare's Troy* 58 and Feerick, "Botanical Shakespeares" 93.

13 The *OED* defines "kind" in the period as the "essential quality or fundamental character as determining the class or type to which a thing belongs; character, nature" (N.I.1.a).

14 For a discussion of the significance of "kind" in *Titus*, see Feerick, "Botanical Shakespeares" 83–93. Feerick notes that Titus "means less that Rome has been 'good' or 'kind' in modern parlance, than that Rome has been 'familial' in protecting his own family member" ("Botanical" 88). She understands "kind" as "difference in relation to qualities of blood" (83).

15 Women were granted the ability to adopt in AD 291 but were only allowed to adopt caregivers (Brosnan 333).

16 See in particular Feerick, "Botanical Shakespeares" 82–3; Fudge, *Perceiving Animals* 3–11; and Feerick and Vin Nardizzi, "Swervings" 3–6.

17 Like other ecocritical scholars of early modern literature, Feerick and Nardizzi identify a "necessary overlap" and "soft boundary separating animals from their human counterparts" (3). What distinguishes their approach to considering cross-species identification, however, is their insistence that animal-human contact and indistinction did not always occasion concern. Instead, "postures of desire, admiration, disappointment, even release" might be observed in representations of the relations between humans and non-humans (4).

18 For a discussion of the role of bees in the period, see Jonathan Woolfson, "The Renaissance of Bees" 281–300.

19 Fudge observes that in Viret, "humans are sent to school not in order to leave the beasts behind but in order to learn from them" (*Brutal* 93).

20 Discussing the "intimate presence of animals in the spaces and routines of the home," Helen Smith argues that "non-humans did not simply offer convenient mechanisms to conceptualize the politic and hierarchies of the family, but became part of the family's social and emotional, as well as bodily, life" (77).

21 Jonathan Bate suggests the allusion in his edition of the play (177).

22 A raven prevents St. Benedict from eating poisoned bread (White 176). Paul of Thebes lives as a hermit and is brought bread daily by a raven (80).

23 A hitwaw, also known as a hickwall, is a green woodpecker. The term and its variants were in use from the fourteenth to the nineteenth century ("hickwall," *OED*, N.1).

24 The Flemish painter Peter Paul Rubens depicts in *Romulus and Remus* (1616) a woodpecker delivering three cherries to one of the boys while the other is suckled by the wolf. Ovid mentions the woodpecker in his *Fasti* (124–5).

25 The boys survive and are eventually found and "brovght vp" by the shepherd Faustulus – described as their "foster-father" (Longus 26) – and his wife Laurentia. They remain ignorant of their biological identities until they are young men.

26 A 2006 Japanese co-production of the play with the Royal Shakespeare Company implied a connection between Shakespeare's text and the Romulus and Remus story by placing a giant replica of the Capitoline Wolf statue on stage. For a review of the production, see Ben Brantley, "Shakespeare in War."

27 Although the statue has long been considered an Etruscan work, the wolf portion dates from the thirteenth century, while the figures of Romulus and Remus were added in the fifteenth century. The statue has been on display in Rome since 1471 (Tuck 3).

28 Pliny the Elder notes in his *Natural History* that the woodpecker was also "important in taking auguries" (317).

29 This passage is also quoted in the introduction.

30 For a detailed description of the ideal qualities that wet nurses were thought to require in order not to negatively affect the children they cared for, see Fildes, *Breasts, Bottles, and Babies* 168–83.

31 Feerick notes that "brethren" and "brothers" appear "as many as 45 times in the play" ("Botanical" 87).

32 Shakespeare depicts elsewhere the amalgamation of the concepts of kindness and kind. As Prospero considers Ariel's sympathetic approach to those men whom Prospero holds prisoner in *The Tempest* (1610–11), for instance, he wonders why he "shall not myself, / One of their kind, that relish all as sharply / Passion as they, be kindlier moved than thou art?" (5.1.22–4). Prospero knows that he should treat those of his kind with kindness, but is incapable of feeling the compassion that Ariel claims to possess.

33 At other times, Shakespeare's characters imagine animals teaching
    humans how to shed their empathy for more aggressive behaviour. In
    Henry VI, Part 3, Clifford implores the King to defend his son by thinking
    and acting like an animal parent, one who nurtures and protects its
    progeny in the face of a threat:

    > Unreasonable creatures feed their young;
    > And though man's face be fearful to their eyes,
    > Yet, in protection of their tender ones,
    > Who hath not seen them, even with those wings
    > Which sometime they have used with fearful flight,
    > Make war with him that climb'd unto their nest,
    > Offer their own lives in their young's defence.
    > For shame, my liege, make them your precedent. (2.2.26–33)

    As opposed to Lavinia, who begs Tamora to exercise a kind of animal-
    inspired pity, Clifford implores the King to learn from animals how to
    lay aside "harmful pity" in the interest of guarding his child from danger
    (2.2.10). He observes that lions, bears, and serpents are all willing to
    use violence if their offspring are threatened. Even worms and doves –
    stereotypically small and peaceful creatures – will "safeguard of their
    brood" (2.2.18). Humans can take such behaviour as "precedent,"
    modelling their own conduct after that found in the natural world.

34 Works of natural history also recounted tales of cross-species interaction.
    In Edward Topsell's *The History of Foure-Footed Beasts*, for instance, several
    species, such as sheep, wolves, and bears, are noted for their propensity
    for feeding abandoned infants. Topsell observes that "it is receiued in
    many Nations, that children haue bene Nursed by beares" and offers
    classical and anecdotal evidence to make his point: "Parris throwne out of
    the cittie, was nourished by a Beare. There is in Fraunce a Noble house of
    the Ursons, whose firste founder is reported to have bene certaine yeares
    togither nourished by a beare, and for that cause was called Urson" (41).

35 Edmund Malone notes that Anthony Munday and Richard Hathwaye wrote
    a play based on the story in 1598 that was never printed and has since been
    lost (385). As Fudge argues, the details of the narrative were altered eventu-
    ally to suit the religious climate of the Reformation (*Perceiving* 58–63).

36 Susan Wiseman argues that in stories of wild children such as that of
    Valentine and Orson, it is the perceived sexual indiscretion of women that
    causes children to be banished or sent out into the wild (161–95).

37 The text and images of the 1555 version, titled *The hystory of the two
    valyaunt brethren Valentyne and Orson*, were reused in many subsequent
    editions. I refer to the 1555 edition here.

38 Bethany Packard identifies Lavinia as an author figure with creative agency
    in "Lavinia as Coauthor of Shakespeare's *Titus Andronicus*" 281–3.

39 Angel Day's text is an English translation of a French translation of Longus' Greek text. *Daphnis and Chloe* was first translated into French by Jacques Amyot in 1559 and was published in several editions. Day's translation of Amyot's French translation appears to be the only known English version of the text until George Thornly's 1657 edition.

40 Jane Hiles argues that "failures of language" occur throughout the play "because characters mistake the context in which they are speaking" (62).

41 Alexander Leggatt has also observed Aaron's genre-bending tendencies and suggests that "for Aaron the play is not a tragedy but a comedy" because of his "ironic detachment" from the horrific events that take place (*Shakespeare's Tragedies* 15).

3. Middleton's *A Chaste Maid in Cheapside* and Adopted Bastards

1 Amy Louise Erickson has shown that primogeniture was at times modified in practice, allowing women to inherit land and goods (62–4). See also Natasha Korda, *Shakespeare's Domestic Economies* 38–51.

2 As many scholars have noted, primogeniture acted as an organizing concept for the family: it preserved and protected the family's economic and social interests. See Lawrence Stone, *The Family, Sex and Marriage* 38, 71–2 and Claire M. Busse, "Profitable Children" 215–19. For a discussion of primogeniture in early modern drama, see Michelle M. Dowd, *The Dynamics of Inheritance on the Shakespearean Stage* 31–75.

3 See, for instance, Northrop Frye, "The Argument of Comedy" 10–11 and Alexander Leggatt, *Shakespeare's Comedy of Love* 166–7. On the fusion of fecundity and the conventions of comedy, see also Arthur F. Marotti, "Fertility and Comic Form in *A Chaste Maid in Cheapside*."

4 For more on city comedy and the development of the middle class, see L.C. Knights, *Drama and Society in the Age of Jonson* 36–54.

5 See also Edward J. Geisweidt's "The Bastard Bomb" on the effects of London's growing population on the play's characters.

6 *A Chaste Maid in Cheapside*, edited by Alan Brissenden. All further citations from the play are taken from this edition.

7 Although the term *economics* now refers to the "production, distribution, consumption, and transfer of wealth" (*OED*, N.2), it is derived from the Greek *oikos*, or "household." The study of *oikonomikē* was the study of "the science or art of household management" ("economics," *OED*, N.1.a). In the early modern period, economics, or oeconomics, did not refer to the modern sense of "economics" alone: the two meanings of the term were often conflated and early modern oeconomics were firmly tied to matters of the family and the household. The term frequently referred to the creation and expenditure of wealth within the practice

of household administration. Thinking about economic matters relied heavily on the microcosmic model of the household to demonstrate the fundamental nature of the macrocosmic order. As a result, the model of household management was representative of larger financial matters; concepts of monetary and familial organization were thus often necessarily intertwined. Early modern economic theorists turned to the works of Aristotle and other classical writers to establish a model for household economy. For classical and humanist discussions of *oikonomikē* translated into English, see Aristotle, *Politiques*, esp. chaps. 3, 5, 7–8; Xenophon, *Xenophons Treatise of House holde*; and Jean Bodin, *Six Bookes of a Common-weale* 1, chap. 2.

8 Alison Findlay suggests that "the natural child is able to confound and confuse the boundary lines between nature and culture in ways which problematise many other binary opposites and, in so doing, reveal the precarious fragility and the oppressive workings of the dominant order. Starting from the living paradox of being both natural and unnatural, the bastard character undoes distinctions between masculine and feminine, sanity and madness, body and spirit, high and low art" (136).

9 See Sandra K. Fischer's catalogues of economic metaphors for procreation in *Econolingua* 18–20.

10 See, for instance, Marc Shell, *The End of Kinship* 29–30. Shell states that "the product of monetary generation, or use, and the product of sexual generation, or a child, have been compared. (The Greek word *tokos*, 'offspring,' referred to both.)" (30).

11 For a detailed description of how children were depicted in economic terms in the drama of the early modern period, see Busse, "Profitable Children" 209–43.

12 For an examination of urban childlessness in early modern drama, see Dowd's chapter on *Volpone* in *The Dynamics of Inheritance on the Shakespearean Stage* 209–55. Dowd argues that the city space "enables Jonson to explore the ways in which the growth of England's urban economy demanded new conceptual approaches to inheritance" (210).

13 See Gail Kern Paster, *The Body Embarrassed* 52–63 for a discussion of female incontinence, "moisture, secretions, and productions as shameful tokens of uncontrol" in the play (52). Paster observes that Lady Kix's "tears are causally linked to her husband's dryness" (61).

14 As Barbara Hanawalt notes, "childless couples do appear among those leaving wills, but they compensated for their lack of immediate family by forming closer bonds with siblings and their children, godchildren, and friends" (252). Historian Lloyd Bonfield also observes that "lurking behind the scenes" of supposedly straightforward inheritance practices were "demographic variables, in particular limited life expectancy and

childlessness, that might require the adaptation of customary rules of inheritance" (158).

15 Patricia Crawford suggests that "barren wives lacked social status and respect, and the higher their social position, the unhappier was their lot" ("Construction" 19). She notes, for instance, that when Catherine of Brayanza, the wife of Charles II, did not bear an heir, "the whole happiness of her life was centred on this single blessing" (19).

16 As David Bevington and Kathleen McLuskie observe, "Mrs. Allwit's childbirth shows ... [Lady Kix's] need for children is ... crucial to her sense of her social status in the city community" (18).

17 Such a wish is in keeping with the experiences of many early modern men. As Helen Berry and Elizabeth Foyster demonstrate, "men of even modest social status" who did not father children in marriage "could be subject to ridicule from their friends, neighbours and family" (167). Berry and Foyster outline four ways in which men could be held responsible for infertility: impotence, or the failure to achieve an erection; "absolute impotence," where an erection could not be followed by penetration; the inability to produce semen; and the incompatibility of the man and woman (169–71).

18 *The Book of Common Prayer* suggests that companionship was an acceptable reason for marrying.

19 As Stone makes clear, the nobility kept good records and were especially concerned with succession and the preservation of estates. It is therefore far easier to track rates of childlessness among the nobility than among the lower classes. The overall rates of sterility are also difficult to determine because of high early death rates (*Crisis* 167–8). Alan Macfarlane argues that infertility was common enough in early modern England to be regarded as a hardship rather than as something ruinous (*Marriage* 51–5).

20 Berry and Foyster describe ways in which city living was believed to be unhealthy and to result in fewer births, especially among those men who suffered from stress and whose focus was primarily on business (174).

21 As Bruce Boehrer argues, "the city's staggering population growth ... finds a fit emblem in the preternatural fecundity of *A Chaste Maid in Cheapside*'s Touchwood Senior" (*Environmental* 42).

22 Marotti observes that "in this play's comic society, [Touchwood's] fertility is initially a victim of economic 'necessity'" (68).

23 Dorothy McLaren notes that the amenorrhoea of lactation, or the period of infertility that occurs during breastfeeding, was the only way in which early modern women could effectively control their own fertility. While breastfeeding could reduce fertility and increase the time between pregnancies, however, women in upper-class households mostly abandoned the practice and engaged in a "reproductive pattern of ever-recurrent births" (27).

For more on the amenorrhoea of lactation, see D. McLaren 22–53. Angus McLaren also suggests that "in some cultures in which stigmas are attached to barrenness and children are highly valued in economic and cultural terms a high birth rate is sought and large families taken as a demonstration of the community's ability to *control*, by promoting, births" (3).

24 As Jacques Gélis suggests in *History of Childbirth*, abundant fertility was often dreaded because parents worried that they might not be able to feed all of their children (xi).

25 As Rachel J. Weil argues, women "had power to exert within a system of hereditary succession" because only they were able to verify legitimacy (82). See also Crawford, *Blood, Bodies and Families in Early Modern England* 113–39.

26 Marianne Novy suggests that modern adoptees reading early modern drama might identify in particular with bastard characters such as Edmund in *King Lear*. "Illegitimacy is handled differently in *Lear* than in modern adoption," she notes, "but there is enough continuity in the issues for an adoptee to find Edmund's words and situation resonant" (*Reading* 79). Novy points to the discrimination that Edmund speaks out against as the "historical antecedent of the discrimination that adoptees experience when their birth certificates are sealed and they cannot get information about their medical and other family history" (81).

27 David Cressy suggests that "one out of every forty babies was born out of wedlock," with the overall rate of bastardy in early modern England around 2 or 3 per cent (*Birth* 73). For further historical information on bastardy in the period, see Richard Adair, *Courtship, Illegitimacy and Marriage in Early Modern England* 80–90; Helen Vella Bonavita, *Illegitimacy and the National Family in Early Modern England*, esp. 21–5; and Eleanor Fox and Martin Ingram, "Bridewell, Bawdy Courts and Bastardy in Early Seventeenth-Century London."

28 See also Macfarlane, "Illegitimacy and Illegitimates in English History" 75–6 and Chris Given-Wilson and Alice Curteis, *The Royal Bastards of Medieval England* 51–3.

29 As Cressy notes, bastards "suffered legal limitations in regard to property and title"; however, "in practice the law allowed bastards to receive legacies through wills" (*Birth* 74). For more on bastards and inheritance, see Findlay, *Illegitimate Power* 30–1.

30 John Webster, Thomas Heywood, and William Rowley's *A Cure for a Cuckold* (1624) stages a problem of succession similar to that of the Kixes in *A Chaste Maid in Cheapside*, and dramatizes a legal situation similar to the one with which Bracton is concerned. Franckford, a wealthy but childless merchant, fathers a bastard child whom he wants to claim as his own for financial reasons. Urse, the woman who bears Franckford his bastard, does so to

provide the wealthy and infertile couple with an heir. Compass, Urse's husband who has been absent for years, however, also wants to lay claim to the child because it is born to his wife. Bradin Cormack argues that *A Cure for a Cuckold* reflects "a relevant historical, legal, and cultural context" in the attention that it pays to the different jurisdictional orders involved in determining who is the lawful father of a particular child (293). Cormack asserts that "the play tests Compass's claim – his attempt to legitimate the child – in terms of competing legal and discursive orders: pitting the mother's rights against the biological father's, for example, but also natural law against human law, central law against local and municipal law, English common law against the Roman civil and canonical orders that together constituted the *ius commune*" (292). For a detailed account of biological versus legal fatherhood in the period, see Cormack, *A Power to Do Justice* 291–329.

31 Joel Welty observes the tendency of the cuckoo to transfer its young to the care of others:

> This characteristic, a nasty and subversive one by human standards, but perfectly natural and biologically "moral" by avian standards, is practiced by representatives of five families … Birds of various genera among these families lay their eggs in nests of other species and abandon them to the care of their foster parents. (323)

32 In French and German, the term was applied to both the adulterer and the husband of the adulteress ("cuckold," *OED*, N.1).

33 Edward Topsell suggests that the term *cuckold* does not stem from the cuckoo bird, but from the curruca bird: "Soe that a Cuckolde is not derived of the Cuckoe but of *Curruca*, a hedge-sparrowe that fostereth the Cuckoes breede in steede of his oune" (*Fowles* 238). This view is not subscribed to by modern etymologists.

34 Boehrer, for instance, notes that Allwit fails "to grasp the extent to which wittolry effeminizes its subject" (*Shakespeare* 93).

35 David Bevington asserts that kneeling expresses "contractual obligation, obedience, homage, submission, fealty, petition, hospitality, parental authority, royal prerogative" (136).

36 As Findlay observes, "bastards were a form of cheap labour." Wat and Nick are dramatic examples of "bastard apprentices or servants" (33).

37 There is, of course, the chance that Allwit and his wife are having sex and producing children despite their deal with Sir Walter. The play could be staged so as to emphasize this reading. The Allwits might, for instance, be physically affectionate when Sir Walter is offstage but cease to be when he comes into view.

38 Boehrer suggests that "Middleton's urban scams illustrate a fundamental change in the ecology of human manners: in the increasingly competitive environment of early modern London, human predatory impulses that,

given less congested circumstances, would primarily be directed toward non-human species begin now, for lack of a better alternative, to take fellow human beings increasingly as their object" (*Environmental* 43).

39 Boehrer provides an extended discussion of this scene's "startling juxtaposition of human and non-human animals, re-staging Christ's redemptive sacrifice within the calendar cycle of Lent and Easter" (*Environmental* 44–5).

4. Adoptive Names in Middleton's *Women Beware Women*

1 *Women Beware Women*, edited by Richard Dutton. All further citations from the play are taken from this edition.

2 Henry VIII's detractors "almost entirely reject the idea that incest aversion is natural; instead they regard it as an institution of divine and canon law, gradually developed to accommodate the shifting needs of a growing human race" (Boehrer, *Monarchy* 33).

3 See, for example, Emily Detmer-Goebel, "What More Could Woman Do?" 141–59; Jennifer L. Heller, "Space, Violence, and Bodies in Middleton and Cary" 425–41; Mark Hutchings, "Middleton's *Women Beware Women*" 366–7; Catherine MacGregor, "Undoing the Body Politic" 14–23; Richard A. Levin, "If Women Should Beware Women, Bianca Should Beware Mother" 371–89; and Anthony G. Dawson, "*Women Beware Women* and the Economy of Rape" 303–20.

4 As Dorothea Krook argues, Livia's immorality is ironically based in affection. See Krook, *Elements of Tragedy* 150–66.

5 Inga-Stina Ewbank also observes the play's focus on familial relations and notes that "the ordinary appellations of kinship are used with more than ordinary care and point." See Ewbank, "Realism and Morality in *Women Beware Women*" 59.

6 Middleton draws on Celio Malespini's *Ducento Novelle* (1609), a historical narrative of Bianca Capello, for the main plot of the play. Hippolito and Isabella are generally believed to be modelled after characters in *The True History of the Tragicke loves of Hipolito and Isabella Neapolitans*, a French novel first published in 1597 and translated into English in 1628. For an account of Middleton's source texts, see William C. Carroll, "Introduction" xiv–xv.

7 See Lynne Magnusson, *Shakespeare and Social Dialogue* 61–90.

8 George Puttenham also comments on epithets in a section of *The Art of English Poesy* (1589) entitled "Of the figures which we call sensable, because they alter and affect the mind by alteration of sense, and first in single words" (262). Puttenham notes that the Greek *antonomasia*, or what he terms "the Surnamer," might be substituted for a term that is "likely to be true" (266). In the same way that the name "father" can be used to refer to someone who is in a position of patriarchal power but who is not in fact the

biological father of the addressee, a person's proper name might be replaced by a new name that is representative of the essence of their position:

> And if this manner of naming of persons or things be not by way of mis-naming as before, but by a convenient difference, and such as is true esteemed and likely to be true it is then called not *metonymy*, but *antonoma-sia*, or the Surnamer (not the Misnamer, which might extend to any other thing as well as to a person). As he that would say not King Philip of Spain, but "the Western King," because his dominion lieth the furthest west of any Christian prince; and the French King "the Great Valois," because so is the name of his house; or the Queen of England, "the Maiden Queen," for that is her highest peculiar among all the queens of the world; or, as we said in one of our *Partheniades*, the "Briton Maid," because she is the most great and famous maiden of all Brittain. (266)

9   It is worth noting that each of these cases is distinct, although they are clearly linked.

10   Historian David Cressy has discovered several epistolary examples from the Restoration period of family members who wrote to distant relatives and exaggerated the degree of their relation – typically using the term *cousin* – "expect[ing] kin-connectedness to pay off" ("Kinship" 45). Cressy suggests that "'the part of a kinsman' is one of the great unexplored areas of early modern social history" (46). The letters that he examines "throw some light on the question of who could invoke it, over what range of family connectedness, in what circumstances, and to what effect" (46), and "demonstrate that kinship, once established, permitted intimacy, and intimacy invited favours. Kinship carried 'clout,' or at least opened doors that might otherwise have remained closed" (47).

11   Leantio's mother is not named in the play but is referred to simply as "Mother."

12   Levin interprets Mother as one of the play's most dangerous characters and takes her interactions with Bianca to be manipulative (371–89).

13   For a discussion of the term *daughter* as signalling relation either by marriage or by birth in the early modern period, see Patricia Parker, "*All's Well That Ends Well*" 365–6.

14   There is an element of recklessness to Bianca's behaviour that is not especially admirable. She relishes having abandoned her previous life, for instance: "I have forsook friends, fortunes, and in country, / And hourly I rejoice in't" (1.1.131–2). As Joost Daalder notes, Bianca has "elope[d] without regard for her parents" (86).

15   This observation is also made in Daniel Dodson, "Middleton's Livia" 379.

16   As Richard Dutton argues, "there is always a sense in which Livia's free-thinking is contained by, and subject to, the patriarchy with which she has reached an accommodation of sorts" (xxiii).

17 Ironically, Isabella urges her uncle to "make [his] love no stranger" later in the same scene – a different usage of the term (2.1.226). She desires the opposite of the distance that Livia establishes with her and hopes for familiarity with Hippolito. But this of course is also the play's problem: Hippolito is no stranger to Isabella but is instead her relative.

18 Livia is not legally correct here. Even if Fabritio were not Isabella's biological father, because he raised her as his daughter she is such according to the law. For a discussion of illegitimacy and legal paternity in early modern drama, see Bradin Cormack, *A Power to Do Justice* 291–330.

19 While Marc Shell cites several classical and medieval sources that suggest that "adoption has the same effect in precluding marriage as does kinship by blood," he goes on to observe that the view of adoption as equal to consanguinity has been contested frequently since the fall of Rome (218). Shell does not cite any early modern sources that speak out against marriage between adoptive relatives, and I have been unable to locate any that treat adoption as a legal barrier to a sexual relationship.

20 As Sybil Wolfram observes, the document treated consanguineous and affinal relatives as similar, and "any affinal relative was forbidden if the same consanguineous relative was expressly prohibited in Leviticus" (26). She notes that "the relatives forbidden to marry were those up to and including third cousins by blood or in-law, or in legal terms relatives in or within the fourth degree of consanguinity and affinity by the canon law reckoning of degrees" (21). The table, which was composed by Archbishop Matthew Parker, was included in *The Book of Common Prayer* in 1662 and was hung in every parish church (Wolfram 26).

21 For an explanation of why the aversion to incest was believed to be natural, see Boehrer, *Monarchy and Incest* 23–4 and 138–42. Boehrer notes that early modern theories of instinct aversion mirror, in some respects, Edward Westermarck's twentieth-century work on incest (24).

22 While guardians typically purchased wardships in order to make a profit or to provide their own sons with wives, they did, on occasion, marry their own wards. An example is Sir Thomas Cheyney, who married his ward Anne Broughton (Ives 126–7). Charles Brandon, Duke of Suffolk is perhaps the most famous case. Only six weeks after the death of his wife, Mary Tudor, he married Katharine Willoughby, his own ward, whom he had originally intended for his son. In a letter dated 22 July 1558, Eustace Chapuys, the Imperial ambassador to England for Charles V, relays information about the match to his master:

> On Sunday next the Duke of Suffolk will be married to the daughter of a Spanish lady named Lady Willoughby. She was promised to the Duke's son, but he is only ten years old, & although it is not worth writing to your Majesty, the novelty of the case made me mention it. The Duke will have

done a service to the ladies who can point to his example, when they are
reproached, as it is usual, with marrying again immediately after the death
of their husbands. (qtd. in Goff 23)

At the time of their marriage, Suffolk was forty-nine years old and
Katherine was fourteen.

23 Joel Hurstfield observes that guardians were granted control of their
wards' lands, but were also given power over the allowance paid by the
Court of Wards to the guardian while the ward was still a minor; the
custodium of the ward, or the possession of the child; and the *maritagium*,
or the right to marry the ward to whomever the guardian chose (89). As
a result, Hurstfield argues, wardships were frequently undertaken for
financial gain alone.

24 For more on women caring for the bodies of others, see Laura Gowing,
Common Bodies 88–96.

25 Daalder suggests that Isabella marries the Ward because, "with the
problem of incest solved, Isabella finds it easier to accommodate her
father's desire that she marry the Ward, to whose money she appears to
be attracted. Her punishment at the end would indicate that her wish for
gold (which is poured into her lap) is the source of her undoing, not incest.
Thus, from this perspective, Middleton appears to view her alliance with
the Ward as a kind of prostitution" (89).

26 Although modern editors agree that Middleton and Rowley worked
closely on the script, Middleton is widely recognized as the author of the
main plot – the scenes between Captain Ager and his mother, Lady Ager,
as well as the scenes between Captain Ager and the Colonel (Gossett 1211).

Afterword: *In loco parentis*

1 In the same interview, the soon to be elected pope compared advancements in
reproductive technology to the development of weapons of mass destruction.

2 In November 2018, He Jiankui, a Chinese scientist, announced that he
had, without ethical approval, manipulated an embryo to make it resistant
to HIV. The statement caused an uproar in the scientific community and
among the public. See, for example, Collier Meyerson, "Crispr Babies,
IVF, and the Ethics of Genetic Class Warfare"; Suzanne Sataline and Ian
Sample, "Scientist in China Defends Human Embryo Gene Editing."

3 Adoption has become increasingly scarce in the face of better access to
contraception and assisted reproductive technologies. American adoption
rates peaked towards the end of the 1960s when adoption had become an
accepted social tool for managing children born out of wedlock. The decline
in adoptions since the 1970s has been fuelled primarily by advancements
in birth control and changing definitions of motherhood, as well as by

the increased use of IVF (Melosh 105–7). The practice has again become relatively rare and unfamiliar. It is, as an article from 2018 in *The Guardian* observes, "competing with lots of other ways of having children" (Press Association). As of 2015, 1.7 per cent of American babies were born with the help of assisted reproductive technologies (Sunderam et al. 1). This is not to say that the response to change has been uniformly positive. As adoption played an increasingly acknowledged and public role in the twentieth and twenty-first centuries, negative responses to it were still common. And Marianne Novy observes that although adoption is now more socially acceptable, adoptive parents often still fear that their adoptive children might want to establish contact with their birth parents (*Reading* 3)

4   Valeria's "Second Suitor" takes Ricardo (another suitor) under his wing and refers to him as adopted. He facilitates the marriage of Valeria and Ricardo by tearing up Ricardo's bonds of debt. The Second Suitor is not entirely benevolent, however: he hopes that the newlyweds will be in constant conflict and will live as beggars. For him it is more "sweet to sow mischief, / Than to receive money" (5.1.352–3).

Bibliography

Ackroyd, Peter. *The Life of Thomas More*. Nan A. Talese, 1998.

Adair, Richard. *Courtship, Illegitimacy and Marriage in Early Modern England*. Manchester UP, 1996.

Akkerman, Nadine, editor. *The Correspondence of Elizabeth Stuart, Queen of Bohemia*, vol. 2, Oxford UP, 2011. 3 vols.

Amussen, Susan Dwyer. *An Ordered Society: Gender and Class in Early Modern England*. Columbia UP, 1988.

Ariès, Philippe. *Centuries of Childhood: A Social History of Family Life*. Translated by Robert Baldick, Knopf, 1962.

Aristotle. *Generation of Animals. Complete Works of Aristotle*, edited by Jonathan Barnes, vol. 1, Princeton UP, 1984, pp. 1111–218. 2 vols.

– *History of Animals. Complete Works of Aristotle*, edited by Jonathan Barnes, vol. 1, Princeton UP, 1984, pp. 774–993. 2 vols.

– *On Rhetoric*. Translated by George Kennedy, Oxford UP, 1991.

– *Politiques*. London, 1598.

Asp, Carolyn. "Subjectivity, Desire, and Female Friendship in *All's Well That Ends Well*." *Shakespeare's Comedies*, edited by Gary Waller, Longman, 1991, pp. 175–92.

Austen, Ralph. *A Treatise of Fruit Trees Shewing the Manner of Planting, Grafting, Pruning*. London, 1665.

Bacon, Francis. *De Augmentis Scientiarum*. Robertson, pp. 413–635.

– *Descriptio globi intellectualis. The Oxford Francis Bacon, Philosophical Studies c.1611–c.1619*, translated and edited by Graham Rees, vol. 6, Clarendon, 1996, pp. 95–170. 16 vols.

– "Of Parents and Children." Robertson, pp. 742–3.

– "On Marriage and the Single Life." Robertson, p. 743.

– *Sylva Sylvarum. The Works of Francis Bacon*, edited by James Spedding, et al., vol. 2, Cambridge UP, 2011, pp. 339–672. 14 vols.

Baker, Susan. "Personating Persons: Rethinking Shakespearean Disguises." *Shakespeare Quarterly*, vol. 43, no. 3, 1992, pp. 303–16.

Bannon, Cynthia Jordan. *The Brothers of Romulus: Fraternal Pietas in Roman Law, Literature, and Society.* Princeton UP, 1997.

Bate, Jonathan. Introduction. *Titus Andronicus,* by William Shakespeare, edited by Bate, Routlege, 1995, pp. 1–121.

Beaumont, Francis, and John Fletcher. *A King and No King.* London, 1619.

Ben-Amos, Ilana Krausman. *Adolescence and Youth in Early Modern England.* Yale UP, 1994.

Bergeron, David M. "'The credit of your father': Absent Fathers in *All's Well, That Ends Well.*" Waller, pp. 169–93.

Berry, Helen, and Elizabeth Foyster. "Childless Men in Early Modern England." *The Family in Early Modern England,* edited by Berry and Foyster, Cambridge UP, 2007, pp. 158–83.

Bevington, David. *Action Is Eloquence: Shakespeare's Language of Gesture.* Harvard UP, 1984.

Bevington, David, and Kathleen McLuskie. *Plays on Women.* Manchester UP, 1999.

The Bible: Authorized King James Version with Apocrypha. Edited by Robert Carroll and Stephen Prickett, Oxford UP, 1998.

Boccaccio, Giovanni. *Genealogy of the Pagan Gods [De Genealogia deorum gentilium].* Edited and translated by Jon Solomon, Harvard UP, 2011–17. 2 vols.

Bodin, Jean. *Six Bookes of a Common-weale.* London, 1606.

Boehrer, Bruce. *Environmental Degradation in Jacobean Drama.* Cambridge UP, 2013.

– *Monarchy and Incest in Renaissance England: Literature, Culture, Kinship, and Kingship.* U of Pennsylvania P, 1992.

– *Shakespeare among the Animals: Nature and Society in the Drama of Early Modern England.* Palgrave, 2002.

Bonfield, Lloyd. Introduction. *The World We Have Gained: Histories of Population and Social Structure,* edited by Bonfield, et al., Basil Blackwell, 1986, pp. 1–36.

Boswell, John. *The Kindness of Strangers: The Abandonment of Children in Western Europe from Late Antiquity to the Renaissance.* Pantheon, 1988.

Bourdieu, Pierre. "The Economics of Linguistic Exchanges." *Social Science Information,* vol. 16, no. 6, 1977, pp. 645–68.

– *Outline of a Theory of Practice.* Translated by Richard Nice, Cambridge UP, 1977.

Bracton, Henry. *On the Laws and Customs of England,* c. 1220. *Bracton Online,* 10 Apr. 2019, amesfoundation.law.harvard.edu/Bracton/.

Braekman, W.L. "Bollard's Middle English Book of Planting and Grafting and Its Background." *Studia Neophilologica,* vol. 57, no. 1, 1985, pp. 19–39.

Brantley, Ben. "Shakespeare in War, More Timely Than Ever." *The New York Times,* 8 Jul. 2006, www.nytimes.com/2006/07/08/theater/shakespeare-in -war-more-timely-than-ever.html.

Bray, Alan. *The Friend.* U of Chicago P, 2006.

Briggs, Julia. "Shakespeare's Bed Tricks." *Essays in Criticism*, vol. 44, no. 4, 1994, pp. 293–314.

Brooks, Douglas A. *Printing and Parenting in Early Modern England*. Ashgate, 2005.

Brosnan, John Francis. "The Law of Adoption." *Columbia Law Review*, vol. 22, no. 4, 1922, pp. 332–42.

Brown, Michael J. *Itinerant Ambassador: The Life of Sir Thomas Roe*. UP of Kentucky, 1970.

Brown, Penelope, and Stephen C. Levinson. *Politeness: Some Universals in Language Usage*. Cambridge UP, 1987.

Buell, Lawrence. *The Environmental Imagination: Thoreau, Nature Writing, and the Formation of American Culture*. Harvard UP, 1996.

Burton, Robert. *The Anatomy of Melancholy*. Edited by Thomas C. Faulkner, et al., Clarendon, 1994. 3 vols.

Bushnell, Rebecca. *Green Desire: Imagining Early Modern Gardens*. Cornell UP, 2003.

Busse, Claire M. "Profitable Children: Children as Commodities in Early Modern England." *Domestic Arrangements in Early Modern England*, edited by Kari Boyd McBride, Duquesne UP, 2002, pp. 209–43.

Butler, Judith. *Undoing Gender*. Routledge, 2004.

Callahan, Cynthia. *Kin of Another Kind: Transracial Adoption in American Literature*. Michigan UP, 2011.

Calvo, Clara. "In Defence of Celia: Discourse Analysis and Women's Discourse in *As You Like It*." *Essays and Studies*, vol. 47, 1994, pp. 91–115.

Campbell, Linda. "Wet Nurses in Early Modern England: Some Evidence from the Townshend Archive." *Medical History*, vol. 33, 1989, pp. 360–70.

Capp, Bernard. *The Ties That Bind: Siblings, Family, and Society in Early Modern England*. Oxford UP, 2018.

Carroll, William C. Introduction. *Women Beware Women*, by Thomas Middleton, edited by Carroll, A & C Black, 1994, pp. xi–xxxiv.

Christensen, Ann C. "Settling House in Middleton's *Women Beware Women*." *Comparative Drama*, vol. 29, no. 4, 1995–6, pp. 493–518.

Church of England. "Table of Kindred and Affinity." *The Book of Common Prayer: The Texts of 1549, 1559, and 1662*, edited by Brian Cummings, Oxford UP, 2011.

Clerke, William. *The Triall of Bastardie*. London, 1594.

Coch, Christine. "'Mother of my Contreye': Elizabeth I and Tudor Constructions of Motherhood." *English Literary Renaissance*, vol. 26, no. 3, 1996, pp. 423–50.

Cole, Howard C. *The All's Well Story from Boccaccio to Shakespeare*. U of Illinois P, 1981.

Conn, Peter. *Adoption: A Brief Social and Cultural History*. Palgrave Macmillan, 2013.

Cooper, C.H. "Ben Jonson's Adopted Sons." *Notes and Queries*, vol. 5, no. 138, 1852, pp. 588–9.

Corbier, Mireille. "Introduction. Adoptés et nourris." *Adoption et fosterage,* edited by Mireille Corbier, De Boccard, 1999, pp. 5–41.

– "Divorce and Adoption as Roman Family Strategies." *Marriage, Divorce, and Children in Ancient Rome,* edited by Beryl Rawson, Oxford UP, 1991, pp. 47–78.

Cormack, Bradin. *A Power to Do Justice: Jurisdiction, English Literature, and the Rise of Common Law, 1509–1625.* U of Chicago P, 2007.

"Cornelio v. Cornelio." CanLII 68884 (2008). *Canadian Legal Information Institute,* 10 Sept. 2009, canlii.ca/t/22190. Accessed 2 Sept. 2019.

Cotgrave, Randle. *A Dictionary of the French and English Tongues.* London, 1611.

The Craft of Graffing and planting of trees. London, 1563.

Crawford, Patricia. *Blood, Bodies and Families in Early Modern England.* Routledge, 2014.

– "The Construction and Experience of Maternity in Seventeenth-Century England." *Women as Mothers in Pre-Industrial England: Essays in Honour of Dorothy McLaren,* edited by Valerie Fildes, Routledge, 1990, pp. 33–8.

Cressy, David. *Birth, Marriage, and Death: Ritual, Religion, and the Life-Cycle in Tudor and Stuart England.* Oxford UP, 1997.

– "Kinship and Kin Interaction in Early Modern England." *Past & Present,* vol. 113, 1986, pp. 38–69.

Crook, John. "Patria Potestas." *Classical Quarterly,* vol. 17, no. 1, 1967, pp. 113–22.

Crooke, Helkiah. *Mikrokosmographia.* London, 1615.

Cunningham, Carole. "Christ's Hospital: Infant and Child Mortality in the Sixteenth Century." *Local Population Studies,* vol. 18, 1977, pp. 37–40.

Daalder, Joost. "The State of the Art." Hiscock, pp. 77–96.

Davis, Joe Lee. *The Sons of Ben: Jonsonian Comedy in Caroline England.* Wayne State UP, 1967.

Dawson, Anthony G. "*Women Beware Women* and the Economy of Rape." *Studies in English Literature 1500–1900,* vol. 27, no. 2, 1987, pp. 303–20.

Deans, Jill R. "Albee's Substitute Children: Reading Adoption as a Perfomative." *Journal of Dramatic Theory and Criticism,* vol. 13, no. 2, 1999, pp. 57–79.

De Grazia, Margreta. "Imprints, Shakespeare, Gutenberg, and Descartes." *Printing and Parenting in Early Modern England,* edited by Douglas A. Brooks, Ashgate, 2005, pp. 29–58.

Dekker, Thomas. *News from Hell.* London, 1606.

Della Porta, Giambattista. *Natural Magick.* London, 1658.

Detmer-Goebel, Emily. "What More Could Woman Do? Dramatizing Consent in Heywood's *Rape of Lucrece* and Middleton's *Women Beware Women.*" *Women's Studies,* vol. 36, no. 3, 2007, pp. 141–59.

Dickson, Arthur. Introduction. *Valentine and Orson,* edited by Dickson, Oxford UP, 1937, pp. ix–xvi.

Diefendorf, Barbara. "Family Culture, Renaissance Culture." *Renaissance Quarterly*, vol. 40, no. 4, 1987, pp. 661–81.

Dixon, Suzanne. *The Roman Family*. Johns Hopkins UP, 1992.

Dodson, Daniel. "Middleton's Livia." *Philological Quarterly*, vol. 27, 1948, pp. 376–81.

Dowd, Michelle M. *The Dynamics of Inheritance on the Shakespearean Stage*. Cambridge UP, 2015.

Dubrow, Heather. *Shakespeare and Domestic Loss: Forms of Deprivation, Mourning, and Recuperation*. Cambridge UP, 1999.

Duncan, Claire. "'Nature's Bastards': Grafted Generation in Early Modern England," *Renaissance and Reformation*, vol. 38, no. 2, 2015, pp. 121–48.

Dupont, Florence. *Daily Life in Ancient Rome*. Translated by Christopher Woodall, Blackwell, 1992.

Dutton, Richard. Introduction. *Women Beware Women and Other Plays*, by Thomas Middleton, edited by Dutton, Oxford UP, 1999, pp. xx–xxiv.

Duval, Jacques. *Des Hermaphrodits, accouchemens des femmes, et traitement qui est requis pour les relever ensanté, & bien élever leurs enfants*. Rouen, 1612.

Egan, Robert. "'The Art Itself Is Nature': *The Winter's Tale*." *Drama within Drama: Shakespeare's Sense of His Art in King Lear, The Winter's Tale, and The Tempest*, edited by Egan, Columbia UP, 1975, pp. 56–89.

Ellerbeck, Erin. "'A Bett'ring of Nature': Grafting and Embryonic Development in *The Duchess of Malfi*." *The Indistinct Human in Renaissance Literature*, edited by Jean E. Feerick and Vin Nardizzi, Palgrave, 2012, pp. 85–102.

Enterline, Lynn. *The Rhetoric of the Body from Ovid to Shakespeare*. Cambridge UP, 2000.

Erasmus. "On the Writing of Letters." *Collected Works of Erasmus*, edited by J.K. Sowards, translated by Charles Fantazzi, vol. 25, U of Toronto P, 1985, pp. 10–254. 89 vols.

Erickson, Amy Louise. *Women and Property in Early Modern England*. Routledge, 1993.

Estok, Simon C. *Ecocriticism and Shakespeare: Reading Ecophobia*. Palgrave, 2011.

– "Theory from the Fringes: Animals, Ecocriticism, Shakespeare." *Mosaic: A Journal for the Interdisciplinary Study of Literature*, vol. 4, no. 1, 2007, pp. 61–78.

Estrin, Barbara L. *The Raven and the Lark: Lost Children in Literature of the English Renaissance*. Associated UP, 1985.

– *Shakespeare and Contemporary Fiction: Theorizing the Foundling and Lyric Plots*. U of Delaware P, 2012.

Ewbank, Inga-Stina. "Realism and Morality in *Women Beware Women*." *Essays and Studies*, vol. 22, 1969, pp. 57–70.

Fawcett, Mary L. "Arms/Words/Tears: Language and the Body in *Titus Andronicus*." *ELH*, vol. 52, no. 2, 1983, pp. 261–77.

Feerick, Jean E. "Botanical Shakespeares: The Racial Logic of Plant Life in *Titus Andronicus*." *South Central Review*, vol. 26, no. 1/2, 2009, pp. 82–102.

– "The Imperial Graft: Horticulture, Hybridity, and the Art of Mingling Races in *Henry V* and *Cymbeline*." *The Oxford Handbook of Shakespeare and Embodiment: Gender, Sexuality, and Race*, edited by Valerie Traub, Oxford UP, 2016, pp. 211–27.

Feerick, Jean E., and Vin Nardizzi. "Swervings: On Human Indistinction." Introduction. *The Indistinct Human in Renaissance Literature*, edited by Feerick and Nardizzi, Palgrave, 2012.

Field, Catherine. "'Sweet Practicer, thy Physic I will try': Helena and Her 'Good Receipt' in *All's Well, That Ends Well*." Waller, pp. 194–208.

Fildes, Valerie. *Breasts, Bottles, and Babies: A History of Infant Feeding*. Edinburgh UP, 1986.

– "The English Wet-Nurse and Her Role in Infant Care 1538–1800." *Medical History*, vol. 32, no. 2, 1988, pp. 142–73.

– *Wet Nursing: A History from Antiquity to the Present*. Basil Blackwell, 1988.

Findlay, Alison. *Illegitimate Power: Bastards in Renaissance Literature*. Manchester UP, 1984.

Fischer, Sandra K. *Econolingua: A Glossary of Coins and Economic Language in Renaissance Drama*. Associated UP, 1985.

Fitzherbert, John. *Here begynneth a newe tract or treatyse moost profytable for all husbande men and very frutefull for all other persones to rede newly correcte & amended, by the auctour with dyverse other thynges added therunto*. London, 1530.

Fleming, Anne Taylor. "New Frontiers in Conception." *The New York Times*, 20 Jul. 1980, p. 14.

Fletcher, Anthony, and Peter Roberts, editors. *Religion, Culture and Society in Early Modern Britain: Essays in Honour of Patrick Collinson*. Cambridge, 1994.

Fletcher, John. *The Chances*. London, 1647.

– *Monsieur Thomas. The Dramatic Works in the Beaumont and Fletcher Canon*, edited by Fredson Bowers, vol. 4, Cambridge UP, 2008, pp. 415–540. 10 vols.

Forbes, Thomas Rogers. *Chronicle from Aldgate: Life and Death in Shakespeare's London*. Yale UP, 1971.

Fox, Eleanor, and Martin Ingram. "Bridewell, Bawdy Courts and Bastardy in Early Seventeenth-Century London." *Cohabitation and Non-Marital Births in England and Wales, 1600–2012*, edited by Rebecca Probert, Palgrave, 2014.

Frye, Northrop. "The Argument of Comedy." *Northrop Frye's Writings on Shakespeare and the Renaissance. Collected Works of Northrop Frye*, edited by Troni Y. Grande and Garry Sherbert, vol. 28, U of Toronto P, 2010, pp. 3–13. 30 vols.

Frye, Susan. *Elizabeth I: The Competition for Representation*. Oxford UP, 1993.

Fudge, Erica. *Brutal Reasoning: Animals, Rationality, and Humanity in Early Modern England*. Cornell UP, 2006.

– *Perceiving Animals: Humans and Beasts in Early Modern English Culture*. U of Illinois P, 2002.

– "Saying Nothing Concerning the Same: On Dominion, Purity, and Meat in Early Modern England." *Renaissance Beasts: Of Animals, Humans, and Other Wonderful Creatures*, edited by Fudge, U of Illinois P, 2004, pp. 70–86.

Gager, Kristin Elizabeth. *Blood Ties and Fictive Ties: Adoption and Family Life in Early Modern France*. Princeton UP, 1996.

Gardner, Jane F. *Family and Familia in Roman Law and Life*. Clarendon, 1998.

– "Status, Sentiment, and Strategy in Roman Adoption." *Adoption et fosterage*, edited by Mireille Corbier, De Boccard, 1999, pp. 63–80.

– *Women in Roman Law and Society*. Indiana UP, 1991.

Geisweidt, Edward J. "The Bastard Bomb: Illegitimacy and Population in Thomas Middleton's *A Chaste Maid in Cheapside*." Munroe, et al., pp. 121–30.

Gélis, Jacques. *History of Childbirth: Fertility, Pregnancy, and Birth in Early Modern Europe*. Translated by Rosemary Morris, Polity, 1991.

Gibbons, Brian. *Jacobean City Comedy: A Study of Satire Plays by Jonson, Marston, and Middleton*. Harvard UP, 1968.

Gill, Roma. Introduction. *Women Beware Women*, by Thomas Middleton, edited by Gill, Benn, 1968, pp. i–xlvii.

Given-Wilson, Chris, and Alice Curteis. *The Royal Bastards of Medieval England*. Routledge, 1984.

Goff, Cecilie. *A Woman of the Tudor Age*. J. Murray, 1930.

Goldberg, Jonathan. *James I and the Politics of Literature: Jonson, Shakespeare, Donne, and Their Contemporaries*. Johns Hopkins UP, 1983.

Goody, E.N. "Forms of Pro-Parenthood: The Sharing and Substitution of Parental Roles." *Kinship: Selected Readings*, edited by Jack Goody, Penguin, 1971, pp. 331–45.

Goody, Jack. *The Development of the Family and Marriage in Europe*. Cambridge UP, 1983.

Gossett, Suzanne. Introduction. *A Fair Quarrel*, by William Rowley and Thomas Middleton. Taylor and Lavagnino, pp. 1209–15.

Gottlieb, Beatrice. *The Family in the Western World from the Black Death to the Industrial Age*. Oxford UP, 1993.

Gowing, Laura. *Common Bodies: Women, Touch, and Power in Seventeenth-Century England*. Yale UP, 2003.

Granger, Thomas. *A Looking-Glasse for Christians; or, The Comfortable Doctrine of Adoption Wherein Euery True Beleeuer May Behold his Blessed Estate in the Kingdome of Grace*. London, 1620.

Greene, Robert. *Pandosto*. 1595. *The Winter's Tale*, by William Shakespeare, edited by J.H.P. Pafford, Thomson Learning, 2006, pp. 181–225.

Griffith, Paul. *Youth and Authority: Formative Experiences in England, 1560–1640*. Clarendon, 1996.

Grubbs, Judith Evans. *Women and the Law in the Roman Empire: A Sourcebook on Marriage, Divorce and Widowhood*. Routledge, 2002.

Guillemeau, Jacques. *Child-Birth or, The Happy Delivery of Women*. London, 1612.

Guy, John. *A Daughter's Love: Thomas More and His Dearest Meg*. Houghton Mifflin Harcourt, 2009.

Hanawalt, Barbara. *The Ties That Bound: Peasant Families in Medieval England*. Oxford UP, 1986.

Harvey, Elizabeth D. "Sensational Bodies, Consenting Organs: Helkiah Crooke's Incorporation of Spenser." *Spenser Studies: A Renaissance Poetry Annual*, vol. 18, 2003, pp. 295–314.

Heller, Jennifer L. "Space, Violence, and Bodies in Middleton and Cary." *Studies in English Literature 1500–1900*, vol. 45, no. 2, 2005, pp. 425–41.

Heminge, John, and Henry Condell. "Epistle Dedicatorie." *Mr. William Shakespeare's Comedies, Histories, and Tragedies*. London, 1623.

Henrey, Blanche. *British Botanical and Horticultural Literature before 1800*. Oxford UP, 1975. 3 vols.

Hiles, Jane. "A Margin for Error: Rhetorical Context in *Titus Andronicus*." *Style*, vol. 21, no. 1, 1987, pp. 62–75.

Hill, Thomas. *Naturall and Artificiall Conclusions*. London, 1581.

– *The Profitable Arte of Gardening*. London, 1574.

Hippocrates. *On the Nature of the Child. Hippocratic Writings*. Edited by G.E.R. Lloyd, translated by I.M. Lonie and E.T. Withington, Penguin, 1978, pp. 317–46.

Hiscock, Andrew, editor. *Women Beware Women: A Critical Guide*. A&C Black, 2011.

Holbein, Hans the Younger. "The Family of Thomas More." 1787. Royal Collection Trust. RCIN 659104.

Homans, Margaret. "Adoption Narratives, Trauma, and Origins." *Narrative*, vol. 14, no. 1, 2006, pp. 4–26.

Hooke, Christopher. *The Child-birth or Womans Lecture*. London, 1590.

Hopkins, Lisa. *The Female Hero in English Renaissance Tragedy*. Palgrave MacMillan, 2002.

Houlbrooke, Ralph. *The English Family, 1450–1750: Themes in British Social History*. Longman, 1984.

Howard, Jean. "Female Agency in *All's Well That Ends Well*." *Journal of the Australasian Universities Language and Literature Association*, vol. 106, no. 106, 2006, pp. 43–60.

Huard, Leo Albert. "The Law of Adoption: Ancient and Modern." *Vanderbilt Law Review*, vol. 9, 1955–6, pp. 743–63.

Hulse, S. Clark. "Wresting the Alphabet: Oratory and Action in *Titus Andronicus*." *Criticism*, vol. 21, no. 2, 1979, pp. 106–18.

Hurstfield, Joel. *The Queen's Wards: Wardship and Marriage under Elizabeth I*. Harvard UP, 1958.

Hutchings, Mark. "Middleton's *Women Beware Women*: Rape, Seduction – or Power, Simply?" *Notes and Queries*, vol. 45, no. 3, 1998, pp. 366–7.

The hystory of the two valyaunt brethren Valentyne and Orson. Translated by Henry Watson, London, 1555.

Ives, E.W. *Anne Boleyn*. Blackwell, 1986.

Jacobson, Miriam, and Vin Nardizzi. "The Secrets of Grafting in Wroth's *Urania*." *Ecofeminist Approaches to Early Modernity*, edited by Jennfier Munroe and Rebecca Laroche, Palgrave, 2011, pp. 175–94.

James, Heather. *Shakespeare's Troy: Drama, Politics, and the Translation of Empire*. Cambridge UP, 1997.

Jonson, Ben. *The Complete Plays of Ben Jonson*. Edited by G.A. Wilkes, Oxford UP, 1981–82. 4 vols.

Kahn, Coppélia. "New Directions: 'Two kings on one throne': Lust, Love, and Marriage in *Women Beware Women*." Hiscock, pp. 156–70.

Knight, G. Wilson. *The Crown of Life*. Oxford UP, 1947.

Knight, Leah. *Reading Green in Early Modern England*. Ashgate, 2014.

Knights, L.C. *Drama and Society in the Age of Jonson*. Chatto, 1951.

Korda, Natasha. *Shakespeare's Domestic Economies*. U of Pennsylvania P, 2002.

Krook, Dorothea. *Elements of Tragedy*. Yale UP, 1969.

Leggatt, Alexander. *English Stage Comedy 1490–1990: Five Centuries of a Genre*. Routledge, 1998.

– *Shakespeare's Comedy of Love*. Routledge, 1974.

– *Shakespeare's Tragedies: Violation and Identity*. Cambridge UP, 2005.

Levin, Richard A. "If Women Should Beware Women, Bianca Should Beware Mother." *Studies in English Literature 1500–1900*, vol. 37, no. 2, 1997, pp. 371–89.

Lindsay, Hugh. *Adoption in the Roman World*. Cambridge UP, 2009.

Longus. *Daphnis and Chloe*. Translated by Angel Day, London, 1587.

Loomba, Ania. *Shakespeare, Race, and Colonialism*. Oxford UP, 2002.

Lupton, Julia Reinhard. *Citizen-Saints: Shakespeare and Political Theology*. U of Chicago P, 2005.

Lyly, John. *Mother Bombie. Four Tudor Comedies*, edited by William Tydeman, Penguin, 1984, pp. 330–420.

Macfarlane, Alan. *The Family Life of Ralph Josselin, a Seventeenth-Century Clergyman: An Essay in Historical Anthropology*. Cambridge UP, 1970.

– "Illegitimacy and Illegitimates in English History." *Bastardy and Its Comparative History*, edited by Peter Laslett, et al., Edward Arnold, 1980, pp. 71–85.

– *Marriage and Love in England: Modes of Reproduction, 1300–1840*. Oxford UP, 1985.

MacGregor, Catherine. "Undoing the Body Politic: Representing Rape in *Women Beware Women*." *Theatre Research International*, vol. 23, no. 1, 1998, pp. 14–23.

Magnusson, Lynne. *Shakespeare and Social Dialogue: Dramatic Language and Elizabethan Letters*. Cambridge UP, 1999.

Malone, Edmund. *Historical Account of the Rise and Progress of the English Stage.* J.J. Tourneisen, 1800.

Marcus, Leah S., et al., editors. *Elizabeth I: Collected Works.* U of Chicago P, 2000.

Marotti, Arthur F. "Fertility and Comic Form in *A Chaste Maid in Cheapside.*" *Comparative Drama*, vol. 3, no. 1, 1969, pp. 65–74.

Marvell, Andrew. "The Mower against Gardens." *The Complete Poems*, edited by Elizabeth Story Donno, Penguin, 1977, p. 105.

Mascall, Leonard. *A Booke of the Arte and maner, howe to plant and graffe all sortes of trees, howe to set stones, and sowe pepines to make wylde trees to graffe on, as also remedies and mediicnes.* London, 1572.

McIlwain, Charles Howard. *The Political Works of James I.* Harvard UP, 1918.

McLaren, Angus. *Reproductive Rituals: The Perception of Fertility in England from the Sixteenth to the Nineteenth Century.* Taylor and Francis, 1984.

McLaren, Dorothy. "Marital Fertility and Lactation 1570–1720." *Women in English Society 1500–1800*, edited by Mary Prior, Methuen, 1985, pp. 22–53.

McLeod, John. *Life Lines: Writing Transcultural Adoption.* Bloomsbury, 2015.

Melosh, Barbara. *Strangers and Kin: The American Way of Adoption.* Harvard UP, 2002.

Merbecke, John. *Book of Notes and Common Places.* London, 1581.

Meyerson, Collier. "Crispr Babies, IVF, and the Ethics of Genetic Class Warfare." *Wired*, 16 Dec. 2018, www.wired.com/story/crispr-babies-ivf-and -the-ethics-of-genetic-class-warfare/.

Middleton, Thomas. *A Chaste Maid in Cheapside.* Edited by Alan Brissenden, Bloomsbury, 2014.

– *No Wit, No Help Like a Woman's.* Edited by John Jowett. Taylor and Lavagnio, pp. 783–832.

– *The Revenger's Tragedy.* Edited by MacDonald P. Jackson. Taylor and Lavagnino, pp. 543–93.

– *The Widow.* Edited by Gary Taylor. Taylor and Lavagnino, pp. 1078–123.

– *The Witch.* Edited by Marion O'Connor. Taylor and Lavagnino, pp. 1124–64.

– *Women Beware Women. Women Beware Women and Other Plays*, edited by Richard Dutton, Oxford UP, 1999, pp. 73–164.

Middleton, Thomas, and John Webster. *Anything for a Quiet Life.* Edited by Leslie Thomson. Taylor and Lavagnino, pp. 1596–631.

Milanich, Nara. *Paternity: The Elusive Quest for the Father.* Harvard UP, 2019.

Miller, Mara. *The Garden as an Art.* State U of New York P, 1993.

Moffet, Robin. "*Cymbeline* and the Nativity." *Shakespeare Quarterly*, vol. 13, no. 2, 1962, pp. 207–18.

Montaigne, Michel de. *The Essays or Morall, Politike, and Millitarie Discourses of Lo: Michaell de Montaigne.* 1580. Translated by John Florio, London, 1603.

More, Thomas. *Utopia.* Edited by George M. Logan and Robert M. Adams, Cambridge UP, 2016.

Morton, A.G. *History of Botanical Science: An Account of the Development of Botany from Ancient Times to the Present Day*. Academic, 1981.

Munroe, Jennifer. "Is It Really Ecocritical If It Isn't Feminist? The Dangers of 'Speaking For' in Ecological Studies and Shakespeare's *Titus Andronicus*." Munroe, et al., pp. 37–47.

– "It's all about the gillyvors: Engendering Art and Nature in *The Winter's Tale*." *Ecocritical Shakespeare*, edited by Lynne Bruckner and Dan Brayton, Ashgate, 2011, pp. 139–54.

Munroe, Jennifer, et al., editors. *Ecological Approaches to Early Modern English Texts: A Field Guide to Reading and Teaching*. Ashgate, 2015.

Nardizzi, Vin. "Shakespeare's Penknife: Grafting and Seedless Generation in the Procreation Sonnets." *Renaissance and Reformation*, vol. 32, no. 1, 2009, pp. 83–106.

– *Wooden Os: Shakespeare's Theatres and England's Trees*. U of Toronto P, 2013.

Neill, Michael. *Putting History to the Question: Power, Politics, and Society in English Renaissance Drama*. Columbia UP, 2000.

Nelson, Claudia. "Nontraditional Adoption in Progressive-Era Orphan Narratives." *Mosaic*, vol. 34, no. 2, 2001, pp. 181–97.

N.F. *The Fruiterers Secrets*. London, 1604.

Ng, Su Fang. *Literature and the Politics of the Family in Seventeenth-Century England*. Cambridge UP, 2007.

Notestein, Wallace. *The House of Commons, 1604–1610*. Yale UP, 1971.

Novy, Marianne. "Adopted Children and Constructions of Heredity, Nurture, and Parenthood in Shakespeare's Romances." *Childhood and Children's Books in Early Modern Europe, 1550–1800*, edited by Andrea Immel and Michael Witmore, Routledge, 2006, pp. 55–74.

– "Adoption and Shakespearean Families: Nature, Nurture, and Resemblance." Novy, *Reading*, pp. 56–86.

–, editor. *Imagining Adoption: Essays on Literature and Culture*. U of Michigan P, 2004.

– "Multiple Parenting in *Pericles*." *Pericles: Critical Essays*, edited by David Skeele, Garland, 2000, pp. 238–48.

– "Multiple Parenting in Shakespeare's Romances." *Domestic Arrangements in Early Modern England*, edited by Kari Boyd McBride, Duquesne UP, 2002, pp. 188–208.

– *Reading Adoption: Family and Difference in Fiction and Drama*. U of Michigan P, 2005.

OED: Oxford English Dictionary. Oxford UP. www.oed.com.

The Orchard, and the Garden Containing Certaine necessarie, secret, and ordinarie knowledges in Grafting and Gardening. London, 1594.

Osherow, Michele. "She Is in the Right: Biblical Maternity and *All's Well, That Ends Well*." Waller, pp. 155–68.

Ovid. *Fasti*. Translated by James G. Frazer, Loeb-Harvard UP, 1931.

Oxford Dictionary of National Biography. Oxford UP. oxforddnb.com.

Ozment, Steven. *When Fathers Ruled: Family Life in Reformation Europe*. Harvard UP, 1983.

Packard, Bethany. "Lavinia as Coauthor of Shakespeare's *Titus Andronicus*." *Studies in English Literature 1500–1900*, vol. 50, no. 2, pp. 281–300.

Painter, William. *The Palace of Pleasure*. 1566. *All's Well That Ends Well*, by William Shakespeare, edited by G.K. Hunter, Oxford UP, 1994, pp. 145–216.

Parker, Patricia. "*All's Well That Ends Well*: Increase and Multiply." *Creative Imitation: New Essays on Renaissance Literature in Honor of Thomas M. Greene*, edited by David Quint, et al., 1992, pp. 355–90.

– *Shakespeare from the Margins: Language, Culture, Context*. Chicago UP, 1996.

Paster, Gail Kern. *The Body Embarrassed: Drama and the Disciplines of Shame in Early Modern England*. Cornell UP, 1993.

Peacham, Henry. *The Garden of Eloquence*. 1593. Scholars' Facsimiles and Reprints, 1954.

Peppard, Michael. *The Son of God in the Roman World: Divine Sonship in Its Social and Political Context*. Oxford UP, 2011.

Perkins, William. *Christian Oeconomy*. London, 1609.

Pettigrew, Todd H.J. *Shakespeare and the Practice of Physic: Medical Narratives on the Early Modern English Stage*. U of Delaware P, 2007.

Pliny the Elder. *Natural History*. Translated by Harris Rackham, vol. 1, Loeb-Harvard UP, 1938. 10 vols.

Plutarch. *Lives of the Noble Grecians and Romans*. Translated by Thomas North, London, 1579.

Pollock, Linda A. *Forgotten Children: Parent-Child Relations from 1500 to 1900*. Cambridge UP, 1983.

Press Association. "England Adoption Rates Falling as IVF Improves, Says Senior Official." *The Guardian*, 3 Nov. 2018, www.theguardian.com/society/2018/nov/03/england-adoption-rates-falling-as-ivf-improves-says-senior-official.

Puttenham, George. *The Art of English Poesy*. 1589. Edited by Frank Whigham and Wayne A. Rebhorn, Cornell UP, 2007.

Raine, James, editor. *Wills and Inventories Illustrative of the History, Manners, Language, Statistics, &c. of the Northern Counties of England from the Eleventh Century Onward*. Part 1, London, 1834.

Ranald, Margaret Loftus. "'As Marriage Binds, and Blood Breaks': English Marriage and Shakespeare." *Shakespeare Quarterly*, vol. 30, no. 1, 1979, pp. 68–81.

Randolph, Thomas. "A Gratulatory to Master Ben Johnson, for His Adopting of Him to Be His Son." *Poetical and Dramatic Works of Thomas Randolph of Trinity, Cambridge*, edited by W. Carew Hazlitt, Benjamin Blom, 1968, pp. 537–9.

Reilly, Terry. "*All's Well, That Ends Well* and the 1604 Controversy Concerning the Court of Wards and Liveries." Waller, pp. 209–20.

– "'Doctor She': Helena and Sisterhood in William Shakespeare's *All's Well That Ends Well* (ca. 1602–1603)." *Women in Literature: Reading Through the Lens of Gender*, edited by Jerilyn Fisher and Ellen S. Silber, Greenwood, 2003, pp. 8–11.

Ricoeur, Paul. *The Rule of Metaphor: Multi-Disciplinary Studies of the Creation of Meaning in Language*. Translated by Robert Czerny, et al., U of Toronto P, 1981.

Robertson, John M., editor. *The Philosophical Works of Francis Bacon*. Routledge, 2011.

Robinson, John V. "Helena's Living Mother: *All's Well That Ends Well* 5.3.314." *English Studies*, vol. 80, no. 5, 1999, pp. 423–7.

Rogers, John. *The Glasse of Godly Loue*. London, 1569.

Rosenberg, Jessica. "The Point of the Couplet: Shakespeare's Sonnets and Tusser's *A Hundreth Good Pointes of Husbandrie*." *ELH*, vol. 83, no. 1, 2016, pp. 1–41.

Rowe, Katharine. "Dismembering and Forgetting in *Titus Andronicus*." *Shakespeare Quarterly*, vol. 45, no. 3, 1994, pp. 279–303.

Rowley, William, and Thomas Middleton. *A Fair Quarrel*. Edited by Suzanne Gossett. Taylor and Lavagnino, pp. 1209–50.

Royster, Francesca T. "White-Limed Walls: Whiteness and Gothic Extremism in Shakespeare's *Titus Andronicus*." *Shakespeare Quarterly*, vol. 51, no. 4, 2000, pp. 432–55.

Rutkoski, Marie. "'Arm the Minds of Infants': Interpreting Childhood in *Titus Andronicus*." *Criticism*, vol. 48, no. 2, pp. 203–26.

Sacks, Elizabeth. *Shakespeare's Images of Pregnancy*. Macmillan, 1980.

Salvian. *The Writings of Salvian, the Presbyter*. Translated by Jeremiah F. O'Sullivan, Catholic U of America P, 2008.

Sataline, Suzanne, and Ian Sample. "Scientist in China Defends Human Embryo Gene Editing." *The Guardian*, 28 Nov. 2018, www.theguardian.com/science /2018/nov/28/scientist-in-china-defends-human-embryo-gene-editing.

Schoenbaum, Samuel. "*A Chaste Maid in Cheapside* and City Comedy." *Studies in English Renaissance Drama*, edited by Josephine Waters Bennett, et al., New York UP, 1959, pp. 287–309.

Schwarz, Kathryn. "'My intents are fix'd': Constant Will in *All's Well That Ends Well*." *Shakespeare Quarterly*, vol. 58, no. 2, 2007, pp. 200–27.

"Science." *Time*, vol. 44, no. 7, Aug. 1944, p. 74.

Scott, Charlotte. *Shakespeare's Nature: From Cultivation to Culture*. Oxford UP, 2014.

Seneca the Elder. *Declamations*. Translated by Michael Winterbottom, vol. 1, Loeb-Harvard UP, 1974. 2 vols.

Shackleton, Mark. *International Adoption in North American Literature and Culture*. Palgrave, 2017.

Shakespeare, William. *All's Well That Ends Well*. Edited by G.K. Hunter, Methuen, 2004.

– *Antony and Cleopatra*. Edited by Walter Cohen. *The Norton Shakespeare*, edited by Stephen Greenblatt, et al., W.W. Norton, 1997, pp. 2619–708.
– *As You Like It*. Edited by Alan Brissenden, Oxford UP, 2008.
– *Cymbeline*. Edited by Martin Butler, Cambridge UP, 2005.
– *Hamlet*. Edited by G.R. Hibbard, Oxford UP, 1998.
– *Henry IV, Part 1*. Edited by David M. Bevington, Oxford UP, 1994.
– *Henry IV, Part 2*. Edited by René Weis, Oxford UP, 1998.
– *Henry V*. Edited by Gary Taylor, Oxford UP, 1998.
– *Henry VI, Part 3*. Edited by Randall Martin, Oxford UP, 2008.
– *Julius Caesar*. Edited by Arthur Humphreys, Oxford UP, 2008.
– *King Lear*. Edited by R.A. Foakes, Thomas Nelson and Sons, 1997.
– *Love's Labour's Lost*. Edited by G.R. Hibbard, Oxford UP, 1990.
– *Macbeth*. Edited by Nicholas Brooke, Oxford UP, 1998.
– *A Midsummer Night's Dream*. Edited by Peter Holland, Oxford UP, 1994.
– *Much Ado about Nothing*. Edited by Sheldon P. Zitner, Oxford UP, 1993.
– *Othello*. Edited by Michael Neill, Oxford UP, 2008.
– *Pericles*. Edited by Suzanne Gossett, Thomas Nelson and Sons, 2004
– *Richard II*. Edited by Charles R. Forker, Arden, 2002.
– *Richard III*. Edited by Janis Lull, Cambridge UP, 1999.
– "Sonnet 15." *Shakespeare's Sonnets and Poems*, edited by Barbara A. Mowat and Paul Werstine, Folger Shakespeare Library, 2006, p. 49.
– *The Tempest*. Edited by Stephen Orgel, Oxford UP, 1987.
– *Titus Andronicus*. Edited by Jonathan Bate, Routledge, 1995.
– *The Winter's Tale*. Edited by J.H.P. Pafford, Thomson Learning, 2006.
Shannon, Laurie. *The Accommodated Animal: Cosmopolity in Shakespearean Locales*. U of Chicago P, 2013.
– *Sovereign Amity: Figures of Friendship in Shakespearean Contexts*. U of Chicago P, 2002.
Shell, Marc. *The End of Kinship: "Measure for Measure," Incest, and the Ideal of Universal Siblinghood*. Stanford UP, 1988.
Sidney, Sir Philip. *A Defence of Poesy*. *Miscellaneous Prose of Sir Philip Sidney*, edited by Katherine Duncan-Jones and Jan van Dorsten, Oxford UP, 1973.
Simpson, Percy. "Ben Jonson and the Devil Tavern." *Modern Language Review*, vol. 34, 1939, pp. 367–73.
Singley, Carol J. *Adopting America: Childhood, Kinship, and National Identity in Literature*. Oxford UP, 2011.
Smith, Helen. "Animal Families." *Family Politics in Early Modern Literature*, edited by Hannah Crawforth and Sarah Lewis, Palgrave, 2017, pp. 75–83.
Smith, Jeremy L. *Thomas East and Music Publishing in Renaissance England*. Oxford UP, 2003.
Sommerlad, Joe. "World's First Test Tube Baby at 40: How the Public Reacted to the IVF Breakthrough of the Century." *Independent*, 24 Jul. 2018,

www.independent.co.uk/news/health/test-tube-baby-40th-anniversary
-world-first-reaction-ivf-louise-brown-a8454021.html.

Standish, Arthur. *The Commons Complaint*. London, 1611.

Stone, Lawrence. *Crisis of the Aristocracy, 1558–1641*. Clarendon, 1965.

– *The Family, Sex and Marriage in England 1500–1800*. Weidenfeld & Nicolson, 1977.

Summers, Claude J., and Ted-Larry Pebworth, editors. *Classic and Cavalier: Essays on Jonson and the Sons of Ben*. U of Pittsburgh P, 1982.

Sunderam, Saswati, et al. "Assisted Reproductive Technology Surveillance – United States, 2015." *MMWR Surveillance Summaries*, vol. 67, no. 3, 2018, pp. 1–28, https://doi.org/10.15585/mmwr.ss6703a1.

Surtz, Edward, and Virginia Murphy, editors. *The Divorce Tracts of Henry VIII*. Moreana, 1988.

Tadmore, Naomi. *Family and Friends in Eighteenth-Century England: Household, Kinship and Patronage*. Cambridge UP, 2011.

Taylor, Gary. "The Orphan Playwright." *The Guardian*, 17 Nov. 2007, www.theguardian.com/books/2007/nov/17/classics.theatre.

Taylor, Gary, and John Lavagnino, editors. *Thomas Middleton: The Collected Works*. Oxford UP, 2007.

Thacker, Christopher. *The History of Gardens*. U of California P, 1985.

Theophrastus. *De Causis plantarum*. Edited and translated by Benedict Einarson and George K. Link, vol. 1, Loeb-Harvard UP, 1976. 3 vols.

Tilley, M.P. *A Dictionary of the Proverbs in England in the Sixteenth and Seventeenth Centuries*. U of Michigan P, 1950.

Todd, Barbara J. "The Remarrying Widow: A Stereotype Reconsidered." *Women in English Society 1500–1800*, edited by Mary Prior, Methuen, 1985, pp. 54–92.

Topsell, Edward. *The Fowles of Heaven; or History of Birdes*. 1613–14. Edited by Thomas P. Harrison and F. David Hoeniger, U of Texas P, 1972.

– *The History of Foure-Footed Beastes*. London, 1607.

– *The Reward of Religion. Delivered in Sundrie Lectures upon the Booke of Ruth*. London, 1613.

Traister, Barbara. "'Doctor She': Healing and Sex in *All's Well That Ends Well*." *A Companion to Shakespeare's Works: The Poems, Problem Comedies, Late Plays*, edited by Richard Dutton and Jean E. Howard, Blackwell, 2006, pp. 333–47.

Tromly, Fred B. *Fathers and Sons in Shakespeare: The Debt Never Promised*. U of Toronto P, 2010.

Tuck, Steven L. *A History of Roman Art*. Wiley Blackwell, 2015.

Tucker, Anthony. "The Brave New World of Test Tube Babies." *The Guardian*, 27 Jul. 1978, www.theguardian.com/society/1978/jul/27/health.lifeandhealth.

Vella Bonavita, Helen. *Illegitimacy and the National Family in Early Modern England*. Routledge, 2017.

Viret, Pierre. *The Schoole of Beastes, Intituled, the good Householder, or the Oeconomickes*. London, 1585.

Virgil. *Georgics*. Translated by David Ferry, Farrar, Straus and Giroux, 2005.

Wall, Wendy. *Staging Domesticity: Household Work and English Identity in Early Modern Drama*. Cambridge UP, 2002.

Waller, Gary, editor. *All's Well, That Ends Well: New Critical Essays*. Routledge, 2007.

– "From 'the Unfortunate Comedy' to 'this Infinitely Fascinating Play': The Critical and Theatrical Emergence of *All's Well, That Ends Well*." Waller, pp. 1–56.

Wallis, Patrick. "Apprenticeship and Training in Premodern England." *The Journal of Economic History*, vol. 68, no. 3, 2008, pp. 832–61.

Watson, Alan. *The Law of Persons in the Later Roman Republic*. Oxford UP, 1967.

Webber, Ronald. *The Early Horticulturalists*. Augustus M. Kelly, 1968.

Webster, John, Thomas Heywood, and William Rowley. *A Cure for a Cuckold*. London, 1624.

Weil, Rachel J. "The Politics of Legitimacy: Women and the Warming-Pan Scandal." *The Revolution of 1688–1689: Changing Perspectives*, edited by Lois G. Schwoerer, Cambridge UP, 1992.

Welty, Joel. *The Life of Birds*. Thomson Brooks/Cole, 1979.

White, Caroline, translator. *Early Christian Lives*. Penguin, 1998.

Wilkins, Ernest H. "The Genealogy of the Genealogical Trees of the 'Genealogia Deorum.'" *Modern Philology*, vol. 23, no. 1, 1925, pp. 61–5.

Wilson, Chris. "The Determinants of Marital Fertility." *The World We Have Gained*, edited by Lloyd Bonfield, et al., Oxford, 1986, pp. 203–30.

Wilson, Harold S. "'Nature and Art' in *The Winter's Tale* IV, iv, 86 ff." *Shakespeare Association Bulletin*, vol. 18, no. 3, 1943, pp. 114–20.

Wilson, Miranda. "Bastard Grafts, Crafted Fruits: Shakespeare's Planted Families." *The Indistinct Human in Renaissance Literature*, edited by Jean E. Feerick and Vin Nardizzi, Palgrave, 2012, pp. 103–17.

Winstanley, William. *The Lives of the Most Famous English Poets*. London, 1687.

Wiseman, Susan. *Writing Metamorphosis in the English Renaissance: 1550–1700*. Cambridge UP, 2014.

Wolfram, Sybil. *In-Laws and Outlaws: Kinship and Marriage in England*. St. Martin's, 1987.

Woolfson, Jonathan. "The Renaissance of Bees." *Renaissance Studies*, vol. 24, no. 2, 2010, pp. 281–300.

Wrightson, Keith. "Household and Kinship in Sixteenth-Century England." *History Workshop Journal*, vol. 12, 1981, pp. 151–8.

Xenophon. *Xenophons Treatise of House holde*. London, 1573.

Zitner, Sheldon P. *All's Well That Ends Well*. Harvester Wheatsheaf, 1989.

Zunshine, Lisa. *Bastards and Foundlings: Illegitimacy in Eighteenth-Century England*. Ohio State UP, 2005.

Index

Figures are indicated by page numbers in italics.

abandoned and orphaned children: adoption of, 21–2; institutional care for, 12, 119n19, 120n21, 120nn23–5; mother's sexual indiscretion and, 134n36; surreptitious abandonment, 86–9; wardships and, 10–11, 21, 50–1, 106–7, 129n46, 142n22, 143n23; wet-nursing and, 11–12, 88, 120n20

adoption: about, 3, 6–7, 14–15, 24, 116; agency and choice, 12–13, 23, 25–6, 55–6; bastards and, 82, 83, 138n26; Christianity and, 18, 121n33, 122n34; citizenship and, 55, 57–8, 132n11; concealment of, 19, 123n48; contemporary decline of, 143n3; contracts for, 19, 122n35; in early modern English theatre, 7, 8–10; early modern practices, 6–7, 19, 20–2; genetic testing and, 115; as human intervention in the natural world, 7–8, 113–14; Jonson's adoption of "Tribe of Ben," 22–3, 123nn49–50, 124n51; legality of, 6, 117nn4–5; marriage and, 105–7, 129n44, 142nn19–20; patronage and, 124n52; Roman practices, 19–20, 55, 57–8, 122n38, 122nn40–2, 132n15; scholarship on, 13–14, 120n26, 121n27; self-making and, 114; service (fostering out) and, 10, 117n6, 118n11; spiritual adoption, 16–18, 19, 128n36; sworn brotherhood and, 10, 119n13; theatrical qualities of, 23–4, 124n53, 125n54; wardships and, 10–11, 21, 50–1, 106–7, 129n46, 142n22, 143n23; wet-nursing and, 11–12, 62, 88, 119n15, 119nn17–18, 120n20. *See also* animals and animal parenting; familial relations; grafting and grafting metaphors

adoptive names (familial honorifics), 96–9, 100, 103, 141n10

affection, familial, 6, 8–9, 59, 114, 118n8

agency and choice: adoption and altering relations, 12–13, 23, 25–6, 55–6; of women, 13, 47–8, 52, 53

Albee, Edward, 124n53

All's Well That Ends Well (Shakespeare), 47–53; about, 14, 27–8; comparison to Shakespeare's romances, 53; emotional ties and